Adequately Explained by Stupidity?

Lockerbie, luggage and lies

Adequately Explained by Stupidity?

Lockerbie, luggage and lies

Morag G. Kerr

Matador
9 Priory Business Park
Kibworth Beauchamp
Leicestershire LE8 0RX, UK
Tel: (+44) 116 279 2299
Fax: (+44) 116 279 2277
Email: books@troubador.co.uk
Web: www.troubador.co.uk/matador

ISBN 978 1783062 508

British Library Cataloguing in Publication Data.
A catalogue record for this book is available from the British Library.

Typeset in Aldine by Troubador Publishing Ltd
Printed and bound in the UK by TJ International, Padstow, Cornwall

Matador is an imprint of Troubador Publishing Ltd

Never attribute to malice
what can be adequately explained by stupidity

Robert J. Hanlon

CONTENTS

FOREWORD

No one can pick up this book without remembering the family and friends of those who died so tragically on the fateful night of 21st December 1988. The explosion aboard Pan Am 103, over the small town of Lockerbie in Scotland, was an event that horrified people right across the world. Twenty-five years later those close to the victims still bear the scars of that dreadful event.

Although to a certain extent the passing of time enables some healing to take place, that process has not been helped by the multitude of speculative theories regarding the individual, or individuals, responsible for the act. Twenty-five years on, speculation continues. It is well known that the Crown prosecuted a case which resulted in the conviction and sentence of a Libyan subject, Mr. Abdelbaset al-Megrahi. There were many who felt profoundly uncomfortable about the safety of the conviction, and across the years they have raised their concerns in books and articles. Dr. Morag Kerr was one such individual, and in her quest to understand the anomalies and contradictions in the official narrative she sought out primary evidence which has not, until now, been publicly available. The result is this book which is a masterpiece of forensic investigation.

The book is highly detailed and examines with faultless logic the essential elements of the case. Dr. Kerr sticks clearly to the facts and leaves the reader seriously questioning the safety of the conviction. Given her analysis one is forced to ask – how could the explosive device have been planted in the luggage other than at Heathrow? In addition to a detailed and devastating scrutiny of the provenance of the bomb suitcase, she also explores the uncertainty surrounding the allegation that Mr. al-Megrahi was the individual who bought the clothing packed in the suitcase with the bomb, some of which was later recovered in a fingertip search following the explosion. She raises vital questions about the competence of both the police and the expert witnesses.

In short, any reasonable person following her analysis will be left in little doubt that there are far too many uncertainties surrounding this case for the conviction of Mr. al-Megrahi to be considered safe.

Dr. Kerr wisely steers clear of making allegations other than what can be demonstrated by the application of rigorous logic. It is in the interest of all who value justice and fair dealing, and especially those affected by the disaster, to read this book carefully and, if convinced by its argument, to press for a thorough review of this whole sorry affair.

Terry Waite CBE, August 2013.

INTRODUCTION

Sometimes what they don't tell you is more revealing than what they do. The Lockerbie trial at Camp Zeist was one of those times.

Do you want to know exactly which heading *Maid of the Seas* was on as she left Heathrow airport on the evening of 21st December 1988, which FM frequencies the various air traffic controllers used to talk to the cockpit, and what banal greetings were exchanged between the ground staff and the doomed flight? It's all there. Does it have any bearing on who planted the bomb? None at all.

Do you want to know what a member of the public who was driving north on the A69, or another member of the public who was waiting for his daughter at the railway station in Lockerbie, heard and saw when the plane came down? Their testimony is there. Does it have any bearing on who planted the bomb? None at all.

Do you want to know the names of all the passengers on KM180 from Malta to Frankfurt that morning, where they were going and why, and exactly what luggage they were carrying with them? That's all there too, mostly in their own words in the witness box. Does that help us decide who planted the bomb? Maybe, but over twenty separate witnesses called to testify to essentially the same thing is gross overkill, and it's anybody's guess what the prosecution thought had been proved by the exercise.

Do you want to know exactly how the twenty-four legitimate items of transfer luggage on the computer printout from the Frankfurt baggage system were reconciled to their owners, so that the twenty-fifth item could confidently be shown to be the bomb suitcase flying in from Malta? Good luck with that. Is that important in determining who planted the bomb? Extremely.

Do you want to know the names of the passengers who joined Pan Am 103 from other incoming flights at Heathrow that afternoon, which of them were discovered to have had their luggage loaded into baggage container AVE4041 in the interline shed before quarter past four, how many items there were and what these looked like? Not a chance. Is that important in determining who planted the bomb? It is absolutely vital.

Do you want to know what the baggage handler who took that container out to the tarmac said he did with these items when he was adding the transfer luggage from the delayed feeder flight from Frankfurt? Too bad. Is that important in determining who planted the bomb? It is the most important thing there is.

Of course some evidence is required to set the scene and establish the facts of what happened, even uncontentious facts. The striking thing about Camp Zeist, though, is the abundance of minute, obsessive detail presented in areas where in the final analysis it frankly doesn't matter a damn, contrasted with the fog of uncertainty that descends as soon as the evidence gets anywhere close to the crux of the matter – where exactly did that brown Samsonite hardshell that blew up in a corner of AVE4041 at three minutes past seven begin its journey?

An important thing to remember about this trial is that virtually all the evidence introduced in court was led by the prosecution. The defence were entirely reactive. They called only three witnesses, who between them occupied the witness box for less than a day on days seventy-six and seventy-seven of the trial, with the Crown summing-up beginning on day seventy-eight. Only one of these three witnesses testified in relation to baggage transfers, and his testimony was in fact of peripheral relevance. As a result, the Crown had almost total control over what was presented to the court and what was not.

What they didn't tell the judges was far more important than what they did.

1

A CASE ABOUT CASES

Although on paper Pan Am 103 flew from Frankfurt to Detroit with stopovers in London and New York, the three stages were flown by different aircraft, with different flight crews. Boeing 727s were used for the two short connecting legs at either end, while the long-haul transatlantic leg was flown by a Boeing 747 'Jumbo' jet, *Maid of the Seas*.

Maid of the Seas herself flew in to Heathrow from San Francisco at noon on 21st December 1988. She was unloaded, cleaned, serviced, refuelled and made ready for the return trip to the USA during a six-hour turnover, and there was no luggage in any of the holds at that time. Thus, however it happened, the suitcase containing the explosive device that brought down Pan Am 103 was loaded into the aircraft at Heathrow airport.

The aircraft carried its cargo in holds situated under the floor of the passenger compartment. Baggage containers were loaded in two rows, one either side of the central line. Eight of these carried passenger luggage, six in the forward hold and two in the aft hold.

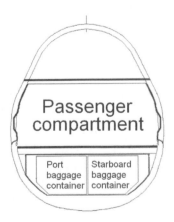

Figure 1
Cross-section of aircraft body (front-facing) showing the positions of the baggage containers when loaded.

The containers were aluminium or fibreglass cubes about five feet in each dimension, with an extra overhang section to one side which maximised the amount of luggage that could be carried by shaping the containers to the curve of the plane's hull.

Figure 2
Aluminium AVE-type baggage container as carried on Boeing 747 aircraft.

Seven of the eight containers of passenger luggage had been filled in the busy baggage build-up shed at Heathrow Terminal 3, with luggage belonging to passengers joining the flight through the check-in desks at that terminal. The eighth contained the luggage transferred from the 727 which flew in from Frankfurt.

The feeder flight was timetabled to arrive at Heathrow at 17.20 GMT, allowing at best only forty minutes for the transfer of passengers and their luggage to the transatlantic leg, which was scheduled to push off from the gate at 18.00. Standard practice was therefore to take a baggage container out on to the tarmac to meet the aircraft, which was routinely parked at the adjacent stand to the transatlantic aircraft, load that with the luggage bound for the USA, then tow it directly over to the transatlantic flight for loading. No security screening of the transfer luggage was carried out at that stage, on the assumption that this luggage had all been adequately screened at Frankfurt airport.

On Christmas Eve 1988, the third day of the investigation into the disaster, an important piece of debris was brought in from the fields around Lockerbie. It was a section of one of the aluminium AVE baggage containers, and it had clearly been very close to an explosive blast. Further pieces of the same container were recovered over the next few days, including sections bearing the serial number AVE4041PA. The container recorded as having held the luggage from the feeder flight. Partial reconstruction revealed all too clearly that the explosive blast had occurred inside the container itself.

Figure 3
Left is the reconstructed superstructure of the container, seen from the back with the overhang section to the right. Right is the reconstructed floor, with the front to the bottom of the picture and the side bordering the overhang section to the left.

The UK newspapers cottoned on to the implications of this almost at once, closely followed by the foreign press. The headline in the *Times* on 31st December, "Disaster bomb was 'placed on board Jumbo in Frankfurt'", was factually inaccurate, but conveyed the message well enough. The security breach had occurred in Germany, not in London. Contemporary accounts suggest the relief on the British side of the investigation was palpable.

It wasn't quite that simple of course. The West German authorities had recognised from the outset that the Frankfurt origin of the flight potentially made it their problem, and indeed it is unclear whether the German police (the Bundeskriminalamt, or BKA) actually realised at the very beginning that there had been a change of planes at Heathrow, or that only forty-nine of the Jumbo's 243 passengers had transferred from the feeder flight. Their officers were in Frankfurt airport by Christmas Day (which was a Sunday), interviewing baggage handlers. However by the following Sunday, New Year's Day, the mood was different. A spokesman from the German Ministry of the Interior insisted that there was no proof the bomb had come from Frankfurt, and indeed claimed to have evidence to the contrary.

This set the scene for a conflict that continued for the next eight months. The British side of the investigation insisted that the bomb must have come from Frankfurt on the feeder flight, while the Germans insisted, equally vehemently, that it had originated at Heathrow. Nevertheless the message conveyed by the reconstructed baggage container, a dozen or so blast-damaged pieces of luggage, and residues of the components of Semtex identified on these items and on the adjacent section of the airframe, was clear. Wherever it had come from, the explosion that had brought down Pan Am 103 had occurred inside a piece of passenger luggage, and that piece of passenger luggage had been inside container AVE4041, low down, to the extreme left of the container as seen from the open (aft-facing) side.

A graphic little sketch in a BKA memo dated 7th January 1989 shows the first approximate estimate of the position of the exploding suitcase within the container.

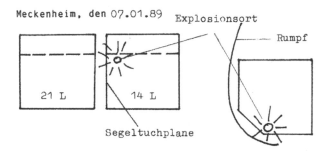

Figure 4
German estimate of the location of the explosion.

14L was the loading position of AVE4041, and 21L was the adjacent container AVN7511, which was one of those containing luggage belonging to passengers who had checked in at Heathrow. The diagrams below from the Air Accident Investigation Branch report into the crash illustrate how the explosion in the container related to the airframe itself.

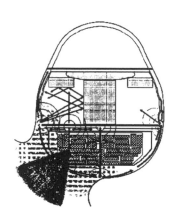

Figure 5
AAIB diagram of the explosive blast. The position is however merely approximate, as the centre of the explosion was determined to have been only ten inches above the floor of the container.

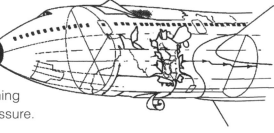

Figure 6
Petalling of the fuselage skins around the small hole created by the explosion, and the skin beginning to lift off elsewhere due to overpressure.

Subsequent forensic investigation identified the exploding suitcase as a Samsonite 'Silhouette 4000' hardshell in 'antique copper', actually a simulated leather finish in a colour variously described as brown, bronze, maroon and even burgundy. The bomb itself was determined to have been hidden inside a Toshiba RT-SF16 radio-cassette recorder packed in the case with a selection of clothes. Exactly where that suitcase came from, and how it had circumvented the security screens designed to detect its lethal contents, became a major focus of the inquiry.

2

LUQA AIRPORT, MALTA

The ugly game of diplomatic ping-pong between Britain and Germany, and their respective police and forensics departments, continued into the late summer of 1989. A number of lines of inquiry were communicated (or perhaps leaked) to the press during that time, including the possibility that the bomb had been unwittingly carried by an American student returning from a term studying in Vienna, who had befriended a young Jordanian man during her stay. Other suspicions centred around another passenger who carried dual US/Lebanese nationality and who had been staying with friends in Frankfurt on his way home to Michigan from a visit to his grandmother in the Lebanon.

These suggestions all came to nothing, although various theories surrounding Khaled Jaafar, the young man from the Lebanese family, proved remarkably tenacious. However they had one thing in common; they all concerned luggage that would have travelled on the feeder flight. At no time was there the slightest hint that anything suspicious might have occurred in the Heathrow terminal buildings, or that anyone was looking into any possibility other than a suitcase that had been transferred across the tarmac from the 727.

In mid-August 1989 the focus of the investigation shifted dramatically. The Scottish police suddenly became intensely interested in the Mediterranean island of Malta, and a group of detectives secretly flew out there at the beginning of September. They became increasingly convinced that the bomb had flown into Frankfurt on Air Malta flight KM180, which had left Luqa airport at 9.45 local time with thirty-nine passengers on board. The theory was that the suitcase had been carried on that flight as illegitimate unaccompanied luggage, complete with Air Malta tags directing it to be transferred to the Pan Am 103 feeder flight at Frankfurt, and thence to Pan Am 103 itself at Heathrow.

This conviction never wavered thereafter. The belief that the bomb had begun its journey on Malta was crucial to the Camp Zeist verdict in 2001 in which Abdelbaset al-Megrahi was found guilty of the bombing. He was at Luqa airport that morning catching the 10.20 flight to Tripoli which was open for check-in at the same time as KM180, and he was travelling on a passport with a false name. His presence in the airport at the very time the bomb was believed to have been smuggled on board the Frankfurt flight was central to the court's finding that he was 'the Lockerbie bomber'.

The security system at Luqa airport was explained in some detail in court by Wilfred Borg, the general manager for ground operations, who was in the witness box for a day and a half. Malta occupies a strategic position in the Mediterranean, quite close to several middle eastern trouble spots. Only three years previously the airport had been the scene of a major hijacking incident which resulted in the deaths of fifty-eight passengers. As a result the airport authorities had developed their own security system which at that time was unique in the world.

The Maltese military was heavily involved at the airport, both in guarding the aircraft and in checking luggage for explosives. Airline staff rotas were irregular and not published in advance, so that the check-in clerks and baggage handlers only found out which flights they would be dealing with on any particular day when they arrived to begin their shift.

Luggage was checked in and entered into the computer system in the usual manner, and tagged for the appropriate flight. Suitcases were then placed by the check-in clerk on a continuous moving belt which ran behind the check-in desks and delivered the luggage piecemeal through a hatch on to the tarmac. There, everything was checked for explosives by military personnel using a hand-held 'sniffer' device of indeterminate functionality or efficacy. Once that was completed the luggage was sorted according to which flight it was intended for, and transported to the appropriate aircraft.

Then came the clever part. The head loader was required to count the items of luggage as they were loaded into the aircraft. Once that was completed he communicated this figure to the flight dispatcher, who radioed independently to the terminal building to ascertain how many items were recorded in the computer as having been checked in for that flight. Only if the two numbers tallied was the flight departure allowed to proceed. If they didn't, steps were taken to reconcile the discrepancy, culminating in the passengers being asked to disembark and identify their own luggage if necessary. Triple head counts of passengers on board were also used to confirm that everyone who had checked in luggage was physically present on the aircraft. Very few things in life are foolproof, but this seems to have been pretty good. Mr. Borg testified that the baggage mishandling rate from Luqa at that time was only 20% of the rate experienced by other airports.

Airport records showed that fifty-five items of luggage were checked in for KM180 at Luqa on the morning of 21st December 1988, and fifty-five items were counted into the hold by the head loader. All thirty-nine checked-in passengers were on board. The flight was good to go.

Additional evidence heard in court revealed that the Boeing 737 which became KM180 that morning had been in for repair and was being worked on overnight the previous night. Nobody could have known in advance that the aircraft was even going to fly on 21st December, let alone which flight it would be allocated to. Evidence was also given that the hold had been checked before loading began, and there were no suitcases present at that time.

No doubt the system could be subverted. One obvious ploy might be for a terrorist to make a booking to travel to New York via KM180 and PA103, using a false name and false documents. He could check in the bomb suitcase as his luggage for the flight, and assuming he was prepared to fly across the Mediterranean in an aircraft with an unexploded bomb in the hold, all he then had to do was slope off at Frankfurt and allow the suitcase to continue without him. So long as the IED's disguise fooled the x-ray operator there, the plan would work, as Pan Am didn't reconcile passengers with luggage when dispatching flights. However, that didn't happen. There was no such booking.

A terrorist who was able to gain access to the airside area at Luqa might conceivably manage to switch the ready-tagged bomb suitcase for a legitimate item of luggage, so that the overall tally remained correct. However, that would result in a passenger reporting a piece of lost luggage. That didn't happen either. All the passengers on KM180 reported picking up their luggage at their destinations, with nothing going astray.

Or perhaps a terrorist might have an accomplice prepared to check in an extra item of luggage, which would be substituted for the bomb airside, then lie about having picked it up at his destination. Did that happen? The passengers who travelled on KM180 that day were investigated until their pips squeaked, and no such allegation was made in court against any of them. Table 1 (opposite) lists the thirty-nine people who flew on that flight.

'Interline' simply means that these passengers were booked on connecting flights, and checked their luggage to be conveyed all the way to their final destinations rather than collecting and rechecking it when changing planes. This luggage was handled by the airports separately from check-in luggage, and the minutiae and security of these internal transfer systems became very important in the Lockerbie inquiry because the bomb suitcase was believed to have made two such transfers – once as interline luggage from KM180 to the

Party	Names	Destination	Items of luggage	Interline?
1	**Emmanuel**, Josephine, Daniella and Lavinia **Caruana**	Miami	1	Yes
2	**Ulrich Schauen, Peter Mann, Andreas Köhle**r and **Agostino Iaia**	Köln (air)	17	Yes
3	**Zdeněk Krajnik, Jiři Stursa, Antoni Kostal** and **Jaroslav Burianek**	Prague	4	Yes
4	Ferdinand Lohbeck and Mrs. E. Lohbeck	Munster	4	Yes
5	**Manuel Farrugia**	Bremen	1	Yes
6	**Klaus Schickedanz**	Düsseldorf	1	Yes
7	**Günter Fricke**	Hanover	1	Yes
8	**Astrid Vella** (Camilleri)	Köln (rail)	1	Yes
9	Saviour Mallia and Louise Attard (Mallia)	Madeira	3	No
10	**Albert Schmid**	Hanover	0	No
11	**Peter Rothenpieler**	Hamburg	0	No
12	**Johannes Malz** and Mrs. P. Malz	Frankfurt	2	No
13	**Albert Bachmann** and **Michael Griesfeller**	Frankfurt	4 (?)	No
14	**Rolf Schneider**	Frankfurt	0	No
15	**Maria Ko**	Frankfurt	1	No
16	**Anna Brincat** (Poque)	Frankfurt	1	No
17	**Joseph Bonello**	Frankfurt	0	No
18	**Klaus Leibnitz**	Frankfurt	1	No
19	**Evelin Steinwandt**	Frankfurt	1	No
20	Michael Pernak and Mrs. C. Pernak	Frankfurt	3	No
21	Robert Lockett	Frankfurt	4	No
22	Edith Brünner	Frankfurt	1	No
23	Christine Calleja (Gauci-Maistre)	Frankfurt	1	No
24	Mr. B. and Mrs. C. Seliger	Frankfurt (?)	3	No (?)

Table 1: Passengers on flight KM180.

PA103 feeder flight at Frankfurt, and a second time as online luggage from the feeder flight to the transatlantic flight at Heathrow. Pedantically, 'interline' luggage denotes luggage transferring from one airline to another, while transfer luggage heading for another flight run by the same airline is termed 'online'.

No less than twenty-four of the KM180 passengers (names in bold) showed up at Camp Zeist, entered the witness box, and gave an account of their journey and the luggage they were carrying that day. The little vignettes of business travel, holidays, visits to girlfriends and boyfriends and grandmothers and so on can all be read in the court transcripts. Nobody from parties 4, 20, 21, 22 or 23 was available to give evidence, but accounts of their travels were entered into the record as uncontested. Inexplicably, Mr. and Mrs. Seliger were not mentioned in court at all, although they are recorded on the passenger list as being on the flight and having three items of luggage between them. It seems they were simply overlooked by the prosecution, who called all these witnesses.

This rather invites the question, if it was so important to have virtually every single passenger testify regarding their journey that morning, to the point of calling every member of a four-man TV crew and all four of a party of Czech businessmen individually, how come the Seligers and their three items of luggage were just forgotten about?

The number of checked-in items on the passenger list certainly adds up to fifty-five.

Mr. Griesfeller was recorded as having three checked-in items, but his ticket noted only two items. He himself didn't remember. He was a frequent traveller who had gone to Malta to repair some sort of machine. The records of his outgoing flight definitely showed three items, but he was uncertain whether he had brought all three back with him, as it was possible a spare part had been carried on the outbound flight. Nobody seems to have thought of asking his colleague Mr. Bachmann whether he could clear up the mystery.

Party 2 consisted of the director, two cameramen and a sound technician from Cologne, who had been in Malta making a travel documentary. They arrived at the airport together, but the director Ulrich Schauen took their hired minibus back to the car rental company while the other three went ahead to the check-in with their equipment. Each man had only one suitcase of personal belongings, but they shared out the film equipment between them for check-in. Some particularly valuable camera equipment was also carried as hand luggage.

The passenger list records Peter Mann and Andreas Köhler as having five checked-in items each, while Agostino Iaia had six. Ulrich Schauen, the last passenger to check in, only had his own suitcase. Nearly twelve years later at Camp Zeist the TV crew were all fairly hazy about exactly what had and what hadn't been checked in, however statements taken by the BKA in September of 1989 appeared to confirm the seventeen-item total. There was no evidence that the figure of seventeen items between them was in any way wrong, and all four men confirmed that everything had arrived safely on the connecting flight to Cologne as expected. Agostino Iaia, the sound technician, pointed out that if they had lost any equipment belonging to West Deutscher Rundfunk there would have been hell to pay.

The Caruana family, who were the only passengers on the flight booked to travel to the USA, were a particular focus of the early police inquiry. Someone, at some point, seems to have believed that their single suitcase was in fact the bomb, and communicated as much to the press. In the autumn of 1989 a newspaper report declared that the bomb suitcase was recorded on the KM180 passenger list as having been booked through to Miami from Malta via PA103 – which was complete nonsense.

Emmanuel Caruana was a manager with Air Malta who dealt with travel agency bookings and related matters, including staff discount travel applications. He was a fluent Arabic speaker (and gave evidence at Camp Zeist in English), who had worked in Libya for four years. He had a number of transatlantic tickets in his possession valid for late December, including one route to Florida which involved the PA103 feeder flight (but not the transatlantic leg) on 24th December. The Scottish police evidently regarded the whole story as highly suspicious.

However, the Caruana family was entirely innocent. Mr. Caruana was entitled to very generous staff discount travel, and had decided to take his wife and two little daughters (aged eight and five) to Disneyworld in Orlando for Christmas. Thanks to his position in Air Malta he was able to check out a variety of different routes, and because the flights were essentially free he had reserved more than one set of tickets. In the end he had settled on KM180 to Frankfurt then LH462 from Frankfurt to Miami on 21st December as being the best itinerary, and cancelled the rest. The family had gone straight from the KM180 arrival gate to the Lufthansa gate, as their Miami flight was already boarding by the time KM180 came on-block. Their suitcase was waiting for them in the baggage reclaim hall at Miami. There was no possibility that the Caruanas were mixed up in anything.

Saviour Mallia was perhaps a different story.

Saviour Mallia, a cargo officer to trade, was one of four other Air Malta employees who travelled on KM180. Anna Brincat, who by 2000 was married to a German citizen and living in Germany, gave evidence at Camp Zeist about her Christmas 1988 trip to visit her future husband, in an entirely straightforward manner. Christine Calleja (by then married to a Maltese citizen and still living in Malta) and Saviour Mallia both refused repeated witness citations, and the Scottish court had no power to compel foreign nationals to attend. In the end, however, Miss Calleja's evidence was accepted on the same basis as the evidence of a handful of German passengers who were unable to attend court. There was no mention of whether Louise Attard (by then Mrs. Saviour Mallia) had also declined to attend, but it appears likely.

The reason behind this blanket refusal, which extended to almost all the rank-and-file Air Malta staff, was the heavy-handed nature of the police investigation on Malta during 1989 and 1990. Having failed to find any trace in the KM180 baggage records to show that an unaccompanied suitcase had been illegitimately smuggled on to the plane, the police became convinced that one or more of the Maltese ground staff had conspired with the terrorists to cover up the introduction of the bomb at Luqa. Following complaints about telephone tapping and general harassment, the Maltese government twice asked the Lockerbie investigators to leave the island, and the situation for a time was very tense.

Matters were smoothed over and the investigation continued. However in 1993 the BBC Scotland documentary *Silence over Lockerbie* included explicit accusations from Vincent Cannistraro, a senior CIA officer involved in the Lockerbie inquiry, that the entire Luqa Airport operation had been suborned by Libya with wholesale forgery of the flight documentation. Nothing had changed by 2000 when the case came to trial, so it's hardly surprising the Maltese airport workers looked at the direction the Crown case was taking and declined to attend a court which seemed likely to be asked to consider that they were co-conspirators with the accused.

Bear in mind that it was the prosecution who were attempting to call the baggage handlers, not the defence. However the Crown appears to have had no particular theory about how the bomb suitcase had ended up on KM180 that it wished to demonstrate by presenting these witnesses. It seems likely the prosecution were merely hoping for a qualifying statement or a "maybe" from someone that could be spun as casting doubt on the main thrust of their evidence, as they achieved from Wilfred Borg, Sulkash Kamboj the Heathrow x-ray operator, Joseph Mifsud the Maltese meteorologist and Lawrence Whittaker the FBI agent. Nevertheless the majority of the Air Malta staff were having none of it.

Saviour Mallia had perhaps more reason to be concerned than most, given the details of his evidence concerning the luggage he had with him on the flight that morning. He did however provide a police statement which was read out in court. In it he confirmed that he and his fiancée Louise, also an Air Malta employee, had decided to spend Christmas 1988 in Madeira. Unlike the

Caruanas, who had pre-booked, they had chosen to fly on staff standby tickets which were subject to some restrictions. First, they would not be checked in until it was certain the flight was not full (that is, they would not know in advance whether they would indeed be on that particular flight), and second, they were not permitted to book luggage through to their final destination by the interline system, but would have to collect it and re-check it for each stage of their journey.

Saviour and Louise were almost the last to be checked in for the flight, with only Mr. Schauen the car-hire-returnee coming after them. The passenger list notes one item of checked-in luggage for Saviour and two for Louise. The problem was that when Saviour was first interviewed by Scottish detectives on 18th September 1989 he told them that the couple had only two suitcases between them. The discrepancy was noted by the police, leading to a request for a re-interview ten days later. At that interview Saviour admitted to three items in total. When asked why he had changed his story he replied that after the first interview he had spoken on the telephone to Louise, and this had reminded him of the third suitcase which did not belong to either of them but which he had agreed to take to Frankfurt as a favour for a friend.

The story that then emerged was nothing if not suspicious. Saviour had been asked by another Air Malta employee based in Frankfurt to carry a suitcase to Frankfurt on his behalf. This colleague was called Edwin Caruana, apparently no relation to Emmanuel. (The Maltese population seems to have only about a dozen surnames to go round, and the same few names reappear again and again throughout the Malta narrative. When one of them also turns up attached to the eminent Professor of Forensic Medicine at Edinburgh University who oversaw the post mortem examinations of the disaster victims, it all begins to seem a little surreal.)

Saviour had picked up the suitcase from Edwin's father at his house in Naxxar, on the evening of 20th December. He had no memory of what sort of case it was. He was told it contained clothes, but hadn't opened it to check the contents. The case was locked, and although he was given keys along with the suitcase, he hadn't even tried them in the lock.

The case apparently having been checked in by Louise rather than Saviour was never referred to, with Saviour's statement implying that he had been responsible for all three items carried by the couple. He testified to having picked the case up from the carousel at Frankfurt baggage reclaim, carried it through customs, and passed it over in the arrivals hall – either to Edwin Caruana himself, or to "another person by the name of Olensio" who was also an Air Malta employee, and like Edwin Caruana hailed from the adjacent island of Gozo. 'Olensio' was later identified as one Lorenzo Grazias, a Portuguese national. After handing over the suitcase, Saviour and Louise proceeded to board their onward flight to Lisbon.

On the way back from their holiday the couple (or perhaps Saviour alone) had in fact stayed with Edwin Caruana in his flat in Frankfurt for a few days. Saviour didn't remember Edwin having mentioned the suitcase at that time, but he supposed that if there had been any problem with it, Edwin would have told him. Oddly, Saviour had included an account of his return stopover in his original police statement, even though he completely "forgot" all about the mysterious locked suitcase and its earlier handover.

What are we supposed to make of this tale? Could the third Mallia suitcase have been the bomb, with the belated, rambling account of the Frankfurt handover invented in September to explain a discrepancy in the passenger list the conspirators had only just realised could be a problem?

It seems vanishingly unlikely. Even if Saviour could have been reasonably sure he would be on that flight, and was either fully complicit and prepared to fly to Frankfurt in a plane carrying an unexploded bomb or had in some way been duped into "forgetting" the extra suitcase and not picking it up at Frankfurt, the plan would also have depended on having an airside accomplice at Luqa able to switch the Frankfurt-destination tags on the case for interline tags directing it to PA103 as transfer baggage. It's also a racing certainty that the cover story would have been perfectly prepared and perfectly rehearsed, rather than calling attention to itself with incorrect statements unconvincingly 'corrected' by a complicated and disjointed narrative. Another racing certainty is that the Scottish police probed the backgrounds and contacts of Saviour, Louise, Edwin, Edwin's father and Lorenzo Grazias with particular care. Nothing was ever reported about this, which makes it pretty certain nothing relevant to the Lockerbie case was uncovered.

Perhaps the locked suitcase really did contain nothing more than warm clothes for a native of the Mediterranean condemned to spend winter in northern Europe. On the other hand, one has to bear in mind that Malta in the 1980s had something of a reputation as a conduit for drug smuggling from sources further east. It's not impossible that Saviour Mallia really did have something to hide from the cops, something he wasn't expecting to have to explain, hence his original injudicious "forgetting" about the locked suitcase which a moment's thought (possibly provided by Louise) would have demonstrated must have been recorded on the passenger list. Something to hide – but probably not the something that blew up over Lockerbie.

The Scottish detectives were right about one thing. If the bomb suitcase had been carried on KM180, there must have been an organised conspiracy involving several Air Malta airside staff to introduce it and ensure that the double-counting of the suitcases still tallied.

Perhaps the head loader for the flight had been bribed to report one item fewer than he really counted? The head loader for KM180 on 21st December 1988 was Michael Darmanin, who did not give evidence at Camp Zeist, but Wilfred Borg in his evidence vouched for him as a reliable employee. Like Saviour Mallia, he was still working for Air Malta in 2000.

Perhaps the ramp dispatcher had been bribed to 'hear' a different number from the number Darmanin communicated to him? Perhaps the check-in clerk had been bribed to record one more item of luggage from one party than was actually presented for check-in? This last would be very hit-and-miss, relying on a party such as the TV crew with an unusually large number of items to check in, or Mr. Griesfeller and his uncertainty over his luggage details, not only being present but being identifiable by the check-in agent.

One problem with this line of speculation is that none of these staff members had any idea they would be dealing with KM180 on the morning of 21st December 1988 until they came on-shift. Another is that a deliberate mis-count on its own would not have been sufficient to get the bomb suitcase on board – someone would have had to take the thing physically airside and add it to the luggage for the flight. It was repeatedly emphasised by Mr. Borg that this would have been an essentially impossible undertaking in view of the number of staff dealing with the baggage and the constant presence of the military airport guards.

Another problem is that all these possibilities were vigorously investigated by the police inquiry on Malta not just for months but for years, and no evidence of any dishonestly or complicity was ever discovered. Most of the Air Malta staff were Maltese nationals, and Malta is a devoutly Catholic country. No terrorist connections or sympathies were ever discovered, and the baggage handlers willingly testified in the civil action against Pan Am in the USA in 1992. Twenty-five years later, and still nobody on Malta has come forward with any relevant information or even suspicions.

Despite the years of effort and intrusive investigation, the police could present nothing but unsubstantiated speculation and baseless innuendo to explain the alleged introduction of the Lockerbie bomb into the hold of KM180 at Luqa. In court the Crown advanced no particular explanation for the alleged presence of the bomb suitcase on that flight, accused none of the passengers or the Air Malta staff of complicity in the atrocity, and failed even to mention Saviour Mallia's name in their closing submissions.

They were unable to show that Abdelbaset al-Megrahi had done anything while at the airport that morning other than catch his flight home. There was certainly no evidence he had gone airside, where he would have stuck out like a sore thumb, and he didn't even check in any luggage for his Tripoli flight. The trial judges at Camp Zeist noted this in their written judgement, acknowledging that "the absence of any explanation of the method by which the primary suitcase might have been placed on board KM180 is a major difficulty for the Crown case." They offered no explanation as to how they had overcome that difficulty.

The same difficulty was noted during Megrahi's first appeal (held at Camp Zeist in 2002) by Lord Osborne, who remarked, "there is considerable and quite convincing evidence that that [the smuggling of an unaccompanied suitcase on board KM180] could not have happened." He continued, "Now, it's quite difficult rationally to follow how the Court can take the step of saying, 'Well, we don't know how it got on to the flight. We can't say that. But it must have been there.' On the face of it, it may not be a rational conclusion."

Nevertheless the appeal judgement glossed over this point in much the same terms as the trial court, noting only that "it was to be remembered that the Crown case was that the security measures at Luqa had been deliberately circumvented by a criminal act." Exactly what this is supposed to mean is anybody's guess.

The Crown's original case was that Lamin Fhimah, the former Libyan Arab Airlines station manager at Luqa, who still had his airside pass despite having recently left his job, had actually introduced the bomb into the baggage chain. Fhimah had flown into Malta with Megrahi on the afternoon of 20th December and spent most of the day with him. However the prosecution failed to show that Fhimah had even been at the airport on the morning of the 21st, let alone that he had gone airside, and he was found not guilty of all charges.

It's often said that "you can't prove a negative". That's a reasonable rule of thumb, but there is a corollary. In certain circumstances, if a particular event has really occurred, a sufficiently diligent inquiry by competent investigators would be expected to discover evidence of it. If no such evidence is uncovered, it is perfectly reasonable to take the absence of evidence as a positive indication of the event's non-occurrence. Whether the Lockerbie investigators were competent or not is a matter for debate, but there is no doubt their inquiries on Malta were extremely diligent.

Despite all this, the judges decided that Megrahi's mere presence at the airport that morning proved that he had in some way engineered the levitation of the invisible unaccompanied fifty-sixth suitcase into the hold of KM180, and was thus guilty of mass murder.

3

FRANKFURT AM MAIN

The explanation for the Lockerbie investigation's obsession with Malta and KM180 is to be found not in the uneventful and unsuspicious departure of that flight from Luqa, but in a single piece of paper which emerged in Frankfurt in late January 1989. Several items of evidence have been described as the central key to this case, in particular the fragment of printed circuit board referred to as PT/35b, but that accolade belongs without a doubt to the computer database query printed out by IT technician Bogomira Erac the evening after the disaster, and kept by her as a souvenir of the event.

Frankfurt am Main was and is a major international hub airport, about as different from the backwater that was Luqa in the 1980s as it was possible to get. Rather than relying on muscle-power and trolleys to move the luggage to the planes, the airport had installed one of the first automated computer-controlled baggage transfer systems in the world. It was primitive compared to today's systems, designed only to forward luggage to the correct plane without any reference to whose it was or where it came from, but it was still way ahead of its time.

Figure 7
Inside the Frankfurt baggage transfer system, showing the bar-coded trays running on rails through the conduits which led all round the airport.

Understanding the operation of this system is essential to understanding how it came to be believed that an item of luggage had been unloaded from KM180 on its arrival at Frankfurt and transferred to the PA103 feeder flight, despite there being no record at Malta of any suitcase tagged to travel by that route.

On arrival at Frankfurt, luggage was unloaded from the aircraft by baggage handlers employed by the German airport, and sorted into two groups. Most of the passengers were terminating their journeys at Frankfurt, and their luggage was taken directly to baggage reclaim to be collected. This included the suitcases checked in by Saviour Mallia and Louise Attard, whose standby tickets didn't permit through booking of luggage. The luggage belonging to the rest of the passengers with through tickets to onward destinations was loaded into a wagon to be taken to the automated transit system. Due to the unusually large amount of luggage being carried by the television crew, who were booked through on a flight to Cologne, a total of thirty of the fifty-five items from KM180 were in this group. The system had a spur leading to the railway station, allowing Astrid Vella's suitcase to be handled as well, even though her ticket to Cologne was by train.

Luggage was entered into the automated system by coders who worked in pairs, one heaving the suitcases while the other entered the requisite details into the computer terminal, switching roles every wagon or two. There were twelve coding stations dealing with transfer luggage; five in the central hall of the airport (Halle Mitte) and seven at a temporary facility set up on the apron (Vorfeld), referred to as V3. The central hall stations were designated HM1 to HM5 and the V3 stations 201 to 207. Other coding stations at the check-in desks dealt with the luggage belonging to passengers beginning their journeys at Frankfurt.

Each item of luggage was placed in an individual bar-coded tray. The computer terminal automatically read the bar code and entered that number, the current time and the identity of the particular coding station. All the coder had to do was check the luggage tag and key in the correct code for the outgoing flight that item was due to travel on. Once in the system codes were added documenting the tray's journey through the conduits, culminating in its delivery to the correct baggage room to be loaded on to its outgoing flight.

In addition to entering the outgoing flight numbers, the staff operating the transfer coding stations were required to complete worksheets recording the incoming flight numbers of the wagons they were dealing with, and the start and finish times for dealing with each flight. They were also supposed to note the incoming flight number and time of any single stray items being entered. The primary purpose of the worksheets was to allow the various airline companies to be billed for the baggage handling services they received, however this also allowed the incoming flight to be figured out for individual entries in the computer system, by checking the appropriate worksheet for the number of the flight whose luggage was being coded at the time in question. The worksheet below is the one recording the unloading of KM180.

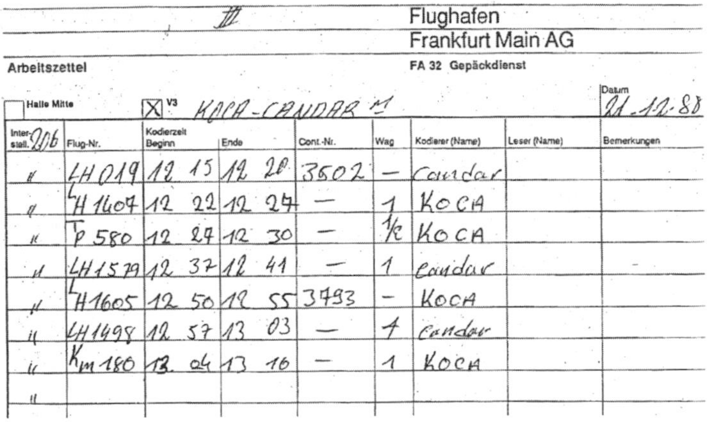

Flughafen Frankfurt Main AG									Datum 21.12.88
Arbeitszettel					FA 32 Gepäckdienst				
☐ Halle Mitte		☒ V3 KOCA-CONDAR M							
Inter-stell. 206	Flug-Nr.	Kodierzeit Beginn	Ende	Cont.-Nr.	Wag	Kodierer (Name)	Leser (Name)	Bemerkungen	
ḥ	LH019	12 15	12 20	3502	—	Condar			
ḥ	H1607	12 22	12 24	—	1	KOCA			
ḥ	P580	12 27	12 30	—	½	KOCA			
ḥ	LH1579	12 37	12 41	—	1	Condar		—	
ḥ	H1605	12 50	12 55	3493	—	KOCA			
ḥ	LH1498	12 57	13 03	—	4	Condar			
ḥ	KM180	13 04	13 16	—	1	KOCA			
ḥ									

Figure 8
Worksheet for V3 coding station 206, early afternoon.

These handwritten worksheets were naturally not perfect. Coders sometimes made errors, completed entries retrospectively, or wrote in illegible handwriting. In addition, it was known that the times entered might be slightly out of synchronisation with the computer clock, especially later in the day. It was also entirely possible for luggage to be entered into the system without any paper record being made, and as this would have no effect on the luggage's onward journey (so long as the correct flight had been entered into the computer), it was impossible to say how often it happened. Nevertheless the system worked with tolerable efficiency and was used from time to time to trace luggage which had become misrouted.

It should therefore have been possible to compile a detailed map of everything going through the automated baggage transfer system before 16.50 on 21st December 1988, when the PA103 feeder flight left Frankfurt for Heathrow. Unfortunately that didn't happen. The system had very limited data storage capacity, and by the time anyone on the German side of the inquiry realised the baggage records stored in the computer might be relevant, the information was gone, automatically over-written after a week.

That's right. Despite the doomed flight's Frankfurt origin being recognised from the earliest hours of the disaster, and the German police conducting interviews with baggage handlers only four days after the crash, nobody – not the police, not airport security, not the employees in the baggage handling department and not the baggage handlers themselves – recognised the importance of securing a back-up copy of that day's computer records. Nobody.

Various people familiar with the Frankfurt system have mentioned routine off-system back-ups, the possibility of saving data to floppy disc on demand, and routine hard-copy teletype printouts made for every flight and usually discarded after the flight had departed, but the fact remains, nothing of that sort was available to the inquiry. And without the computer data, the worksheets and other written records were so much waste paper.

The reaction within the German inquiry when this was discovered is not documented, but the Scottish detectives were seriously displeased when they were informed blandly that all the baggage records from the airport of origin of the flight they believed had carried the bomb into Heathrow had been lost. The debacle was a major cause of the poisonous distrust that marked the relationship between the two teams for the first eight or nine months of the inquiry.

In fact not all potentially useful information had been lost. Checked-in baggage was recorded on some ticket stubs and Pan Am had its own passenger list, but the potential for detecting the presence of a rogue or illegitimate bag from these data was limited. Passenger transfer message (PTM) telexes notifying the feeder flight crew of baggage from three Pan Am shuttle flights from Berlin which was normally transferred directly across the tarmac rather than being entered into the automated system were available, but their numbers appeared to tally and none of these passengers had transferred to the transatlantic flight.

One record of luggage transferred from other airlines (interline luggage) was preserved. It was Pan Am's practice to screen all such items by x-ray before they were loaded on to the flight, and it saw this practice as an acceptable substitute for physical baggage reconciliation and checking that the owners of these items were actually on board the plane. The x-ray operator Kurt Maier maintained a log of everything he x-rayed, and his log for PA103 on 21st December recorded thirteen items. He listed ten suitcases, two holdalls and a carton he believed contained half a dozen bottles of wine.

This information was utilised by the US Federal Aviation Authority inquiry which was carried out at Frankfurt in January 1989. The FAA report, as reprised by the President's Commission on Aircraft Security and Terrorism (PCAST) investigation which reported in May the following year, noted as follows:

This list shows that 13 parcels (including two garment bags and a box appearing to contain six wine bottles) passed through the machine on the way to the flight. Other records, however, account for only 12 parcels (11 checked by passengers who boarded the flight and one so called 'rush' bag of a passenger who had left on an earlier flight of another carrier).

This analysis is incorrect in its detail, but it is the first expression of a theme which surfaced again in the 1992 civil action in the USA, that Kurt Maier had x-rayed one more interline item than could be accounted for from the records of legitimate transfer luggage. Notably, the conclusion appears to have been reached without benefit of the crucial piece of evidence that surfaced at the end of January 1989.

The German investigators believed the computer data to be lost and gone forever, but this turned out not to be the case. Unbeknown to them, a small but vital extract had in fact been preserved in hard-copy form.

Bogomira Erac was an IT technician in the airport baggage handling department. In the witness box she described hearing about the crash of Pan Am 103 on her car radio as she drove home from work that evening. The following day, it was "virtually all that people talked about." (And it seems to have been assumed that the disaster plane had been a direct flight from Frankfurt, but absolutely nobody appears to have thought about saving the previous day's computer records.)

In the evening, when work was quiet, Bogomira gave in to an urge to play amateur detective. She interrogated the computer database for 21st December, which was of course still in existence at that time, and produced a printout of all the luggage trays that had been coded to be loaded on to PA103. She looked at the result, and unsurprisingly couldn't deduce much from it. She noted that no luggage appeared to have been left behind, and that there was a surprisingly small load for a transatlantic flight, and that was that.

In a later television interview Bogomira described being about to toss the printout in the waste paper basket, as would normally be done with the routine daily teletext printouts when they were finished with, but she hesitated, and laid it on the table instead. She thought about the passengers on the doomed flight, the owners of the bags enumerated on the printout, and decided to keep it as a memorial. She put it in her locker and forgot all about it.

A few days later she went on holiday to visit her family in Slovenia, as she did every year at New Year – her birthday was on 10th January. She returned on 15th or 16th January, but it was about a week later, she said, some time between 20th and 25th January, before she realised that her ghoulish little souvenir might in fact be the only surviving remnant of the vital computer data for the day of the Lockerbie disaster.

In this context it may be relevant to note that Michael Jones of Pan Am security in London travelled to Frankfurt on Monday 23rd January "to look for the documents in relation to the preparation of flight 103 from Frankfurt to London, in particular the cargo and baggage loading plan, who was responsible for loading the plane and what their duties were." He failed to find what he was looking for, possibly because the FAA investigators had got there before him. It may be however that it was his visit that prompted Bogomira's realisation that the computer data had been overwritten without any copy being secured.

Having come to this realisation, she went to her supervisor Kurt Berg with her story, and handed over the printout from her locker. His reaction was one of surprise, but also quite surprising. He asked Bogomira to make a further check of the filing cabinets to see whether any of the routine teletype printouts for 21st December still remained.

In late January? Had he not been involved in an exhaustive search when the loss was first discovered? Had the filing cabinets not been turned inside out at that time? Had nobody tried going through the rubbish for the discarded teletypes? It would seem perhaps not.

Be that as it may, Kurt Berg did the obvious thing and took the printout to the German police.

The essence of the printout is shown in figure 9, with the headers and the tray that turned out to be of such importance to the Lockerbie investigation displayed. (The printout itself is reproduced in full in Appendix A.)

Tray 8849, lower highlight, is the entire reason for the Lockerbie investigation moving to Malta. Using that line as an example, the code is

Figure 9

Detail of KIK computer printout saved by Bogomira Erac on 22nd December.

interpreted as follows. F1042 was the designation of the PA103 feeder flight, also referred to as PA103A (or occasionally PA103B). S0009 identified the coding station which dealt with the item, in this case the V3 station 206, and Z (zeit, time) 13.07 was the time the tray was coded into the system. TO stood for 'Tunnel Ost', the transit tunnel linking the V3 coding stations with the main system. HS33 designated the internal store where the tray was parked to await the call for the baggage for the appropriate flight, and Z15.17 was the time the tray left the store in response to the call for the PA103A baggage which was given to the system at 15.12. B044 was the baggage room designated for the bulk of the luggage for that flight, although a few late-arriving items were directed straight to B041 after the baggage handling was switched there for operational reasons. Z15.23 was the time the tray was actually delivered to the baggage room.

The first analysis of the printout was carried out by German police officer Jürgen Fuhl, assisted by Kurt Berg. After a skeletal report on 2nd February 1989 which merely noted the presence of twenty-five transfer bags, a more detailed report was submitted on 21st February. This was a seriously flawed analysis, to put it politely.

There were 111 trays listed on the printout altogether, eighty-six being entered at coding stations located at the check-in desks and the remaining twenty-five entered at coding stations in either the central hall or the V3 location – transfer luggage from other flights. Little information is available about the eighty-six check-in items other than that the BKA believed they tallied with the information they already had from other sources. Whether or not that is true, it is the twenty-five transfer items that are important, because these are the group whose analysis eventually led the Scottish investigators to Malta over six months later.

You'd think all Fuhl and Berg had to do was check which coding station had coded each of the twenty-five transfer trays, check the relevant worksheets to see which flights were being coded at the time, then check the passenger lists for these flights to see which passengers were booked to travel on PA103A, job done. They did that, but it didn't work out as expected.

The nine flights listed in the report dated 21st February were as follows.

AI (Air India) 465	Sydney – Singapore – Bombay	2 items
AI 165	Bombay – Delhi – Frankfurt	5 items
LH (Lufthansa) 631	Kuwait – Frankfurt	3 items
LH 1453	Vienna – Frankfurt	5 items
LH 177	Nürnberg – Frankfurt	6 items
AZ (Alitalia) 422	Rome – Frankfurt	1 item

KM (Air Malta) 180	Malta – Frankfurt	1 item
PA 643	Berlin – Frankfurt	1 item
PA 647	Berlin – Frankfurt	1 item

The problem with this is that about half of it is simply wrong. The report didn't mention how these flights related to passengers transferring to PA103A, but the fact is that KM180 is far from the only one with no legitimate luggage for the feeder flight. *Half the flights on the list* weren't carrying any transfer passengers, and indeed the first flight listed doesn't actually seem to go to Frankfurt! In terms of reconciling the twenty-five items of transfer baggage this exercise was an abject failure, with fourteen or fifteen of the trays not matched to luggage destined for the feeder flight.

There was another problem Fuhl didn't even seem to notice, despite interviewing Kurt Maier three times about the x-ray screen. While Maier had recorded x-raying only thirteen items of luggage which arrived in the PA103A departure baggage room bearing luggage tags from other airlines, the analysis above records no less than twenty-three of the transfer items against non-Pan Am flight numbers. This is grossly at variance with the findings of the FAA investigation which was carried out about the same time, where it was concluded from an examination of the incoming passenger records that only twelve legitimate interline items could be identified.

Despite the uncertainty the BKA tried to follow up the flights identified as apparently carrying unaccompanied luggage for PA103A. One of these was found to be quite straightforward, with paperwork provided by Alitalia showing a legitimate item of lost luggage being sent to catch up with its owner in the USA. That still left four flights and fourteen items of luggage. Wilfred Borg provided the 'ship's papers' for KM180, and Emmanuel Caruana was interviewed about his booking to Miami, but everything there appeared to be in order.

Not only could no bag from Malta be discovered, at least thirteen more items remained unaccounted for. Given the sheer number of untraceable baggage trays there was really no reason to believe any particular one of them was the bomb, and the German police gave up. They appear to have been so thrown by the impenetrability of the worksheets they decided the whole thing was a complete waste of time. They didn't share the printout with the Scottish police, and simply held to the line that no useful baggage records had been preserved at Frankfurt.

Nothing else happened for six months.

* * * * * * *

The Scottish investigators appear to have been seriously frustrated during the first half of 1989. They were entirely certain that the bomb suitcase had been transferred across the tarmac from the feeder flight, but their investigations were not going well. Initial suspicions that student Karen Noonan had been duped into carrying the bomb in her luggage, possibly as a favour for her Jordanian acquaintance, came to nothing. Not only that, but forensic examination of the recovered luggage seemed to suggest that the bomb had been in a brown plastic simulated leather hardshell case which was proving impossible to reconcile to any of the legitimate passengers and certainly hadn't belonged to either Karen or her friend Patricia Coyle.

In early August a group of Scottish detectives travelled to the forensics laboratory in Kent to examine the blast-damaged clothing recovered from the crash scene. The forensic scientists had attempted to divide it into two groups – items which appeared to have been in the bomb suitcase itself, packed with the bomb, and items (like Karen's clothes) which appeared to have been in luggage loaded right up against the bomb suitcase.

They returned to Scotland after a few days with photographs and descriptions of a number of miscellaneous items, including a pair of pyjamas, a cardigan, a tweed jacket and a pair of checked trousers. The checked trousers were interesting, in that the maker's name was visible on a label – 'Yorkie'. This was an unfamiliar brand, and despite its English connotations did not appear to be an English company.

After following up some dead ends someone remembered that another piece of blast-damaged clothing, a badly shredded Babygro identified in May 1989, carried the label 'Made in Malta'. Inquiries on Malta in May had come to nothing because the distributor had no records of the retail outlets the garments had been supplied to. This time the Maltese inquiries were more fruitful, and in early September the trousers were traced not just to their manufacturer but to the shop which had sold them to a customer.

This line of investigation was developing fast when one of the periodic international case conferences was convened, this time in Meckenheim, West Germany, with detectives from the different forces meeting in person to compare notes. The Scottish detectives told their BKA counterparts about the clothes, and their Maltese provenance. The BKA detectives shuffled in embarrassment, then went to find Jürgen Fuhl's report. This time, the tray linked to KM180 from Malta seemed to leap out with special significance.

The Scottish detectives were understandably furious, then galvanised. Nobody seems to have asked just how reliable the conclusions from the printout actually were, or whether there were other trays that couldn't be reconciled to legitimate passenger luggage and might be worth investigating.

Malta was where the clothes had come from, Malta was where KM180 had come from, and it was the answer they had been looking for.

The German investigators seem to have realised there was a problem though, and as the investigation in Malta ramped up, Jürgen Fuhl was told to go back and have another go. The tortuous saga of this exercise, the dead ends and the missed opportunities and the wasted effort, is frankly painful to relate.

The full story, the 'director's cut', if you like, is laid out in Appendix A. The short version is that Fuhl's February report had misidentified many of the flights – four of the nine listed were complete red herrings. However, rather than reconsider whether his interpretation of the printout and worksheets was mistaken, he expended an enormous amount of time and effort following up a couple of flights that quite obviously had nothing to do with the case. It wasn't until about December 1989 that it occurred to him to look at the *passengers* on flights PA103A/PA103 and the actual luggage recovered at Lockerbie, to ascertain whether some of the transfer items could be identified by that method. At this point he finally caught on to a number of relevant pieces of information that both the FAA and the Scottish investigators had been aware of since the earliest days and weeks of the inquiry.

His final report, dated 2nd July 1990, is anything but a literary masterpiece. It is rambling, repetitive, riddled with errors and in places close to incoherent, but it documents what was in the end a thorough and painstaking investigation. Fuhl wasn't an uncritical adherent of the "there must have been an unaccompanied bag on KM180" school of thought, and once he finally found the right track he pursued it conscientiously. He identified two more flights which really did have transfer baggage for PA103A. He doggedly hunted for some legitimate item of luggage that might have been in tray 8849. He failed – but then, he also failed to trace anything that might have been in at least five of the other trays on the printout, which puts *that* into a bit of perspective.

The twenty-five transfer items on the printout actually fall into eight groups, corresponding to eight incoming flights, not nine. Summarising the information laboriously tracked down by Fuhl over many months, the final tally can be seen in Table 2 opposite (names of Lockerbie victims in bold).

Flights A and B, the first two groups to arrive, relate to delayed incoming flights. This luggage was supposed to be carried on the previous Pan Am flight taking a similar route to 103, PA107 which flew Frankfurt–Heathrow–Washington–Detroit and departed at 11.00. Both LH241 and PA637 landed late at about 10.40, which simply wasn't enough time for the baggage to make the connection.

Adolf Weinacker, who was travelling to Detroit, missed his connection to PA107 and was re-booked by Pan Am on to PA103. When he discovered that

	Number coded	Flight	From	Passengers	Number identified
A	2	LH241	Munich	Adolf Weinacker (2)	2
B	11	PA637	Berlin	Fiona Leckie, Thomas Trautmann, Gerd Pilz (2), **Kenneth Gibson**, John Hubbard (2)	7
C	5	LH1453	Vienna	**Karen Noonan** (3), **Patricia Coyle** (2)	5
D	1	[KM180]	[Malta]		0
E	1	PA643	Berlin	Wiebke Wagenführ	1
F	1	AZ422	Rome	Susan Costa	1
G	3	LH631	Kuwait	**Thomas Walker** (3)	3
H	1	[LH1071]	[Warsaw]		0

Table 2: Reconciliation of transfer items to arriving flights.

103 didn't leave until 16.50 he complained to Lufthansa, who booked him on one of their own flights to Chicago, connecting to Detroit. It was however impossible to do anything about his luggage, which had already been entered into the automated system coded for PA103A, and wouldn't be regurgitated until the baggage for that flight was called for about quarter past three. His two suitcases therefore travelled unaccompanied on the feeder flight, were transferred to *Maid of the Seas* at Heathrow, and ended up on the ground at Lockerbie.

Fiona Leckie, Thomas Trautmann and Gerd Pilz were all on board PA637. They were able to make the connection to PA107 by running for the departure gate, but at the cost of becoming separated from their suitcases. As they were only booked as far as Heathrow their re-booked luggage wasn't transferred to the transatlantic flight from PA103A, and lost-and-found records were traced in London documenting the ensuing lost luggage claims.

Kenneth Gibson, a young US serviceman stationed in Berlin who was returning home for Christmas, inexplicably missed PA637 after checking in for the flight. He arrived at Frankfurt on the next shuttle, PA639, which landed well after PA107 had left. Pan Am booked him on PA103 at his own request, although there was an earlier flight available which would have taken him to his destination. Sadly, he was attracted by the idea of flying via London, a city he had never visited. Thus he was travelling almost by chance on the same flight as the suit carrier he had become separated from at Berlin Tegel airport, which had preceded him on PA637 and been re-booked with the above group.

John Hubbard was a Pan Am pilot, also based in Berlin, who needed to send two suitcases of personal possessions home to Seattle, although his duty rota required him to fly to Karachi. Staff members were permitted to send personal items unaccompanied through the 'rush tag' system, and Mr. Hubbard decided to send his suitcases from Berlin to Heathrow on 21st December to fly on the direct Pan Am flight from London to Seattle on 22nd December. One case did exactly that, and was delivered to his house on the afternoon of the 22nd. The other one was inexplicably found on the grass at Lockerbie. The most probable explanation is that the case was mistakenly sent to the transfer luggage container during the rushed unloading of the delayed feeder flight, by a baggage handler who noticed the US destination on the tag and mistakenly thought it was intended for the New York flight.

There is no record on the relevant worksheets of the coding of either group A or group B. The worksheets were primarily intended as a record for internal billing purposes, and the potential for tracing individual items of luggage through the system was merely a handy side-effect. It was commonplace for items being re-booked after having missed their outgoing flight not to be recorded on the paperwork, as in this case.

Flight C represents the text-book example where everything does what it's supposed to do, and was the one presented in detail at Camp Zeist as an example to show how the printout should be analysed. The two passengers in question were Karen Noonan and Patricia Coyle, both only twenty years old, friends from Maryland and Connecticut respectively who were studying education at Boston College in Massachusetts. Their ambition was to become primary school teachers, and as part of their studies they had spent the autumn term of 1988 on an exchange programme in Vienna. They had originally booked to return home on 21st December on a direct flight from Vienna to New York, however when they showed up together at the Pan Am office in Vienna on 20th December to confirm their flight they were informed that it had been taken off the winter timetable. The office re-booked them on PA103, and arranged tickets with Lufthansa to take them to meet up with that flight at Frankfurt.

Karen was carrying three holdalls (two blue ones and a green one) and Tricia had a navy-blue canvas American Tourister suitcase with maroon trim, and a maroon holdall. Five lines in the computer printout document the passage of these items through the Frankfurt baggage transfer system. Later, one of Karen's holdalls and Tricia's suitcase were loaded right up against the bomb suitcase in

AVE4041, and some of Karen's clothes were found singed by the explosion that destroyed the plane. That was the reason behind the early suspicions that she had been duped into carrying the bomb in her luggage, suspicions which caused her family enormous distress on top of the loss of their much-loved daughter.

Tricia's suitcase became crucial at a much later stage, and was eventually of seminal importance in supporting the case for the bomb having travelled from Malta, as it was presented at Camp Zeist.

Flight D is the single item which was a worksheet match for KM180 from Malta. The worksheet reconciliation is correct, with the tray in question (no. 8849) being coded right in the middle of the KM180 coding window. However, as we know, there was no luggage carried on KM180 which was tagged to be transferred to PA103A.

Flight E was another of the hourly Pan Am shuttle flights from Berlin. Luggage coming in on these shuttles for other Pan Am flights was usually sent straight over the tarmac in wagons without going through the automated system, as noted above. However the single item carried by PA643, arriving before the outgoing flight even had a confirmed departure gate, was entered into the central system. Because of this, the single suitcase arriving on PA643 appears twice in the written records – once on the PTM telex, and a second time as tray 8042 on the computer printout. This case belonged to Wiebke Wagenführ, who disembarked from the feeder flight at Heathrow.

Flight F, AZ422, was not carrying any passengers for PA103, but it did have an item of legitimate unaccompanied luggage. Susan Costa had flown from Rimini to New York via Rome on 19th December, but when she arrived in the USA she discovered that one of her suitcases was missing. The missing item was identified by Alitalia and tagged to be sent on to her two days later. Lost luggage being returned to its owner like this was dealt with by attaching a conspicuous 'rush tag' to the item which identified it as legitimately unaccompanied, and to be sent to its destination by the most expedient route irrespective of which carrier it had originally been booked to travel with. The Costa item initially caused some confusion to the Lockerbie forensic team, because *two* suitcases appeared to reconcile to this single item. It was eventually discovered that the suitcases had been packed one inside the other, and had been blown apart by the explosion in AVE4041.

Flight G is another text-book example where the worksheet match for the computer data identified a passenger transferring to PA103 from the incoming flight. Thomas Walker, a first class passenger who also hailed from Massachusetts, was an engineering specialist who had flown to Kuwait to repair a complex piece of medical equipment. He was carrying a black suitcase, a black briefcase, and a carton containing ophthalmological instruments.

Flight H represents another serious mistake in the initial analysis of the printout. This was another single tray, tray 5620, and the worksheet match for the computer data is undoubtedly flight LH1071 from Warsaw. The tray was coded at the same coding station as Mr. Walker's luggage and the two flights appear on the same worksheet as illustrated in figure 10. However, just as with KM180, there was no luggage on LH1071 tagged to be transferred to PA103A.

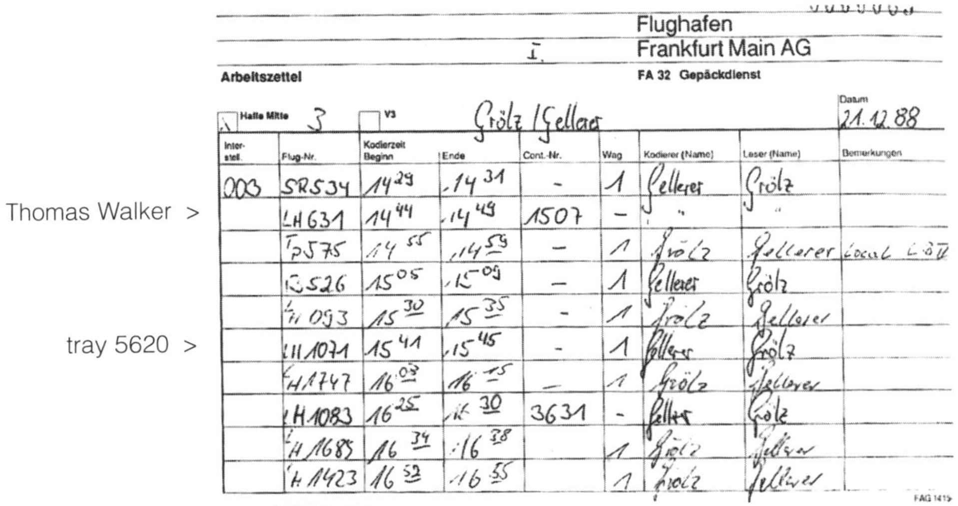

Figure 10
Worksheet for coding station HM3, afternoon.

Fuhl's February report didn't mention LH1071. Instead tray 5620 was attributed to another Berlin shuttle, PA647. The luggage from PA647, twenty-one items altogether, was transferred across the tarmac. It's presumably not entirely impossible that a stray suitcase might have been taken to the coding stations by mistake, but PA647 was coded at a different coding station from LH1071, and its coding window ended two minutes before tray 5620 was entered into the system. This error was corrected at the beginning of Fuhl's October do-over, but the result was that the Warsaw flight was not identified as being of interest to the inquiry until after the Lockerbie investigators were already committed to the Malta flight as the one with the bomb in it. Luqa airport was turned over by the cops. There is no record of a single Scottish policeman going anywhere near Warsaw.

Once he realised that passenger movements were important, Jürgen Fuhl extended his inquiries in that department. In addition to the twenty passengers on the later Berlin shuttles whose luggage was transferred across the tarmac, seventeen more passengers were identified as having arrived at Frankfurt on other incoming flights. Francis Boyer, who flew in from Toulouse on a Lufthansa flight which landed about three o'clock, was at one point believed to have interlined his luggage, at least by the US branch of the inquiry. This however turned out not to be the case, and like a couple of other passengers he collected his suitcase at the carousel in Frankfurt and re-checked it at the Pan Am check-in desk. The remaining fourteen transfer passengers had no hold luggage on PA103A, for various reasons.

Fuhl also identified another six items of luggage from other incoming Pan Am flights which had missed PA107 for one reason or another. However the lost luggage records at Heathrow indicated that all six had arrived on other flights, not on PA103A. No information seems to be recorded as to whether any other items were left behind on the Heathrow carousel which could not be reconciled to a passenger.

The reconciliation of four of the eight groups, those designated C, E, F and G, is incontrovertible. Legitimate luggage transfers for PA103A were confirmed from the flights identified on the coders' worksheets. Groups A and B are less certain.

While the two-item group A is the probable reconciliation for Mr. Weinacker's two suitcases, it's also possible they could have been amalgamated with the luggage from PA637, which missed PA107 at approximately the same time as LH241. In that case, they were two of the unidentified items in group B, and group A is as big a mystery as groups D and H.

Although seven items which appear to have been carried on PA637 are credited to group B, only two of these are supported by documentary proof. The lost luggage records for Mrs. Leckie's and Mr. Trautmann's suitcases note PA103 (A) as the flight on which they arrived at Heathrow. The equivalent record for Mr. Pilz's cases doesn't. While a checked-in suit carrier was credited to Ken Gibson in the overall Lockerbie baggage reconciliation, it wasn't recovered on the ground, and there is no hold luggage recorded against his name on the PA637 passenger list. There is no paperwork confirming the route taken by Mr. Hubbard's rush-tagged suitcases between Berlin and Heathrow.

Thus, while two of the items in group B are certain, five more are simply in the 'good guess' category. Continuing the guessing game, it seems likely that all eleven items in the group arrived at Frankfurt on PA637, although since the other four passengers on that flight who were booked through to Heathrow had no checked-in luggage, the final four must have been rush-tagged items like Mr. Hubbard's cases.

Mr. Hubbard's mishandled suitcase demonstrates that it was in fact perfectly feasible for an item of luggage to pass through the system without leaving any trace whatsoever apart from a line in the computer record. His other suitcase did exactly that. If one hadn't been erroneously loaded on to *Maid of the Seas*, both would have been delivered to his home in Seattle without any further remark and without any way to figure out how they got there, or that they had anything at all to do with the Lockerbie investigation. It's possible that the four unidentified items in group B were more rush-tagged luggage being sent from Berlin to Heathrow that morning, but in the absence of any records at Berlin Tegel, that remains speculative.

Groups D and H are utterly mysterious. Both were single items apparently coded at a time and a place where no legitimate luggage for PA103A was being handled. We're completely out of legitimate luggage to reconcile to either of them. More lost, misrouted or rush-tagged cases being shuttled to Heathrow? Who knows. The fact is, though, that it has happened twice, and in the context of a significant number of other items being less than conclusively reconciled. Tray 8849 is anything but an isolated anomaly shrieking "bomb here!"

★　★　★　★　★　★　★

The other aspect which might help clarify the nature of the transfer luggage loaded on to the feeder flight is Kurt Maier's x-ray log. Maier was Pan Am's excuse for not bothering with the pesky chore of checking that every item of baggage being transferred to one of its flights from a different airline was actually attached to a live, breathing passenger seated on the plane. Instead, all such luggage was to be x-rayed, and if the minimally-trained low-wage x-ray operator didn't see anything suspicious, well that was all right then.

Everything without a Pan Am check-in tag was pulled out by baggage handler Kilinc Tuzcu and sent to Maier to x-ray. Maier noted in his contemporaneous log that he screened thirteen items – ten suitcases, two holdalls and a carton apparently containing six wine bottles. These were supposedly all the non Pan Am items in the waiting stack.

The eleven known items of interline luggage include four holdalls (three belonging to Karen Noonan and one to Tricia Coyle), a briefcase (belonging to Thomas Walker) and five suitcases, which suggests Maier mistook two of the holdalls and the briefcase for suitcases. He was right about the carton of glassware though. Another of Mr. Walker's three checked-in items was a carton containing ophthalmological instruments – something Jürgen Fuhl inexplicably failed to pick up on, lamenting that … *ein eingecheckter Karton – insbesondere von einem Interline-Passagier – könnte nicht ermittelt werden.* "… a checked-in carton – in particular one from an interline passenger – could not be identified."

Twenty-five items of transfer luggage, but only thirteen x-rayed. That implies that twelve of the transfer items were carrying Pan Am check-in tags, thus classifying them as online rather than interline transfers. Eleven items from PA637 and one from PA643 indeed makes twelve, which rather supports the assumption that the entire eleven-item batch of group B did in fact consist of luggage flown in on the delayed shuttle. This implies that both single mystery items were interline, and so both were x-rayed. It's a reasonable enough assumption, but we're some way down the guesswork channel by this time.

Thinking about rush tags in the context of the x-ray screen invites even more guesswork. Tuzcu stated that he thought there were two rush-tagged items in the group he pulled out for PA103A that afternoon, though it's debatable just how reliable that recollection can really be. Susan Costa's case definitely had a rush tag. Adolf Weinacker's didn't, because he was originally re-booked on to PA103 when he missed PA107. The other eight interline items were accompanied. If Tuzcu's memory was correct that would imply that one of the two mystery cases had a rush tag and one didn't, but by this point, who knows?

Another little wrinkle is that Pan Am standard operating procedure mandated that *all* rush-tagged luggage be x-rayed, even if it was carrying a Pan Am tag. Pan Am's defence team used this point in their defence of the civil action for damages raised against them in the US in 1992 by some of the relatives of the victims. Their argument was that there was no discrepancy in the x-ray log, because the additional x-rayed item would have been Mr. Hubbard's rush-tagged online case. This doesn't really fly, though. Whichever way you slice it, there must have been more than one rush-tagged suitcase on PA637, probably six in total, and there simply isn't room in the x-ray log for them all to have been screened. Tuzcu initially wasn't clear whether he'd pulled out the online rush-tagged luggage, though he became more 'certain' as it dawned on him that he was actually supposed to be doing that. However, the numbers just don't add up. The online rush-tagged items *can't* have been x-rayed.

The crucial question as regards the x-ray screen, however, is this – if the bomb suitcase was indeed among the thirteen x-rayed items, would Maier have spotted the booby-trapped radio-cassette recorder? There is really no satisfactory answer to this question.

The main reason for disguising an improvised explosive device as a radio-cassette player is to fool a security inspection. Nevertheless it should not have fooled that security inspection on that day. A major recurring theme in all discussions of the Lockerbie disaster is the Frankfurt police operation codenamed *Herbstlaub* ('Autumn Leaves'), which took place in October 1988. The BKA had become aware that a number of known terrorists associated with a group known as the Popular Front for the Liberation of Palestine – General Command were congregating in the town of Neuss, a suburb of Düsseldorf, about 230 km from Frankfurt. This group had been responsible for a number of aircraft bombings in the 1970s, using devices triggered to explode by the fall in internal pressure that occurs in the first few minutes after takeoff. Fearful that further attacks in the same vein were being planned, the BKA swooped on 26th October. An entire arsenal of bomb-making paraphernalia was discovered, including – in the boot of a Ford Cortina – a Toshiba RT-F453D radio-cassette player which proved to have been modified into an IED triggered by an altitude-sensitive device. The convoluted and bizarre circumstances of the arrest and subsequent release of the PFLP-GC gang are outwith the scope of this book, but the saga is recounted in detail elsewhere, with *The Fall of Pan Am 103* by Steven Emerson and Brian Duffy (1990) containing a wealth of information.

The relevance to the PA103A interline luggage is that as a result of this incident, the security staff at Frankfurt airport were issued with a specific warning to look out for IEDs disguised as radio-cassette recorders. Kurt Maier had received that warning and seen the illustrations of the Toshiba in question, and he was well aware that radios and other consumer electronics in suitcases were potential trouble. The thing that muddied the waters in this respect was that in his police interviews Maier indicated that he had devised his own little system to decide whether a radio was likely to be a bomb or not. He looked for apparent modifications to the set, and in particular seemed to believe that if the mains plug of the radio was present, it was safe.

This was simply wrong. The IEDs produced by Marwan Khreesat, the PFLP-GC's bomb-maker, were almost impossible to distinguish from unmodified sets on a security screen, and indeed were actually capable of functioning as radios. And any radio, no matter how lethal, can have a mains plug attached. Would Maier have allowed a radio-cassette player to pass without comment if he had seen the all-important mains plug, or would he have called his supervisor regardless, or at the very least made a note of having seen such an item in his log-book?

This point became crucial when the civil action came to court. Maier was the sole defence against a bomb being infiltrated on to that aircraft in the way the police investigation believed the Lockerbie bomb had been infiltrated, and it was in the interests of the plaintiffs to prove that this defence was inadequate. Pan Am's lawyers, of course, were keen to demonstrate that Maier was a dependable, impregnable barrier.

Maier's evidence wasn't wholly reassuring, and without doubt he had not received adequate training. However, as discussed in the following chapter, there were language difficulties, and in any case Maier was on a hiding to nothing. The US court had already decided that the bomb had flown in from Malta, relying on the precedents of the Scottish Fatal Accident Inquiry findings, and most crucially the dual US/Scottish indictments of Abdelbaset al-Megrahi and Lamin Fhimah, which had been issued in 1991 and which explicitly alleged that precise *modus operandi*. The question really boiled down to whether or not Pan Am's actions in substituting suitcase x-ray for passenger reconciliation and then just leaving Maier to get on with it as best he could amounted to wilful misconduct.

Maier, for his part, appeared to be trying to say that in the light of the Autumn Leaves warning he would have regarded any radio-cassette player as suspicious, plug or not, and pulled it out for further investigation. It's hard to be sure, though, that this wasn't just the same sort of hindsight that saw Tuzcu become convinced he'd pulled the online rush-tag luggage out for screening.

Nevertheless the fact is that the Lockerbie investigation's pet theory required a bomb disguised as a Toshiba radio-cassette recorder to have passed through a security check manned by someone who had been specifically warned of the danger of bombs disguised as Toshiba radio-cassette recorders, and that person recorded in his log book, *im Monitor sah man keine besonderen Kennzeichen*. "Nothing of particular note was seen on the monitor."

★ ★ ★ ★ ★ ★ ★

Fuhl's final conclusions as they appear in his report are largely an exercise in fence-sitting, but the sting is in the tail.

Reasons in favour of the transfer from KM180

This conclusion is rendered significant by the findings of RARDE (the Royal Armament Research and Development Establishment, where the Lockerbie evidence was examined) who reported that the bomb suitcase contained textiles which had been purchased in a shop on Malta.

It was always technically possible that a detonation system had been used which exploded after a predetermined number of flights, assuming that a simple countdown timer was not employed.

Accomplices would not be required in either London or Frankfurt.

By smuggling a suitcase containing explosives from Malta, the perpetrator would have had a good chance of succeeding.

The computer printout lists an item of luggage coded for PA103A in hall V3 at 13.07.

Reasons against the transfer from KM180

This item of luggage cannot be said with certainty to originate from KM180 for the following reasons.

- In several cases the interline writers' records were not found in the worksheets
- Entries in the worksheets did not always agree with the input point
- The recorded start and end times of the coding sometimes varied from the computer clock
- Baggage inputs were not consistently documented in the worksheets
- Human error, in that baggage is not always loaded on to the intended aircraft. In order to conceal such a mistake, the person responsible might load this baggage on to the next aircraft, without involving the other Pan Am stations
- Errors occurred due to the direct transfer of online baggage from aircraft to aircraft. The absence of documentation of these items makes a definite conclusion impossible
- Erroneous routing via the forwarding system can only be detected by the responsible baggage worker at the point of exiting the system if that person recognises that falsely routed piece of baggage

In particular the workers directly related with baggage for PA103A were questioned, and none of them could remember a case from Malta.

In relation to this the Alert x-ray operator stated that prior to 21st December 1988, he had been informed about a transistor radio bomb and had at that time seen an illustration in regard to this. Since then he has paid attention to radio sets he sees, to establish if additional parts have been fitted and if the set is operational.

If he is in any doubt the item of baggage is secured and the passenger is brought by the supervisor, who must then identify his baggage and open it. If further doubt exists then the owner must operate the set.

During the x-raying of the baggage for PA103A he did not notice any suspicious item, which he would otherwise have checked according to his knowledge for a radio-bomb and recorded in his duty report (see the interview of Kurt Maier).

The former Alert tutor stated that he had informed the x-ray operator about the Toshiba radio warning bulletin and shown him the informational material (see interview of Oliver Koch).

Throughout the inquiries into the baggage for PA103A there was no evidence that the bomb suitcase had been transferred with the luggage either from or via Frankfurt Main to London.

This report is anything but a ringing endorsement of the theory that tray 8849 contained the Lockerbie bomb being transferred to PA103A from KM180. The "reasons in favour" are merely a re-hash of the Scottish detectives' original rationale for believing that the bomb had come from Malta – in essence, that the coincidence of the clothes in the bomb suitcase having been purchased on Malta and the computer printout appearing to show an item of luggage being transferred from a flight from Malta must be significant. The "reasons against" boil down to two points. The documentary evidence is far too confusing to prove anything, and Kurt Maier didn't see anything significant when he x-rayed the interline luggage for the feeder flight.

Jürgen Fuhl certainly took the scenic route, and dropped more than a few stitches on the way, but it's difficult to argue with the overall thrust of his conclusions on the basis of the evidence available to him. His analysis ultimately ran into the sand not through lack of application, but through lack of essential information. It is simply not possible to figure out what was in tray 8849 – it can't be shown to be an item of legitimate passenger luggage, but equally, it can't be shown to be the bomb.

The elephant in this particular room is of course the missing data. Not just the missing Pan Am records of transferred and re-booked baggage, referred to repeatedly in Fuhl's report, but the missing 99% of the computer records for 21st December 1988, lost in the very first days of the inquiry. It is the absence of these data that necessitates the guesswork and speculation Fuhl resorted to in his attempts to find some way to explain the unidentified luggage trays, as described in Appendix A.

It should not be necessary to stare at the V3 206 worksheet and wonder whether Yaser Koca intended to write 13.10 or 13.16. It should not be necessary to speculate whether luggage from LH669 might or might not have been coded at station 206 at about that time. It should not even be necessary to count cameras and sound consoles to figure out whether the TV crew from Cologne really did check in seventeen items of luggage.

The onward destinations of all thirty interline items documented as having been carried on KM180 were known. The computer loading list relating to LH140 Frankfurt–Köln would have answered a huge number of questions all by itself. What times were recorded for the coding of the seventeen items carried by the TV crew, and indeed the rest of the thirty interline items from Malta? Did they match the worksheet record or not? Were all thirty items coded as a discrete batch, or were other items interspersed? Were there indeed thirty items, as documented?

The simple fact is that if a back-up disc or tape of the computer data for the day of the disaster had been secured by the German police or Frankfurt airport security before the whole thing was irretrievably over-written a week later, it would have been possible to see exactly what had been coded at station 206 in the minutes either side of 13.07. It should have been these 30 items from KM180, but was it? In the context of the full dataset, would tray 8849 still look like part of the Malta group, or not? We can never know, now. We can speculate with Jürgen Fuhl until hell freezes over, but the knowledge is forever out of reach.

It should not be necessary to wonder whether only four, or seven, or eleven items carried on PA637 missed their connection to PA107 that morning. There should have been a PTM telex from the Berlin flight, notifying the earlier Heathrow flight of passengers and luggage to be transferred. There were also Pan Am re-booking records at Frankfurt detailing what was done with luggage that missed its connection. Either would have confirmed the number of transfer items in an instant – if they had been requested when they should have been requested, in February 1989, rather than a year after the event when Fuhl finally realised that PA637 was important. The latter documentation might also have shown other re-booked items that were carried on PA103, and must therefore have been in trays 8849 and 5629. We will never know.

It is tempting to heap the blame for this entire debacle on the head of the hapless Jürgen Fuhl, but this would be a short-sighted reaction. For a start, it is highly unlikely that Fuhl was the man responsible, singlehandedly, for the loss of the computerised data in 1988. In 1989 and 1990 Fuhl was simply doing the job he had been assigned to do by his superior officers, and he was doing it to the best of his ability. At the beginning it probably seemed like a simple enough exercise, and Kurt Berg, Bogomira Erac's supervisor, was also providing assistance. How on earth did *Berg* fail to realise that the eleven-item group could not possibly have come from AI165 and LH177? It's incomprehensible.

Later, however, when it was plain that Bogomira's souvenir printout was potentially the key to the entire case, the whole thing seems to have been turned over to Fuhl and his assistant, an officer named Siegburg. If their abilities were insufficient to the task, is that their fault, or the fault of those who simply left them to it?

The analysis of the very incomplete transfer baggage dataset is not a job for someone who thinks in straight lines. It needs lateral thinking and brainstorming. It needs detectives prepared to go out and search for additional information, rather than doggedly ferreting away down blind alleys long after it should be patently obvious there's absolutely nothing there. In the final analysis this was a failure of management – a failure to realise that this was a bigger mouthful than Fuhl should have been expected to have to chew on his own. But Fuhl's 1990 report, on which the entire case for the bomb having been loaded at Malta eventually rested, wasn't even proof-read for elementary mistakes.

The final conclusion, however, bears repeating, because it is absolutely on the money.

In den gesamten Ermittlungen zum Gepäck PA103A ergeben sich keine Beweise, daß mit dem Gepäck der Bombenkoffer von oder über Frankfurt/Main nach London befördert würde.

Throughout the inquiries into the baggage for PA103A there was no evidence that the bomb suitcase had been transferred with the luggage either from or via Frankfurt Main to London.

The Scottish branch of the Lockerbie investigation, despite having found nothing on Malta to contradict that position, simply ignored him.

4

INQUIRIES AND TRIBUNALS

FAA and PCAST

The first inquiry into the Lockerbie luggage transfers was conducted by the US Federal Aviation Authority, which began an investigation at Frankfurt immediately after the disaster that continued until 31st January 1989. It's unclear whether there was equal scrutiny of the Heathrow operation, despite that being the airport where the doomed aircraft had begun its journey. The FAA report, published in May, proposed fines totalling $630,000 against Pan Am for violations of regulations, both on 21st December and during the five-week period thereafter.

The report of the President's Commission on Aircraft Security and Terrorism (PCAST), which was published almost exactly a year after the FAA report, presents extensive detail of the FAA inquiry, covering both the investigation of the disaster itself and the significant number of security violations committed by Pan Am both before and after the incident. While recognising that there were multiple vulnerabilities in Pan Am's security procedures at both Frankfurt and Heathrow, only one specific baggage discrepancy was documented in relation to PA103 on 21st December 1988 – the finding that "one interline bag loaded on at Frankfurt could not be accounted for through any passenger records."

> [Maier's x-ray log] shows that 13 parcels (including two garment bags and a box appearing to contain six wine bottles) passed through the machine on the way to the flight. Other records, however, account for only 12 parcels (11 checked by passengers

who boarded the flight and one so called 'rush' bag of a passenger who had left on an earlier flight of another carrier).

It's unclear how this tally was arrived at. In total only eleven legitimate interline items were identified by Jürgen Fuhl's investigation, and of these, only eight belonged to passengers who boarded the flight. Adolf Weinacker, the "passenger who had left on an earlier flight of another carrier" had two suitcases, not one, but these were not carrying rush tags. The only identified interline item which was rush-tagged was Susan Costa's unaccompanied suitcase.

The most probable explanation is that the FAA believed Francis Boyer had interlined his suitcase from Toulouse, but even that addition doesn't entirely explain the arithmetic as presented. Nevertheless it is interesting to note that the US investigators attempted this reconciliation at an early stage using only the incoming passenger records and the x-ray log, without apparently being aware of the existence of the computer printout (which only came to light in the last week of January 1989). In contrast the European side of the inquiry seems to have placed relatively little weight on Maier's thirteen-item list, and Fuhl's report makes no serious attempt to assign identities to the two extra x-rayed suitcases. The possibility of an unaccompanied 'rogue' suitcase having been transferred to the feeder flight at Frankfurt as interline luggage wasn't seriously considered by the Scottish or the German police until August.

By the time of the PCAST investigation itself the criminal inquiry was already focussed on Malta. Nevertheless the report makes no mention of the Mediterranean island, and indeed appears to be keeping an open mind as regards the actual route of introduction of the bomb. Possibilities explicitly mentioned in the executive summary are an unaccompanied checked-in item being allowed to board the flight at Frankfurt, potential "tampering that may have occurred with baggage left in a partially filled, unguarded baggage container that was later loaded on the flight at Heathrow," and the risk of an "unknowing 'dupe' or saboteur checking a bomb into the plane at either airport."

The Commission made one very pertinent point. Obviously the bomb had been introduced into the baggage system in one way and one way only. However the sheer number of security vulnerabilities which plagued Pan Am's operation compounded the difficulty of figuring out which way this was. Even if the interline baggage wasn't the route of entry, the absence of passenger reconciliation meant that it couldn't be easily excluded and had to be probed in tedious and time-consuming detail.

Having said that however, the Commission was informed by "law enforcement authorities" that "the balance of probabilities was that the device had been loaded on to the initial leg of Flight 103, which began in Frankfurt,

Germany." The report covers a number of failings in the passenger screening protocols, but says virtually nothing about failings in relation to baggage container security at Heathrow. The bulk of the text is devoted to a detailed critique of Pan Am's decision in March 1988 to cease reconciling interline luggage to passengers physically on the plane and rely entirely on the x-ray screen to detect explosives, and to criticism of the FAA inspectors for not having taken a harder line about this matter prior to the disaster.

While it is certainly true that Pan Am security at Frankfurt was wide open to criticism, dispassionate comparison of the systems in place at the two airports in fact reveals Heathrow to be even worse. Early-arriving luggage at Frankfurt was safely tucked up in the inaccessible bowels of the automated transit system, only being delivered into 'human space' about ninety minutes before the flight was due to depart. Early-arriving luggage at Heathrow simply hung around the interline shed for hours, wide open to interference by anyone able to pass themselves off as an airport worker. While the FAA inspection at Frankfurt in October 1988 had prompted Kurt Maier to keep a written log of everything he x-rayed, his counterparts at Heathrow kept no such records, and they had no real idea how many interline items they had screened for the transatlantic leg of PA103 that day.

To some extent the PCAST report's concentration on the problems at Frankfurt reflects a frustration with the fact that Frankfurt had actually been inspected by the FAA only two months before the disaster, and yet its security was still markedly deficient. It is difficult to avoid the impression however that the commission's view was coloured by the information from the criminal investigation that they believed the IED had probably flown into Heathrow on the feeder flight, and this encouraged a focus on Frankfurt to the virtual exclusion of the even more serious shortcomings in London.

AAIB

The investigation of the crash of Pan Am 103 by the Air Accident Investigation Branch of the Department of Transport also began immediately. The AAIB inspectors worked side by side with the forensic investigators from the Royal Armament Research and Development Establishment based in Fort Halstead, Kent, England, who were seconded to work with the Scottish police on the inquiry. The AAIB team was concerned primarily with the mechanical cause of the air crash, and whether this was preventable or if its disastrous consequences could have been mitigated, and not at all with the criminal investigation's main focus of figuring out how the sabotage had been accomplished and by whom. Nevertheless, although Allen Feraday of RARDE was later at pains to deny that there had been significant exchange of information, it is clear that there was close collaboration between the two teams.

As far as the luggage loading is concerned, and in particular the central question of where the bomb suitcase had entered the airline baggage system, the only part of the AAIB investigation which is relevant is that relating to the luggage container itself and the part of the airframe immediately adjacent to the explosion. Two reports cover this aspect – a preliminary report signed by Peter Claiden and dated April 1989, which deals only with the two baggage containers showing evidence of having been close to the explosion, and the full AAIB report signed out by Michael Charles and published by the Department of Transport in June 1990.

The former report contains the first precise estimate of the position of the explosion within the container (excluding the rough sketch produced by the German police on 7th January shown in figure 4), however the diagram drawn by Mr. Claiden to illustrate this was never superseded and featured unchanged in both the complete report of 1990 and in the Joint Forensic Report completed by the RARDE scientific team in December 1991.

This position was very very strange indeed. The IED was known to have been hidden inside a fairly large radio-cassette recorder (the sort of thing often referred to as a 'ghetto-blaster'), which was packed along with an assortment of clothes inside a full-size hardshell suitcase. Nevertheless the location of the blast, agreed by both the AAIB inspectors and the RARDE forensic scientists, was low down in the 'overhang' section of the container, pretty much right at the bottom of the angle.

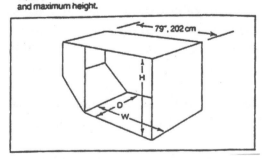

DIMENSIONS   INCHES   CENTIMETERS
  Base Size . . . . 61 D x 62 W   153 D x 156 W
  Maximum Height . . . . . . 64 H   163 H
  Maximum Door Opening 57 W x 62 H   145 W x 157 H
• All dimensions and weights rounded off to nearest whole number.
• Inside dimensions are 3 to 7 inches (8 to 18 cm) less than base and maximum height.

79", 202 cm

Figure 11
Schematic showing the dimensions of the aluminium AVE containers. Note that the quoted figures are outside measurements, and the inside measurements are 8 to 18 cm (3 to 7 inches) less.

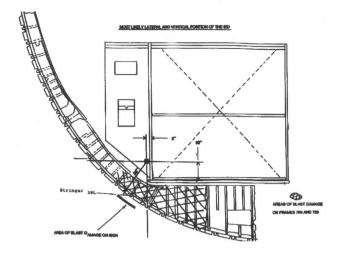

Figure 12
Estimated position of the centre of the explosion in relation to both the container itself and the adjacent blast-damaged airframe.

The distance of the explosion from the open side of the container (not shown in the diagram) is given in the Joint Forensic Report as 50 cm (20 inches). This places the bomb suitcase firmly among the luggage to the front of the container rather than the back, and is not contentious. The height of the explosion, as measured from the flat part of the floor of the container, is shown as 10 inches (25 cm). However the explosion was not actually above the flat part of the floor but 2 inches (5 cm) to the left of the vertical frame section, above the sloping part of the floor.

This is a very peculiar finding. Suitcases were normally loaded in the main cube of the container, with the angled overhang section reserved for holdalls. And irrespective of the usual loading procedure, how do you actually, physically, get a full-size hardshell suitcase into that container in such a way that a lump of Semtex hidden inside a large radio-cassette recorder is positioned right into the angle like that?

This question was not addressed by the AAIB report. It was addressed in the Joint Forensic Report, but that was not presented by the RARDE team until very much later in the investigation. The only illustration in the AAIB report showing the explosion in relation to stacked and loaded suitcases is the one in figure 5, which draws the centre of the blast almost half way up the height of the container and is clearly not intended to be an accurate representation of their proposed scenario.

A single sentence in the text of the April 1989 report deals indirectly with the position of the bomb suitcase relative to other luggage in the container.

The lack of direct blast damage on most of the floor panel in the heavily distorted area, of the type seen on the floor edge member and lower portions of the aft face structural members, would seem to indicate that this had been protected by, presumably, a piece of luggage.

This assessment was repeated verbatim in the full 1990 version of the report, and the point was central to the thinking of the investigators.

Interfor

The word 'bizarre' can be overused in the context of the Lockerbie affair, but the private investigation initiated in the spring of 1989 is definitely in that category. Pan Am's insurance company was feeling the pressure from the FAA and from the bereaved relatives, and commissioned its own inquiry into the disaster. The chosen company was Interfor Inc., a corporate investigations firm based in New York. Interfor was founded in 1979 by Juval Aviv, a controversial Israeli-American who has claimed to have worked for Mossad, but whose actual security experience appears to be in the somewhat more humdrum position of a security guard for El Al. In October 1989 Aviv submitted what was intended to be a preliminary report, explaining what he claimed to have discovered about the introduction of the bomb. It made for interesting reading.

Aviv explained that the US Drug Enforcement Agency was in the habit of allowing shipments of controlled drugs into the USA, often into Detroit, with the aim of tracking the consignment and eventually apprehending the dealers and the middle men. This part actually appears to be true, with the DEA merely denying that any such shipments were carried in December 1988, and specifically not on Pan Am 103 on 21st December. According to Aviv's report, the system in operation was that an accomplice would check in an innocent suitcase which would then pass uneventfully through security. Later, at the departure gate, a complicit baggage handler would switch this innocent suitcase for an identical one packed with heroin, which the accomplice would then retrieve from the carousel in Detroit.

Aviv claimed to have discovered that PA103 was indeed being used for this purpose on the fateful day, and that a German police officer was observing the switch-over of the cases. This officer allegedly filmed the process, and Aviv claimed to have acquired a copy of the videotape, which he passed over to the CIA after which it was never seen again. The film was supposed to show the switch-over, with the baggage handler noting that the suitcase was the "wrong weight" for the expected drugs shipment. The BKA officer is also said to have noted that the suitcase was a different make and colour from the one usually used for the drugs – being in fact a brown Samsonite. The drug courier was said to be Khaled Jaafar and the rogue baggage handler Kilinc Tuzcu, the man who sorted the interline luggage for Kurt Maier to x-ray.

All this and much more was contained in the Aviv's October report. The problem was that the evidence presented to support the allegations – phone numbers and car hire details and so on – simply didn't check out. The story could not be verified. Aviv claimed to have the entire thing on videotape, but didn't keep a copy.

The plan as recounted was also an improbably complicated way to get a suitcase containing contraband on to the plane. There was no bag-count of the luggage accumulating at the departure gate. If it was possible to get a suitcase of contraband airside, and it seems that it was, there was no particular reason to switch it for a legitimate suitcase, which would then have to be disposed of in its turn. An extra case could simply have been added to the waiting stack of luggage to be picked up by the courier at the other end in addition to his own baggage.

It is not the purpose of this book to declare whether Khaled Jaafar was smuggling narcotics or not, and even less so to determine whether this was being done at the behest of the US DEA. One can see why suspicions were raised. He was a frequent traveller between the Lebanon and the USA, and the Bekaa Valley is a notorious hotbed of heroin production. Lester Coleman claimed to have personal knowledge of his connection to the drugs trade and the DEA, as recounted in his 1993 novel *Trail of the Octopus*. While Khaled was recorded on the PA103 passenger list as having two items of checked-in luggage, at least one of the items found at Lockerbie and credited to him appeared to be cabin baggage. There have been persistent rumours that the farmer at Tundergarth Mains at Lockerbie found a suitcase containing packets of white powder on his land, which a policeman told him were probably heroin, but that the suitcase was spirited away by the authorities and the farmer refused to speak about the matter again after another visit from the constabulary.

On the other hand Khaled was only twenty, the same age as Karen Noonan, Tricia Coyle and Ken Gibson, and like them he was killed at Lockerbie. A passenger on the feeder flight who queued behind him at the Frankfurt passport control testified that she believed he was not carrying any cabin baggage – although the reason she remembered him was that he appeared nervous and apprehensive. Khaled's mother showed up at the Fatal Accident Inquiry in 1990, complete with legal representation, and protested vehemently that her son was not a drug smuggler. Her submissions were accepted, and nothing to the contrary has ever been proved.

Be that as it may, the suggestion that the *bomb* was in Khaled Jaafar's luggage is not supported by any evidence whatsoever. If he (or anyone else) was smuggling drugs, the Tundergarth Mains story suggests that the drugs were on the plane, not switched for anything. The variant of the story where Khaled was simply an innocent mule who was induced to carry the booby-trapped radio in his luggage also has no concrete evidence to support it, although it was the main premise of Allan Francovich's 1994 film *The Maltese Double Cross*. The sheer volume and intensity of smoke surrounding Khaled Jaafar is quite extraordinary, but it is impossible to find any associated fire.

One question which has never been satisfactorily answered is this: what was Juval Aviv playing at? With the perspective of nearly twenty-five years it is possible to recognise that his infamous 'Interfor Report' was nothing but a fabrication. But why? He was running a successful private inquiry business, which had been in existence for ten years when he got involved in Lockerbie. Interfor is still trading in 2013, apparently successfully. You don't get where Juval Aviv is today by submitting blatantly fabricated inquiry reports. Was Aviv himself the victim of a hoax? Francovich too? What about Lester Coleman?

What was that all about, indeed?

Air Malta *v.* the *Independent* and Granada Television

Although the police investigation on Malta began on 1st September 1989, the operation on the island was at first conducted in secret. Inevitably however the press got wind of what was going on, and newspaper stories began to appear featuring Malta as the latest Lockerbie news. The story was broken first by the *Sunday Times*, but it was an article published in the *Independent* on 30th October that drew the ire of Air Malta. That article reported that the BKA investigation on the island had discovered that the baggage list for KM180 did not correspond with the items checked in by the passengers. Air Malta brought a court action against the newspaper, which appears not to have been concluded until the spring of 1991. Eventually the *Independent* capitulated, and agreed to an out-of-court settlement in Air Malta's favour. This was reported on 16th April 1991, thus.

> The court was informed that Air Malta had undertaken a careful examination of its security and other procedures in force on the day in question and had shown to the *Independent* the relevant documents concerning the passengers and baggage carried on the flight. The *Independent* accepted Air Malta's assurance that

the quantity of baggage and passengers checked in tallied with the number of pieces and passengers that were carried on the aircraft. It further accepted that the statements referred to above were inaccurate and offered its apologies to Air Malta. It has agreed to pay a substantial sum to Air Malta by way of compensation, together with its costs.

Presumably Granada Television was unaware of these ongoing proceedings when it produced a documentary entitled *Why Malta?*, which was broadcast in November 1990, the month after the start of the Fatal Accident Inquiry in Scotland. The documentary showed a 'reconstruction' of an Arab terrorist arming the bomb in Malta, checking the suitcase in as passenger luggage, and watching the flight take off without him.

Obviously that didn't happen, and Air Malta could prove it. They sued Granada for libel. This case dragged on until 1st November 1992, with Granada producing the Frankfurt evidence as assembled by Jürgen Fuhl to support their contention that the bomb had travelled on KM180 one way or another. Air Malta secured as expert witnesses Denis Phipps, former Head of Security at BA, a former chairman of the Air Transport Association Security Advisory Committee and a former member of the UK National Aviation Committee, and his former colleague from BA Security Operations Nan McCreadie.

Phipps and McCreadie were firmly of the opinion that the Frankfurt baggage records were far too incomplete to prove anything of the sort, and Air Malta again produced its documentation showing that the flight had departed carrying only the fifty-five items of legitimate passenger baggage. Granada eventually settled the case without a formal admission of liability, however Air Malta were satisfied with the outcome, which awarded them £15,005 in damages plus costs, which were estimated to total half a million pounds.

Perversely, almost a year before the case was settled, indictments had been issued in both Scotland and the USA against Megrahi and his former Libyan Arab Airlines colleague Lamin Fhimah, alleging that they had conspired to introduce the Lockerbie bomb into the baggage carried by flight KM180 at Luqa airport on the morning of 21st December 1988.

FAI

The very last thing the Lockerbie investigators wanted was a Fatal Accident Inquiry. Unfortunately for them, there was nothing they could do about it. Scots law mandates that an FAI must be held in every case where someone has died while at work in Scotland. The sixteen members of the flight crew of *Maid of the Seas* had undoubtedly died in Scotland, and they had undoubtedly been at work when they died. There was a some resistance and a bit of foot-dragging, but eventually the proceedings kicked off on 1st October 1990.

By this time the police investigation had been focussed on Malta for over a year, but the name Abdelbaset al-Megrahi had not yet cropped up in relation to the inquiry. For many months the investigators had pursued a theory that a Malta-based cell of the PFLP-GC, the terrorist gang found making aircraft bombs in Neuss, had been responsible for the crime they could still find no proof had been committed at all, but this had more or less run into the sand.

It's likely that Granada's decision to air the *Why Malta?* documentary in November was predicated on the assumption that Malta would figure prominently in the FAI proceedings. It was hardly a secret that the investigation had been pretty much camped there since the autumn of 1989. However, if that was their reasoning, they were wrong. The word 'Malta' was never mentioned, nor 'KM180', nor 'computer printout', nor 'Yorkie trousers', nor 'Mary's House' (the shop where the trousers were purchased). Even the Frankfurt x-ray screening was only hinted at in passing, and the log of x-rayed items was not referred to.

If you can't avoid a Fatal Accident Inquiry, stage-manage it.

A regular court-room was considered to be too small to handle the expected level of interest in such a high-profile case, and the Easterbrook Hall in Dumfries, a former lunatic asylum, was co-opted for the job. In the end however the space was thinly populated for most of the proceedings – apparently a winter in Dumfriesshire wasn't top of the wish list for the metropolitan scribbling classes.

Sheriff John Mowat, who presided over the inquiry, had a choice. He could hear the evidence and find according to where that led, or he could do what the Crown Office wanted him to do. Unfortunately, as is clearly revealed by his written findings, he chose the latter.

The aim of the Crown was to achieve a finding that the bomb had been transferred to *Maid of the Seas* from the feeder flight, and for the cherry on top they would like it to be added that the suitcase had arrived at Frankfurt as interline luggage on another flight. However, they wanted to do that without presenting any of the Frankfurt transfer baggage evidence.

The sheriff's position was entirely clear.

I should say that I had no hesitation in accepting the objections of the Crown to the leading of evidence the publication of which might, in the view of the Lord Advocate, impede the criminal investigation which is still continuing or, perhaps, more importantly, render it impossible to bring the criminals to trial if they were discovered.

Thus, no evidence from Germany, or from Malta.

Nevertheless the Crown in the person of lead advocate Andrew Hardie, plus a succession of representatives of various groups of bereaved relatives, all proposed the finding that the bomb had been transferred to *Maid of the Seas* from the feeder flight, and also indicated their preference for (or at least lack of objection to) the explanation that the suitcase had been transferred to the feeder flight at Frankfurt as interline luggage from an incoming flight. Pan Am's lawyers begged to differ – however, since Pan Am were the *de facto* defendants in the proceedings, this was hardly surprising.

No evidence from Germany, but the evidence from England couldn't be avoided. The Fatal Accident Inquiry was the first time the public got to hear not only that there were a number of suitcases already present in AVE4041 before it was wheeled out on to the tarmac to receive the online transfer luggage from Frankfurt, but that something distinctly odd had happened at Heathrow airport before the feeder flight had even landed. Unfortunately, nobody seems to have been paying attention.

Most of the Heathrow airport staff who had interacted with the luggage heading for PA103 gave evidence at Dumfries, including everyone who had had anything to do with container AVE4041. The airport staff of course appeared in the witness box to give evidence and be cross-examined live, but much of the detail presented was referenced from their police statements, many of which dated back to the first two or three weeks after the disaster. These men had heard the news of the plane crash within a few hours of going off shift that evening – a 'breaking news' flash was broadcast by Channel 4 at about ten to eight, and the horrific story dominated the main BBC *Nine O'Clock News* bulletin. ITN's *News at Ten* had pictures of blazing houses. The baggage handlers knew very well which flight they had been dealing with just before they went home. It's therefore not surprising that recollection was still generally good by the time the police came calling.

A picture emerged of the Heathrow operation, with detail that had not featured in earlier reports of the case. Lacking an automated transit system of the type installed at Frankfurt, luggage arriving at Heathrow booked for direct transfer to outgoing flights was collected from the arrival gates by a company called Whyte's Airport Services. Whyte's personnel drove the luggage to a building in the Terminal 3 complex known as the 'interline shed', but rather than enter the building themselves they placed the suitcases on a conveyor belt that ran along the outside wall. This transported the luggage into the shed and deposited it on a carousel similar to those seen in passenger baggage reclaim halls. It generally took about forty minutes (give or take) for something to arrive in the shed after its incoming flight came on block.

The description of the security in the shed was hardly reassuring. All concerned freely admitted that the place was wide open with no security checks once staff had been admitted to the airside area, and that anyone dressed to blend in could essentially go where he liked and place suitcases anywhere he liked.

Each airline had its own little domain within the shed, and the Pan Am station had a small office in a hut next to its security checkpoint. While there was some co-operation between airlines (Air India was in the habit of borrowing the Pan Am x-ray machine from time to time), airlines' own personnel were responsible for outgoing luggage for their own flights, and the teams didn't share workers.

The Pan Am system was that their baggage handlers, or occasionally the security personnel (who were employees of Alert Security just like their Frankfurt counterpart Kurt Maier), watched for luggage on the carousel destined for a Pan Am flight, and retrieved it. The security guards would then run it through the x-ray screen, and if all was well affix a security sticker to it and leave it beside the x-ray machine for the baggage handler (properly termed a 'loader driver') to load into the appropriate container for its outgoing flight. The only exception to this was luggage which was carrying a Pan Am check-in tag, which was not x-rayed just as the online transfer luggage at Frankfurt was not x-rayed, on the assumption that anything booked in through a Pan Am check-in desk had already been appropriately screened.

The Pan Am station had been very busy in the morning with several outgoing flights, but the last of these left about one o'clock. The normal staff shift finished at two o'clock, but it was usual for a skeleton crew of three to work overtime to deal with the last flight of the day, Pan Am 103 at six o'clock. The three men in question were John Bedford the loader driver and Sulkash Kamboj and Harjot Parmar who were Alert security operatives.

Bedford gave evidence that he selected container AVE4041 for the PA103 transfer luggage just after two o'clock. He took the container at random from a group of about six that were standing idle, but the number stuck in his mind as it related to his wife's and his own dates of birth – 1940 and 1941 respectively. He labelled it to show which flight it was intended to travel on, and then noticed that there was luggage already present for that flight. "One or two" cases had already arrived and been screened, so he loaded them (or it) into the container.

Beford then testified that he loaded another "four or five" cases as they arrived, after they'd been x-rayed, and added them to the collection. All these cases were placed upright (hinge-down, handle-up) in a row across the back of the container, and by quarter past four there was a complete row of suitcases. Bedford didn't remember any holdalls. At quarter past four, all being pretty quiet, he went off for a tea break, and spent about half an hour chatting with his supervisor Peter Walker in Walker's office. Kamboj and Parmar remained behind.

During the conversation Walker remarked that the feeder flight was reported to be running late that afternoon, and that if Bedford stayed to carry out the transfer of the Frankfurt luggage from the feeder flight as he usually did, it would take him past the end of his shift at six o'clock. Walker suggested that he might as well clock off early rather than hang around for the delayed 727.

Bedford returned to the interline shed about quarter to five, and according to his evidence Kamboj then remarked to him that two more suitcases for 103 had arrived during his absence, which he had x-rayed and then placed in the container. Bedford looked into the container and saw two suitcases lying flat in front of the upright row he had already loaded, with the handles pointing to the back of the container. With the addition of these two cases the entire floor area of the container was covered. Something about one of the suitcases seems to have caught his eye. In a statement given to the police on 9th January 1989 he was able to describe it – "a brown hardshell, the kind Samsonite make." He confirmed that the case he was referring to was the one on the left, as seen from the open side of the container.

That's right. Only three weeks after the disaster, well before the bomb suitcase was identified as a brown-ish Samsonite hardshell, John Bedford spontaneously gave a statement in which he described a brown-ish Samsonite hardshell being present in the container an hour before feeder flight landed, in the very corner where the explosion subsequently occurred.

It got worse. When Kamboj was interviewed, he denied having loaded the suitcase, or telling Bedford that he had. It wasn't his job to put luggage into the container. Parmar concurred. Maybe if things were very busy he might lend a hand, but things were anything but busy that afternoon. Loading was the loader's job.

Bedford didn't query the extra items, which he said had security stickers on them. He hitched AVE4041 up to his tug and moved it to a position outside Walker's office, which was next to the baggage build-up shed where all the luggage from the check-in desks was handled. Then he clocked off shift. It appears that the container remained there for about forty-five minutes, unattended. This was the incident which was criticised in the FAA and PCAST reports.

The next baggage handler to see the contents of the container was Tarlochan Sahota, who was asked to check whether there was sufficient room left in that container to accommodate the luggage coming in from Frankfurt. Sahota had a look and reported that there weren't many items there, and there seemed to be plenty of room left. He broadly confirmed Bedford's description of the arrangement of the luggage – a row upright across the back and two cases flat at the front, with the floor area covered and all the suitcases in contact with the floor.

Soon afterwards the container was towed out on to the tarmac to meet the Frankfurt flight which came on-block about twenty minutes late at 17.40.

One wonders who was actually present and awake in the Easterbrook Hall that day. This was (and still is) the biggest terrorist attack on British soil; the biggest loss of life in the west in such an attack before the events of 11th September 2001. It had been public knowledge for about a year that the IED was believed to have been inside an unaccompanied brown or bronze Samsonite hardshell suitcase which had exploded inside baggage container AVE4041. Here was a witness who testified to seeing a brown Samsonite hardshell suitcase appear in the container in circumstances which suggested it might have been introduced by an unauthorised person, and might have circumvented the security check. And the position that case had been seen in, if not the precise location of the explosion, wasn't a gnat's whisker from it.

Where were the headlines? "Mystery bag seen at Heathrow!" "Baggage handler Bedford's shock revelation!" Not a syllable.

Somebody seems to have noticed, though. Bedford was taken through his evidence by Andrew Hardie, lead QC for the Crown, who was later to become Lord Advocate and be heavily involved with the preparation for the trial at Camp Zeist. Mr. Hardie appeared most anxious to persuade him that he had not after all seen a brown Samsonite hardshell in the position in question. He seized on what he claimed was an inconsistency in Bedford's statements, and went on the attack. While Bedford had first described the case as brown, in a later statement he said, "I remember the light shining or reflecting off it. On reflection I am now convinced it was maroon in colour." Mr. Hardie used this as a springboard to put it to Bedford that he actually had no idea what colour the thing was. Was it brown or was it maroon? Could it in fact have been a blue suitcase with a maroon trim?

It's unclear whether Bedford was simply being truthful and admitting that by October 1990, getting on for two years after the event, he no longer had any clear memory of the colour of the case, or whether in fact he was irritated by Mr. Hardie's attempt to undermine his honestly-provided statements, but whatever the reason, he capitulated. He couldn't say what colour the case had been. Could have been blue, maybe.

This was a very disingenuous attack, and a very questionable one. The forensic scientists themselves, who not only had in their possession a selection of pieces of the bomb suitcase itself but also its pristine and undamaged twin provided by the manufacturer, sometimes called it brown, occasionally maroon, often bronze and even burgundy. The manufacturer actually called it 'antique copper'. Are we to disbelieve and disregard the *forensic* evidence because of these inconsistencies in describing the hue of the peculiar metallic finish?

When this was read into the transcript at Camp Zeist it seemed not at all out of place. At Camp Zeist the Crown was prosecuting two accused persons, and an attack on a witness whose evidence tended to undermine the prosecution case is hardly surprising – even one of their own witnesses. However this attack on Bedford occurred during a Fatal Accident Inquiry, a hearing where it is the duty of the Crown simply to seek out the truth.

Nevertheless Bedford's evidence was there, and it has to be addressed. It raises two very specific questions. First, why *wasn't* the suitcase he saw the bomb, and second, if it wasn't the bomb, what was it?

The first question was easily answered. Back in April of 1989 Peter Claiden of the AAIB had recorded his opinion that the floor of the container had been protected from the blast by something, presumably a[nother?] piece of luggage. In the witness box at Dumfries forensic scientist Allen Feraday of RARDE went even further, insisting that he was "adamant" that the bomb suitcase was not on the bottom layer of luggage. Feraday's evidence was heard before Bedford's, which may at least partly account for the singular lack of curiosity about the mysterious brown Samsonite seen on the bottom layer, so near and yet so far.

Nevertheless, the second question remains. If that wasn't the bomb, what was it?

There was no answer to this. Evidence about the luggage loaded into container AVE4041 was given by Derek Henderson, the policeman who had collated the data with the aim of showing that the bomb suitcase had not been legitimate checked-in luggage but must have been an unaccompanied 'rogue bag'. Sheriff Mowat's published findings record that Henderson's evidence demonstrated that "none of the descriptions given by relatives of the baggage which they expected the victims to have been carrying fitted [the bomb] suitcase."

Given that Bedford's description of the mystery suitcase as a brown Samsonite hardshell was a perfect match for the description of the bomb suitcase, what goes for one surely goes for the other. So if none of the baggage being carried by the victims was a brown Samsonite hardshell (and presumably that includes the victims who interlined into Heathrow), *what did Bedford see?*

Nobody seemed to care. That case had been on the bottom, so it wasn't the bomb, because Allen Feraday was "adamant" that the bomb suitcase wasn't on the bottom. No need to inquire any further about it, apparently.

Since none of the luggage loaded into the container in the interline shed had been in either of the two positions Feraday was advancing for the bomb suitcase, the conclusion that the bomb had flown in from Frankfurt wasn't entirely unreasonable. However, what about the conclusion that it had flown into Frankfurt on a flight operated by a different airline?

There were two points to consider. One was that if the suitcase had been checked in at Frankfurt and then the passenger had failed to board, this would have been discovered and the relevant baggage off-loaded. The other was that a disproportionate number of the blast-damaged suitcases were interline items, therefore it could be inferred that the bomb suitcase was in a little enclave of interline items loaded together, therefore it itself was interline luggage.

This reasoning is so tenuous one scarcely knows where to begin. DC Henderson's report provided reasonable grounds for believing that the bomb suitcase had not been checked in by a passenger at Frankfurt. However, there's an excluded middle hovering around somewhere. "Not checked in at Frankfurt" doesn't automatically imply "interline transfer". No evidence was led in relation to airside security at Frankfurt, and the possibility that the suitcase had been introduced at Frankfurt by direct insertion into the baggage system, either at one of the interline coding stations or at the departure gate, was not one the FAI was in a position to exclude.

As regards the second point, there were certainly several Frankfurt interline items among the blast-damaged luggage. There were also several Frankfurt check-in items among the blast-damaged luggage. If the proportion was somewhat skewed towards the former, one might equally argue that the bomb suitcase was more likely *not* to be interline luggage, to balance out the probabilities.

The difficulty at the FAI was that nobody present had any interest whatsoever in probing the Bedford suitcase in more detail. The Crown's interest was in achieving a conclusion that did not contradict the line of inquiry they were pursuing on Malta, and the last thing they wanted, as is made very clear by Andrew Hardie's attack on Bedford, was a finding that the bomb might have been introduced at Heathrow. The relatives of the victims by and large took their cue from the Crown theory, and of course everybody and his budgie knew that the police believed the bomb had come from Malta, thanks to the efforts of the *Sunday Times*, the *Independent*, sundry other newspapers and Granada Television.

Although Pan Am were doing their best to obfuscate the issue and deny liability, they more than anyone had absolutely no interest in turning the spotlight on Bedford's evidence. While they might in the end be found to be at fault if Maier had missed the bomb on his x-ray screen, it was hardly going to help their case to point out that it might in fact been introduced at Heathrow, right under the noses of *two* Alert Security employees.

The result of this was that a crucial point was never scrutinised or challenged by any of the parties. Was it really legitimate to exclude the possibility that the bomb was in the suitcase on the bottom of the stack, purely on the basis of the condition of the recovered parts of the container floor? Exclude it so conclusively that the suitcase Bedford saw could be dismissed out of hand, without even investigating its provenance?

US civil action against Pan Am

The FAI happened at an interesting time for the investigation. Although the police had no suspect when the inquiry began in October 1990, that was about to change. In January 1991 the name Abdelbaset al-Megrahi was passed over to the Scottish investigators by the FBI, together with a couple of photographs. Could they maybe find anything on this guy? Maybe they could. On 13th February 1991, two days before the end of the FAI, Tony Gauci of 'Mary's House' pointed to one of the photographs and agreed that it resembled the man who had bought the Yorkie trousers in his shop back in 1988.

By the time the civil action brought against Pan Am by the bereaved relatives came to court in the USA, formal indictments had been issued against Megrahi and Fhimah by both the US and the Scottish authorities, and pressure was building on Muammar Gaddafi to surrender the two accused for trial.

The civil action was heard by a jury in New York in 1992, with Judge Thomas Platt presiding. Three victims who were residents of that state were named as 'test cases' – Robert Pagnucco and Harry Bainbridge who had flown together into Frankfurt from Rome, and Walter Porter, a Heathrow boarder. The objective of the plaintiffs was to demonstrate wilful misconduct on the part of Pan Am and/or Alert Security, because as the law stood, a finding of wilful misconduct removed the $75,000 per passenger ceiling on compensation and allowed unlimited damages to be awarded.

Much of the legal argument revolved around the extent of Pan Am's negligence, whether that negligence had contributed to the disaster, and whether or not Pan Am and its wholly-owned subsidiary Alert could be treated as separate entities and thus be able to blame each other for the fatal shortcomings. Nevertheless the Frankfurt baggage transfer evidence was presented at this hearing, and indeed was presented in considerably more detail than at Camp Zeist eight years later.

The computer printout assumed pride of place, with Bogomira Erac testifying incognito as 'Mrs. Schmidt', for no readily apparent reason. The twenty-five transfer items were traced, with the jury hearing about Adolf Weinacker and his life-saving change of plans, and the delay to PA637 causing luggage intended for PA107 to be bounced on to PA103A. The plaintiffs' case, obviously, was that tray 8849 held an unaccompanied 'rogue bag' smuggled on to KM180 by terrorists, and that the combination of Pan Am's failure to check that all luggage loaded on the plane was accompanied by a passenger and inadequate training of the x-ray operators had allowed the bomb to be loaded on to the feeder flight.

It was accepted that all interline items had been x-rayed, therefore if the bomb suitcase had indeed been transferred carrying an Air Malta tag, it would have been one of the thirteen items that passed through Kurt Maier's x-ray machine. It is unclear exactly how this was determined. As noted in the previous chapter, at best only seven of the eleven items in the 11.59-12.00 group can be matched to luggage carried on PA637. One might surmise that the other four were also online items carried on the Berlin shuttle, but that's no more than a good guess. They could have been more interline luggage. Another problem should have been tray 5620, apparently coded with a batch of luggage from a flight from Warsaw, but also not matched to any legitimate luggage. With not one but six unidentified trays, how was it possible to declare with certainty that the bomb was in any of them, let alone one in particular?

The evidence from Malta should have put yet another crimp in the argument, as discussed in chapter 2. Wilfred Borg of Air Malta appeared as a defence witness, and spoke to the reliability of the documentary evidence from Luqa showing that only the fifty-five items of legitimate passenger luggage had been carried on KM180 that morning. There was no unaccompanied luggage on the flight, and there was no luggage tagged to be transferred to a Pan Am flight. However, this seems to have cut little ice.

One point seems to have been downright wrong. As in the FAA report in 1989, it was argued that only twelve of the thirteen bags x-rayed by Maier for Flight 103 could be traced to passengers, implying that the thirteenth was an illegitimate 'rogue bag' and hence the bomb. This was 1992. Jürgen Fuhl's report, submitted in July 1990, was entirely clear that only eleven legitimate interline bags could be traced coming through the system. It seems that Francis Boyer was still being classed as an interline passenger, although Fuhl had established he had collected and re-checked his suitcase, and it is not a worksheet match for tray 5620.

The defendants' answer to the problem of the thirteenth x-rayed bag was John Hubbard's misrouted suitcase. It was found at Lockerbie, and it was presumed to have been carried on PA637, and it was carrying a rush tag. Standing orders at Frankfurt were quite clear that all rush-tagged luggage was to be x-rayed, even if it was carrying a Pan Am tag. Therefore the thirteenth x-rayed item was the Hubbard case. All present and correct. No bomb.

The problem with this is something the Platt hearing didn't even seem to realise. As discussed in chapter 3, there must have been more than one online item carrying a rush tag. Despite a thorough inquiry, no more passengers could be traced whose luggage even *might* have been transferred to the feeder flight at Frankfurt. In addition to the *two* Hubbard cases (both rush-tagged) there were four more completely unidentified items in the 11.59-12.00 group. No matter which way you slice it, these things must also have had rush tags. The only possible conclusion is that Tuzcu didn't pull out the online rush-tagged luggage for x-ray, despite the prominent notices announcing that "DIESE VORSCHRIFTEN SIND EIN MUSS!". (These regulations are a must!)

The defence was on a better wicket with the contention that the "contradictory baggage records from varying sources in [Frankfurt airport] contained so many demonstrable errors and omissions that no reliable conclusion could be based on them." Nevertheless none of this appeared to impress the court.

The difficulty for the defence was that by 1992 they had two legal precedents against them. The court noted that the Scottish Fatal Accident Inquiry had determined that the bomb had come into Frankfurt as interline luggage, although it is unclear whether it was realised that the FAI had not heard any of the evidence from Frankfurt or from Malta. The judge also explicitly relied on the fact that in November 1991 a US grand jury had granted indictments against the two Libyan suspects based on the proposition that the bomb had been smuggled on board KM180 at Luqa, and that parallel indictments had also been issued by the Scottish authorities. No matter how strenuously Pan Am's defence team pointed out the flaws and weakness in that evidence, it was never very likely that the Platt court was going to find in their favour on the basis that the bomb could not be proved to have travelled on KM180. The only real question was, accepting that the bomb suitcase was indeed carried on KM180 and transferred through the Frankfurt baggage system in tray 8849, were Pan Am and/or Alert Security guilty of wilful misconduct when they allowed it to be loaded on to the outgoing PA103A?

The jury decided that they were. The relevant paragraph of the court judgement reads as follows.

> The jury listened to overwhelming evidence regarding Alert's failure to employ competently trained and well-informed personnel

to operate the x-ray screeners. In particular, they heard evidence regarding the improper training of Kurt Maier, the Alert employee who was operating the x-ray machine in Frankfurt and who allegedly overlooked the radio cassette player containing the bomb. Mr. Maier himself testified that before his employment by Alert on November 1, 1988, he had no security experience, and that he received no training from Alert except 'on the job' training over a period of two to four days, consisting of random assistance by other Alert employees. Mr. Maier testified further that although he needed his glasses to discern fine detail, he was not wearing them while viewing objects through the x-ray machine on December 21, 1988. Meanwhile, Anthony Cooke, an Alert employee in London, testified that Alert personnel should have had no difficulty recognizing on an x-ray screen a Toshiba radio cassette recorder, such as the one in which the bomb that destroyed Flight 103 was hidden. In short, Alert, by reason of either Mr. Maier not being able to see clearly without his glasses, or not having been trained or advised to pull bags with Toshiba radios for physical inspection, was guilty of wilful misconduct that was a proximate cause of the accident.

At the hearing the American translator had problems with Maier's colloquial German. Maier appears to have been trying to convey the information that his glasses were merely reading glasses, which he didn't need to see something at the distance of the x-ray monitor. Also, that while he could not, in 1992, remember whether he had seen a radio-cassette player on the monitor in 1988, he was sufficiently aware of the 'Autumn Leaves' warning to have called a supervisor if he had seen such an item. The jury, however, was not convinced that his failure to see 'anything in particular' that afternoon proved that the plaintiffs' contention as regards the route of the bomb was unfounded.

Pan Am appealed, with the appeal being heard by a three-judge panel in 1994. One of the grounds of appeal was that the defence testimony challenging the alleged cause of the disaster – the assumption that the bomb had been carried on KM180 – had not been given due consideration. It appears from the text of the lengthy appeal judgement that the decision turned on Pan Am's failure to advance any alternative explanation as to how the bomb could have been loaded on to the plane. Apparently Juval Aviv's assertion that the bomb suitcase had been switched at the departure gate for a suitcase belonging to Khaled Jaafar, and that a German policeman had filmed the entire episode, was not something the airline's lawyers felt confident bringing to court.

It is unclear how much of the Heathrow evidence was presented in the USA, if indeed any of it was. The plaintiffs appear to have relied on Derek Henderson's report to contend that the bomb suitcase had arrived as an unaccompanied 'rogue bag' on the feeder flight. In addition Allen Feraday submitted a statement repeating his assertion at the FAI that it was "physically impossible" for the primary suitcase to be anywhere except the two positions he had specified in his forensic report. However, even if it did occur to Pan Am that the suitcase Bedford described was at least as likely to have been the bomb as the entirely hypothetical 'unaccompanied bag from Malta', they were hardly going to propose a *modus operandi* that left them just as culpable as the one advanced by the plaintiffs. As a result they were forced to argue merely that the method of bombing was not established, without suggesting an alternative theory. The primary hearing didn't buy it, and neither did the majority opinion of the appeal court.

Somebody did buy it, however. One of the three judges, Ellsworth van Graafeiland, entered a lengthy dissenting opinion. He was blisteringly critical of the conduct of the original trial, in which he noted that "plaintiffs' attorneys were permitted to range far and wide with prejudicial, irrelevant testimony, while Pan Am's counsel was precluded time and time again from presenting relevant and probative proof." He was particularly scathing about the Malta-origin theory, which he described as a "house of cards … constructed entirely of opinion testimony", and specifically lambasted Judge Platt's reliance on the indictment of "two unapprehended, unquestioned and unapproachable Middle Eastern terrorists" when deciding to favour the plaintiffs on this point. His opening sally is worth repeating (capitalisation original).

> At the outset, I want to state one clear and uncontrovertible fact: NO ONE KNOWS WHEN, WHERE OR HOW THE BOMB GOT ON THE PAN AM PLANE EXCEPT THE PERSON WHO PUT IT THERE.

Mr. van Graafeiland's two colleagues on the bench begged to differ. The majority judgement went against the defendants and eventually an enormous sum in damages was awarded against Pan Am – or rather against its remaining assets, as the company had been forced to declare bankruptcy in January of 1991.

Pan Am applied for leave to appeal to the US Supreme Court. In June 1995 this application was refused, and payment of the compensation money to the bereaved relatives began.

And there the matter remained, for nearly five years.

5

TRANSFER BAGGAGE, ZEIST STYLE

The 'Lockerbie trial' of 2000–01 was held not in Scotland but at a specially-converted former US air base in the Netherlands, Camp Zeist, which was declared to be Scottish territory for the duration of the proceedings. Uniquely under Scots law, this was not a jury trial but was adjudicated by a bench of three senior judges – Lord Sutherland, Lord Coulsfield and Lord Maclean. Both of these features were concessions to the accused; the former to address fears that they might be in danger of being 'extraordinarily rendered' to the USA from British soil to be tried in a court which had the option of imposing the death penalty, and the second as a result of concerns that it would be impossible to find a Scottish jury whose members were untainted by the wall-to-wall media coverage the case had received since the very day of the disaster. Judges, on the other hand, were believed to be capable of putting aside all prejudice and deciding the case purely on the evidence presented.

All the evidence relating to the luggage transfers and the route of introduction of the bomb suitcase into the baggage system was led by the Crown. Even Wilfred Borg of Air Malta, star witness for the defence in the US hearings, was a prosecution witness in 2000. The Crown was very selective indeed as to what evidence was presented, with certain areas being laid out in great detail while others were barely sketched in.

The evidence from Malta was rehearsed in exhaustive detail. Virtually everything related in chapter 2 above is taken directly from the trial transcripts, with the omission of Mr. and Mrs. Seliger seeming to be no more than an oversight. The court was told exactly who was on the plane, where they were going, what luggage they carried, and what itinerary was followed by each item.

Twenty-four of the thirty-nine passengers gave evidence in person. Saviour Mallia's witness statement was read directly into the transcript. The Crown could not advance any specific theory about how the bomb suitcase had supposedly got itself loaded on to KM180, but they certainly didn't seem to be hiding anything.

Wilfred Borg was in the witness box for the best part of a day and a half. He described the Air Malta operation at Luqa in great detail, both in general terms and in relation to the loading of KM180 on 21st December 1988. He was also taken through the documentation for a number of other flights leaving from Luqa airport around the time in question, apparently to illustrate particular security issues or explore possible areas of insecurity or error. There was a great deal of material available as a result of Granada Television having requested it at the time of the libel case in 1991–92, and the Crown dredged up most of it.

Borg patiently explained the security system, the measures in place to prevent unauthorised luggage being loaded on to aircraft, and the evidence that these measures had not been circumvented on 21st December during the loading of KM180. For a prosecution witness, his evidence-in-chief was very hard going indeed. Alan Turnbull QC for the Crown pressed him hard in an attempt to elicit an admission that a security breach was possible, but this is the best he managed to achieve.

Q Would it have been possible, in 1988, for someone with that knowledge and that access to have deliberately circumvented the checks that you have in place?

A Anything is possible. Whether it is probable is a different story.

Q Yes. You see, plainly, one could imagine any number of ways, perhaps, in which someone could deliberately --

MR. DAVIDSON [junior counsel for Fhimah]: I object to that question in the way it's framed. It's leading the witness. It may be an important matter.

LORD SUTHERLAND: I'm not sure that it got far enough, but it certainly was headed towards being a leading question, Mr. Depute.

MR. TURNBULL: I accept that, My Lords.

Q Taking on board that such things might be possible, Mr. Borg, can you think of any particular ways in which someone could deliberately circumvent the checks that you had in place?

A The possibility is always there. It's the level of difficulty of achieving that possibility. One can also rob a bank.

In the end, despite the difficulty of excluding a theoretical possibility, it was plain that there was no evidence whatsoever of a security breach involving KM180 that morning. More than that, no possible scenario had been suggested whereby someone might have introduced an illicit suitcase on to that flight *in such a way as to leave no evidence that it had been done at all.*

* * * * * * *

While the Malta evidence was positively obsessive in its detail, the Frankfurt evidence was a different matter entirely. The printout again took pride of place, with Bogomira Erac appearing (under her own name this time) to relate the story of how she came to preserve it. But the devil, as they say, is in the detail.

An explanation of how the printout should be interpreted, with the twenty-five items entered at stations with codes in the form "S00xx" representing luggage transferred from incoming flights, was given by Frankfurt airport employee Günter Kasteleiner. Mr. Turnbull led him through the tracing of Karen Noonan and Tricia Coyle's luggage as it arrived on LH1453 from Vienna and was coded at stations 203 and 204 in the V3 hall. He also elicited the information that the input station relating to tray 8849, S0009, referred to station 206 in the V3 hall, and that luggage from KM180 from Malta was being coded there at 13.07, the time recorded for that tray.

And that was that. That's all the Crown wanted the court to know about. The contrast with the prolonged and detailed examination of the Malta evidence is stark. Not even Mr. Walker's luggage was traced, never mind Susan Costa's unaccompanied suitcase. Mr. Weinacker's change of flight and his lucky escape went entirely unremarked. The appearance of a group of eleven items coded in quick succession at HM4 between 11.59 and 12.00 was not something the court was made aware of. The delay to PA637 from Berlin, which resulted in a number of items that should have travelled on PA107 having to be re-booked on PA103, wasn't referred to. While the Passenger Transfer Message relating to one online item to be transferred from PA643 was given in evidence, there was no mention of the fact that this item also appeared on the printout, corresponding to tray 8042 coded at 13.17.

Defence cross-examination of Mr. Kasteleiner was brief, and mainly confined to taking him through four additional entries on the printout. First, the three entries relating to S0074 (HM3) between 14.44 and 14.46 were highlighted, and it was agreed that these entries could be related to flight LH631 (Mr. Walker's flight from Kuwait). Then the other item on the printout which ared on the same coding worksheet was dealt with, that was the item ftered at 15.44 which it was agreed related to flight LH1071.

And again that was that. Additional detail relating to these two flights was confirmed from other witnesses, including the fact that LH1071 was carrying no passengers or legitimate luggage booked to transfer to PA103, but nobody seemed to have any interest in obtaining a comprehensive analysis of all twenty-five transfer items.

This is particularly strange in view of the fact that the majority of the owners of the identified transfer items were still alive. Adolf Weinacker could have been called to tell of his lucky escape, and make it clear that his two suitcases were indeed interlined, and could most plausibly have been re-booked at 11.31. Fiona Leckie, as a Scottish citizen, should have been particularly easy to call to explain how she had sprinted from PA637 to catch the tight connection to PA107 that morning, with the result that her suitcase (containing, among other things, a garden gnome) missed the connection. Wiebke Wagenführ could have confirmed her flight on the later Berlin shuttle. Susan Costa could have explained how her luggage came to be on the flight although she was not, and how it came about that although only one item was recorded on the paperwork, two suitcases belonging to her were found at Lockerbie. John Hubbard could have told the court about the Berlin check-in clerk's suggestion that his rush-tagged cases should fly to Heathrow via Frankfurt on PA637.

Despite having called so many of the KM180 passengers to ensure that flight was fully documented for the court, the Crown failed to call even one of the Frankfurt transfer passengers. Susan Costa's name was noted as appearing on a label attached to a blast-damaged suitcase, but none of the others was mentioned in court at all.

Another notable absentee was Kurt Maier. Maier, whose evidence had been so crucial in the New York hearings, was unable to travel to the Netherlands in 2000. The reason for this was explained in a letter from his physician, which was read out in court in all its highly personal detail. Maier, by now over seventy, had been suffering from bronchial asthma since 1991. On 22nd April 2000, just ten days before the trial began, he had telephoned his doctor to report that he had fallen in his apartment and was unable to rise. The doctor visited him at home and found him in a pitiful state, lying on the floor of his living room surrounded by "hundreds" of empty alcohol bottles. He was severely dehydrated and incoherent.

Worse was to come. He was diagnosed as suffering from inoperable bowel cancer, and complications resulting from palliative surgical treatment led to a worsening of both his physical and mental state. By the end of July, the time at which he was required at Camp Zeist, he was in a nursing home, confined to a wheelchair and intermittently disorientated. He was in no condition to give evidence, and clearly never would be again.

Kurt Maier's evidence was admitted in the form of two written statements. One was a record of an interview he had given to two FAA inspectors who questioned him in English on 5th January 1989. One of these inspectors, Naomi Saunders, was called to the witness box and read out the notes taken at that interview by herself and her colleague David Tiege. The other was the third of three statements taken by Jürgen Fuhl, dated 7th February, which was read into the evidence by Fuhl during his testimony. Both said more or less the same thing.

> Maier further explained when he is assigned to view the monitor, he looks for things that are unusual, like radios, tape recorders, electronic equipment with wires, transistors, et cetera, because they are not easy to recognise on the screen. He stated he looks for a plug in any electrical device. The plug clears his doubt about any explosive device. Maier then stated he could say without question there was no explosives in the bags for Pan Am Flight 103.

In his German interview Maier confirmed that he was aware of the Autumn Leaves warning, and that he understood that explosives were extremely difficult to detect if they were hidden inside a transistor radio. His much more detailed testimony to the 1992 New York trial was not referred to. Under the circumstances there was no possibility for cross-examination to clarify any of these statements. And every possibility to heap the blame for Lockerbie squarely on to Kurt Maier once again, just as had been done by the Platt hearings eight years earlier.

Jürgen Fuhl's sojourn in the witness box was brief, and apart from acting as a conduit for Maier's statement the only matter he was questioned about was his interview of a passenger on the feeder flight who bizarrely turned out to have a connection with one of the addresses used by the PFLP-GC for their bomb-making activities. All that painstaking work tracing passengers and incoming flights – the right ones and the wrong ones – went entirely unacknowledged. His luggage report might as well not have existed.

By adopting this approach the Crown was able to conceal from the court the essentially shambolic nature of the transfer baggage reconciliation. It was never made clear that not just one or two but fifteen of the twenty-five transfer items could not be matched to legitimate baggage for PA103A by the method

...ied by Mr. Kasteleiner; that coding re-booked luggage back into the system ...hout making an entry on the worksheet was commonplace; that although ...ine additional items were identified as legitimate baggage which must have been transferred through the system to PA103A, seven of these were not supported by any documentation and could only be matched to the printout data by assumptions; and that in the final analysis no legitimate luggage could be matched to at least six of the twenty-five items, even by guesswork. The paradox of only thirteen items having been x-rayed was not addressed, with the court being given no information as to how many of the transfer items were identified as online or interline.

The defence could have done something about this, of course. They had the supporting documents, and they had Jürgen Fuhl's report. They could have introduced their own analysis of the transfer baggage, based on Fuhl's findings, and demonstrated all these points. They could at least have called Mr. Weinacker and Mrs. Leckie to show that some transfer luggage wasn't entered on the worksheets. They chose not to.

Instead, during his closing speech for the defence, Megrahi's advocate Bill Taylor indulged in something of a scattergun approach. He nit-picked a number of minor clerical errors. He pointed out that the court had not been told what most of the twenty-five transfer items were, but without showing that many of them were indeed untraceable. He pointed out that there was no reconciliation of the thirteen x-rayed items to any particular subset of the transfer items, without demonstrating that such a reconciliation was highly problematic. He pointed out that the total number of items recorded as being transferred to the feeder flight through the central system and across the tarmac from the Berlin shuttles was greater than the total number of items recorded on the passenger manifest, as if this was somehow sinister.

The rush-tag system was clearly explained to the court by Wilfred Borg, and it is common knowledge that unaccompanied luggage is legitimately carried on many commercial flights. It is therefore difficult to know what Mr. Taylor hoped to achieve by pointing out that the feeder flight was carrying some unaccompanied items. It would surely have been far more effective to have shown that once all the traceable rush-tagged and other unaccompanied luggage was accounted for, at least six of the twenty-five transfer items remained entirely mysterious. Rather than do that, though, he branched off to point out archly that one of the suitcases recovered at Lockerbie carried a luggage label with the name 'Susan Costa' and an address in San Marino. He asked the court to note that there was no Susan Costa named on the PA103 passenger list. This was pure legal trickery. Bill Taylor had Jürgen Fuhl's report, and he knew perfectly well that the Costa case was documented and entirely legitimate.

Taylor demonstrated his familiarity with the Fuhl report by choosing perhaps the worst possible part to explore in detail – the coding of LH669 from Damascus. Fuhl had tried quite hard to figure out whether it was possible that tray 8849 might represent something carried on the Damascus flight, which was entered at station 207 at about the same time as KM180 was being coded at station 206. There were however a lot of problems with this idea, as discussed in Appendix A, not least that there was no legitimate luggage for PA103A on board LH669 either. Fuhl had given the theory up as a bad job, and said so in his report. As reprised by Taylor it came over as contrived special pleading.

Against this background of fluff and irrelevancy Taylor's one solid point, a point that should have well-nigh destroyed the contention that tray 8849 must certainly have contained something carried on KM180, failed to make much impact. Tray 5620, coded at 15.44 at HM3, was a worksheet match for LH1071 from Warsaw – as Mr. Kasteleiner had confirmed during cross-examination. It was also agreed that, just like KM180, LH1071 carried no legitimate luggage for PA103A. Fuhl's report, damningly, had concluded that in view of the utterly negative results from his inquiries into that flight, the tray cannot in fact have contained something flown in from Warsaw, despite the worksheet match.

This point should have been dusted down, polished up, framed, and hung on the wall with a spotlight on it. Instead it was accorded about the same emphasis as the dishonest Costa reference. The opportunity was there to demonstrate to the court what Jürgen Fuhl, Denis Phipps, Nan McCreadie and Ellsworth van Graafeiland had all pointed out in their turn. That the surviving documentation from Frankfurt was far too incomplete and far too ambiguous to support the interpretation the Crown was trying to put on it. Without any supporting evidence from Malta and lacking the full dataset from the computer, tray 8849 was simply one of a number of mystery trays, any one of which might (or might not) have been the bomb. The trick was completely missed.

★　★　★　★　★　★　★

If the Crown's presentation of the Frankfurt evidence could be described as selective, its treatment of the Heathrow evidence was frankly obfuscatory. The only witnesses called who could give any evidence regarding the luggage placed in AVE4041 in the interline shed were John Bedford and Sulkash Kamboj. Unlike Maier, Kamboj kept no record of the luggage he x-rayed, and he had never volunteered any estimate of the number of items in the container.

Bedford merely repeated his evidence about placing a row of suitcases spine-down-handle-up across the back of the container before his half-hour tea break, and then finding the two additional cases flat at the front when he returned. As his direct recollection by 2000 was close to zero, much of the detail was elucidated by taking him through parts of the transcript of his evidence at the Fatal Accident Inquiry.

The question of the number of items loaded into the container was almost completely side-stepped, with Bedford's closest estimate being "eight or ten". (The FAI findings in contrast refer to "six or seven".) He wasn't asked to say in which order he had loaded the items across the back (left to right or right to left, or even at random), or whether the row completely filled the back of the container. He wasn't asked what any of the other items looked like. He wasn't asked whether he had seen security stickers on either or both of the mystery cases. Of course there was essentially no chance he would have remembered any of this by the time of the trial, however there was far more information in the FAI transcript and in his original police statements which could have been introduced, but wasn't.

The story of the mysterious appearance of the two extra suitcases could hardly be avoided, or Bedford's description of the left-hand one as a brown (or maroon) Samsonite hardshell. However Mr. Hardie's suggestion that Bedford really had no idea what colour it was and perhaps it was blue was read into the trial transcript.

Kamboj's evidence mainly covered the usual routine of baggage arrival and screening, and whether he had been aware of the Autumn Leaves warning (he hadn't). He was also pressed once again about whether he had admitted to loading the two extra suitcases, as Bedford said he had. In all his police statements, and again at the FAI, Kamboj had been consistent in his denials. This time, Crown counsel Alan Turnbull managed to throw some doubt on the matter.

> Q Do you remember if you helped him out at all in the later part of that afternoon?
> A I don't remember, sir.
> Q Well, do you remember if you helped him out by putting two suitcases into a container for him?
> A I don't remember, sir.
> Q Doing that, perhaps, whilst he was away for a little while?
> A I don't remember, sir.
> Q All right. Is it possible you might have done that, Mr. Kamboj?
> A Yes, sir, possibility, yes.

Q Do you remember, in fact, telling Mr. Bedford that you had done that for him?

A I don't remember, sir.

Q If Mr. Bedford remembers you telling him that you had helped him out by putting two suitcases into a container, would you quarrel with him over that?

A If he said that, or whatever -- I mean, it's a possibility, as I already said before, and I can't actually remember now. So if he said -- I mean, I will admit that, yes; but if I did, that maybe had to go through the proper security procedure, and then --

Q Of course. Of course. But if Mr. Bedford has a recollection of you telling him that, would you say he was wrong?

A I won't say he was wrong, no.

In cross-examination Kamboj was taken back through his steadfast denials as recorded in three separate police interviews (one mere days after the event) and under oath at the FAI, and agreed that his recollection then was much better than it was in 2000 (hardly contentious, as most of his replies to Mr. Turnbull consisted of "I don't remember"), and that in his police interviews and in the witness box at Dumfries he had told the truth to the best of his ability. Nevertheless this was one more example of clever questioning of a witness succeeding in eliciting an isolated statement that could be spun in such a way as to contradict the main thrust of the witness's evidence.

Although the specific point was never highlighted, one thing was abundantly clear. Just as in Frankfurt, Pan Am had no procedure in place to ensure that luggage coming into the interline shed was legitimate, and was accompanied by a passenger who had boarded the plane. If a case had a tag for a Pan Am flight, and passed the x-ray screen, it was on. It was also virtually certain that Kamboj would have passed a cunningly-disguised radio-cassette bomb if it had been in a suitcase he was given to x-ray. In addition, there was no security in place to ensure luggage was not put into the container by unauthorised persons. While the question was not specifically asked, staff in the shed didn't seem to consider it part of their duties to keep watch on the containers to ensure that this couldn't happen.

In contrast to KM180, where (almost) every passenger and their luggage was examined in detail, and the feeder flight where at least some of the incoming passenger documentation was produced and a number of the transfer items identified as belonging to particular passengers, no incoming passenger records relating to transfers on to PA103 at Heathrow were presented to the court. Astonishingly, the interested researcher can discover more about how many cases were loaded into AVE4041 in the interline shed and which passengers they belonged to by reading David Leppard's 1991 book on the police inquiry, *On the Trail of Terror*, than by searching the court transcript.

The obvious missing feature is of course Derek Henderson's evidence. DC Henderson had been tasked with collating the information available concerning all the luggage which had been or even might have been loaded into AVE4041, including all the interline luggage arriving at Heathrow for PA103 and all the luggage on the feeder flight destined for the transatlantic leg. He compiled two reports, a very detailed one covering all the Heathrow interline luggage and a second which tabulated everything determined to have been in the container; listing owner, description of the item, whether recovered or not, and any explosives damage. His evidence was absolutely central at the FAI, and again in New York. In the latter hearing Pan Am's counsel had attempted to have his testimony ruled inadmissible on the grounds that since he had not personally conducted all the interviews which established the ownership of the various suitcases, but was collating information gathered by other police officers, it should be regarded as hearsay. This application was dismissed on the grounds that DC Henderson was an experienced and competent policeman doing his job, and there was no reason to believe he might be biassed or misrepresenting the evidence. He must surely have expected to be called to Camp Zeist to repeat his performance, however he was not, and his report was not referred to during the trial.

The only luggage described in court was about twenty-five items which featured in the Joint Forensic Report as showing explosives damage. In the witness box Thomas Hayes, the forensic scientist who had examined the luggage recovered at Lockerbie, took the court through his findings relating to these items, reading much of the Joint Forensic Report into the transcript verbatim. His work was purely descriptive and almost completely devoid of interpretation. While he had sketched a few of the items with arrows suggesting the direction from which they had been hit by the blast, there was no attempt to reconstruct the packing of the container or to figure out where each item might have been loaded in relation to the bomb suitcase. The amount of detail presented was impressive, nevertheless it invites the question, what was the point? The prosecution didn't seem to be making one.

Some of the luggage tabulated was identifiable to particular passengers by labels or tags, which were described in the report, however many items had no obvious identification and there was little attempt to demonstrate who owned what. As a result the court was unaware for the most part which items had been loaded in the interline shed and which had been transferred across the tarmac.

Only one point was brought out which touched on the spacial relationship between the bomb bag and another suitcase. This related to a fairly large piece of the bomb suitcase, from either the base or the lid, given the production number PI/911. Dr. Hayes was being questioned by Alistair Campbell for the prosecution, about an examination dated 26th January 1989.

Q   And this is a note of your examination of PI/911. And could I draw your attention to the writing that we see to the right-hand side of the drawing, where you describe the article as: "A severely distorted irregular-shaped sheet of rigid plastics," and go on to say: "Apparently the lower side of a suitcase, compressed and fractured in a manner suggesting it was in contact with a luggage pallet's base and subjected to explosive forces from above." Now, is that an observation that you made when you were examining this article in January of 1989?

A   Yes, it was, sir.

Q   And was that at quite an early stage in the course of examining articles?

A   Yes, it was.

Q   What was it about the item that suggested to you that it was in contact with the luggage pallet's base and subjected to explosive forces from above?

A   On the assumption that it might have been part of the suitcase containing a bomb, firstly the residual size of the fragment, which is quite large, and also the fact it appeared to have been supported in some substantial way by a relatively immoveable surface.

Q   If you assume that the -- this suitcase was not on the floor of the pallet but was on the next level up -- that is to say, on top of other luggage -- are you able to explain what you see here on that basis?

A   Yes, I am. Quite satisfactorily, to my own mind.

Q   How would you do that?

A   By considering that if a suitcase had resided beneath this one, then the surface of that suitcase, whether of a soft material or a hardshell material, could have similarly acted as a relatively immoveable surface if it, in turn, had been supported beneath, and in view of the tremendous speed of the detonation shock front.

EXAMINATION

Ref. PP 8932   Date 26/1/89

PI/911   Plastics bag and contents with attached label marked
" Piece of suitcase with puncture holes".
Contents :—

A severely distorted irregular
shaped sheet of rigid plastic.
Apparently the lower side of a
suitcase compressed and
fractured in a manner
suggesting it was in contact
with the luggage pallet's base
and subjected to explosive
forces from above.

The sheet has an outer thin skin of thin burgundy red
plastics in a simulated leather finish, backed with a
thicker rigid grey plastic — total thickness ≈ 2.5 mm.
The sheet is locally heat affected with blackening, melting.
The?original lining of woven brown cloth with a reticulated
beige coloured foam underlay is adhering in one area.
Elsewhere fragments of partially charred variously coloured
bundles of fibres (red, blue, brown, white) adhere on a carbonised
landscape.
The brown (burgundy) outer surface has been penetrated in
places by materials from the inner surface — is not blackened
and has large to small flecks of foamed blue plastics with
a cross hatched thick blue plastic skin possibly due to
intimate contact with a blue plastic (?lined) suitcase.

PT/42   The items recovered from PI/911 were raised collectively as
PT/42 " ASSORTED MATERIALS RECOVERED FROM SUITCASE
FRAGMENT PI 911 "

PT69   "Fragment of brown lining material removed from PI 911" 28·1·89

Figure 13

Page 25 of Hayes's examination notes, dealing with bomb suitcase fragment
PI/911.

The full entry being referred to is reproduced on the previous page, so let's drill down into this. When Dr. Hayes first examined that fragment of the bomb suitcase, he deduced from its condition that it had been directly in contact with the floor of the container. That, in effect, would put it smack in the position of the case Bedford saw. However, he also noticed something else – some flecks of blue plastic material adherent to the outside surface of the fragment. Both observations appear to have been made at the same time, but obviously the two things are mutually exclusive. If the fragment was in contact with something blue, it wasn't in contact with the floor of the container. Dr. Hayes testified that he had no problem reassessing his analysis to conclude that in fact the bomb suitcase had been on the second layer, with the 'something blue' underneath.

So, is this our evidence that the case Bedford saw was really blue, just as Andrew Hardie had suggested to him in 1990? Well, no. Mr. Campbell didn't pursue the matter further, but Richard Keen, Fhimah's defence advocate, returned to PI/911 in cross-examination. It was at this stage that the identity of the blue suitcase now being presented as having been below the bomb suitcase was revealed. It was Tricia Coyle's navy-blue canvas American Tourister, one of the interline items traced through the Frankfurt baggage transfer system *en route* from Vienna. That's right. The suitcase being proposed as the one on the floor of the container, under the bomb suitcase, in the position where Bedford reported seeing the mysterious brown Samsonite, was one that had come in on the feeder flight.

Wait, *WHAT?*

The fundamental justification for the Fatal Accident Inquiry's dismissal of the 'Bedford bag' as a possible candidate for the bomb suitcase was the assumption that it had remained on the floor of the container, in the position Feraday was adamant the explosion wasn't. However, if the Coyle case was in fact on the floor in that corner of the container, then the Bedford case must have been moved. Why was the FAI not made aware of this? What reason is there now to exclude the mysterious brown Samsonite seen in the interline shed?

Good questions, but answers are very hard to come by.

Mr. Keen pressed Hayes about the timing of his change of mind, from believing that the bomb suitcase was in contact with the floor to believing that it had been on the second layer with the blue item underneath, and why there was no record of this in his notes. Hayes elegantly side-stepped the question in his inimitable style, replying that "other considerations, then the positioning of the fragments, the location, recovery of those fragments, would help to assemble a perhaps rather different picture." However he could produce no record of this assembled picture, and offered no suggestion as to when it had been concluded that a case from the feeder flight had been under the bomb suitcase.

Some things never change, though. At Camp Zeist, Crown witnesses were practically lining up to declare that the bomb suitcase couldn't *possibly* have been on the bottom layer of luggage in the container. Forensic scientist Ian Cullis advanced several arguments to this effect, including the absence of pitting on the floor, the dished appearance of part of the floor, and a claim that he could see indents suggesting that another large suitcase (not the bomb suitcase itself) had been blasted down on to the aluminium base. Allen Feraday maintained that the base would have been more severely damaged than it was if the bomb suitcase had been "in contact with" the floor. Other witnesses made similar or identical points. This evidence however consisted entirely of opinions and assertions which are not at all self-evident from the appearance of the reassembled floor (see figure 3 and plate 2) and which were not supported by any experimental data. The court was simply invited to take the forensic witnesses' word for it.

Allen Feraday went rather further in his contribution to the Joint Forensic Report. He had turned his mind to figuring out just how the bomb suitcase might have been oriented within the container so as to place the centre of the IED in the awkward corner position determined for the explosion, as illustrated in the ubiquitous diagram prepared by Peter Claiden of the AAIB (see figure 12 and plate 3). He had come to the conclusion that only two loading positions for the bomb suitcase were possible, and (surprise, surprise) neither of them was the flat-on-the-floor location. These two positions were as shown in figure 14.

There is a serious problem with these illustrations, which was pointed out in court. The suitcases are drawn far too small. As is clear from Bedford's evidence, and from perusal of the dimensions of the container (figure 11), two suitcases side-by-side would occupy more or less the entire width. Feraday explained that the drawing office at RARDE had misinterpreted his instructions. However, the illustrations had never been corrected.

Although two positions were illustrated, the Crown narrative at Camp Zeist was entirely predicated on the "second postulated position" with the Coyle case represented by the left-hand item in the bottom row. Indeed, it is virtually impossible to see how the PI/911 fragment could have become compressed against the immoveable surface of the Coyle suitcase if the bomb suitcase had been in the overhang section as shown in the "first postulated position". On that basis, the first position seems more theoretical than a practical possibility. In cross-examination Richard Keen tried to demonstrate to Feraday that there

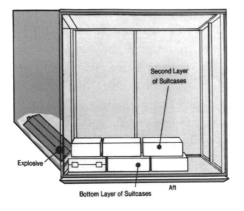 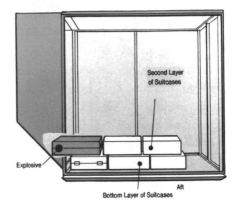

Figure 14
Illustrations from the Joint Forensic Report showing Feraday's two 'postulated positions'.
Left: "First postulated position"
Right: "Second postulated position"

was a third possible position for the bomb suitcase which would also put the IED in the specified corner, but Feraday resisted the suggestion. Lacking a three-dimensional model or at least a properly-scaled diagram the point was difficult to appreciate.

The startling information that the investigators believed the Bedford bag had been moved and replaced by an identified suitcase from the feeder flight throws everything into confusion, however. In that case, the mysterious brown Samsonite could easily have found itself in either of Feraday's two 'postulated positions', and it becomes rather difficult to see the point of the concerted effort to exclude the suitcase on the floor of the container. The bomb was in the brown hardshell, not the blue Tourister.

The inference seemed to be that the necessary rearrangement would have occurred at the time the Frankfurt luggage was added to the container, out on the tarmac beside the incoming 727. In that case, what was to prevent the mysterious brown Samsonite from the interline shed having been replaced right on top of the Coyle case – and being the bomb? Apparently nothing. And yet, it was fairly clear that there had been no serious police investigation into the possibility that the bomb suitcase had been introduced into the container in the interline shed at Heathrow, and the point was not something that had been considered by the Fatal Accident Inquiry.

The concept of a tarmac suitcase-shuffle seems rather improbable on the face of it. The feeder flight was twenty minutes late in landing at Heathrow, which halved the usual time available for the passengers and luggage to be transferred to the transatlantic leg. This was the winter solstice. It was cold and dark and raining and blowing a gale. Airport baggage handlers, like drystone dyke builders, don't waste energy moving something that's already in an acceptable position, and Bedford said the two extra cases were properly loaded. All previous hearings had assumed that the Frankfurt luggage had simply been chucked on top of what was already there, and that seems a pretty reasonable assumption.

The obvious person to ask, clearly, is the man who did the job. What did he say he did?

One loader-driver was indeed asked about the possibility of luggage in a container being rearranged during a tarmac transfer – not by Crown counsel, but by Mr. Davidson, a junior member of Fhimah's legal team.

> Q And again, so far as the loading of such a container was concerned, I take it there was nothing in tablets of stone that dictated how you went about loading such a container?
> A In terms of what, sir?
> Q There was nothing sacrosanct about the way a loader went about loading such a container?
> A No, as long as it was securely loaded, yes.
> Q And different loaders would no doubt employ different methods from time to time?
> A Yes, I suppose so.
> Q Because the object of the exercise [...] within reason, would be to accommodate as many bags as one reasonably could within such a container?
> A Yes.
> Q And to achieve that, it would sometimes be necessary for a loader to initially, perhaps, move bags around in the area of the base of the container so that they would better fit in?
> A During the loading of a container, that is the case, yes.
> Q And you've seen that going on?
> A In this case?
> Q I am talking generally.
> A Generally speaking, yes, sir.
> Q I don't think you saw the loading of the container in this particular --

A   No, sir.

Q   And so, clearly, a loader would improvise, depending on the size of the bags he had to deal with and the number of bags, as to how he positioned them?

A   That is correct.

Q   And he might, on occasion, put some in upright and then decide that it was more effective to stack them in another position?

A   Yes, sir.

Q   And there would be a bit of rejigging of the bags went on to suit the demands; is that correct?

A   Yes, sir.

"I am talking generally." "I don't think you saw the loading of the container in this particular…" That's odd. In fact the baggage handler being cross-examined in this exchange was Terence Crabtree, who was in charge of the team loading *Maid of the Seas*. He didn't even see AVE4041 until it was handed over to him, already fully loaded and with the canvas curtain closed and secured.

Well, that's not much use, is it? Of course a loader *might* rearrange the bags, if he had a particular reason for it. The question is, *did the man who added the Frankfurt luggage to AVE4041 on 21st December 1988 rearrange the bags?* What did *he* say in the witness box?

The witness who testified in relation to the unloading of the 727 was Darshan Sandhu, Crabtree's counterpart for the feeder flight, in charge of the entire crew handling that aircraft. He was brought to Camp Zeist from his retirement home in India to give evidence. His evidence-in-chief was conducted in the most general terms, merely confirming that the luggage for the transatlantic leg had been placed in AVE4041. Again, it was left to defence cross-examination to elicit a bit more detail.

Q   The container which was used to unload luggage from the Frankfurt flight --

A   The container was brought out to us.

Q   You didn't bring it out yourself?

A   I didn't bring it, no.

Q   Do you know who brought it out?

A   Sorry?

Q   Do you know who brought it --

A   Yes, sir, Mr. Sidhu, I. Sidhu.

Q And as regards the unloading of the Frankfurt plane, what part did you actually play in --

A Well, I was on the bulk side of the aircraft, just supervising. I was giving a hand, as well, to put in bags into the container. My function was work on board, tend to the aircraft.

Q So some of the time you were helping put bags in the container, and other times you were moving around that side of the aircraft?

A That's right, sir.

Q Helping out generally?

A Yes, sir.

[...]

Q I'll just read to you what you appear to have said to the police, and perhaps you can confirm if I've read it correctly, and whether you said this to the police: I spent the majority of time assisting Mr. Sidhu load the container, but left occasionally to check the men working on the rear holds. Is that right?

A That's right, sir, as I said.

So Mr. Sandhu isn't the person we need to hear from either. He didn't load AVE4041, he just "gave a hand, generally", while supervising the team. It sounds as if the witness we need is "Mr. I. Sidhu". What did he say he did with the bags from the interline shed? Surely someone asked him?

Well, if they did, nobody at Camp Zeist got to hear about it. "Mr. I. Sidhu" was not called to give evidence.

This is *mindblowingly* frustrating. Here we have evidence of a suitcase perfectly matching the description of the bomb suitcase, seen by a witness in pretty much exactly the position of the explosion, almost an hour before the feeder flight landed. The witness told the police about it less than three weeks after the disaster. And yet the investigators had no coherent explanation as to how they had ruled it out. Not only that, the basic information necessary to figure out whether it *could* actually be ruled out was withheld from the court.

The Crown did not reveal how many passengers interlined into Heathrow for PA103 that day, what luggage they were carrying, which items were the ones placed into AVE4041 in the interline shed, what they looked like, whether all were recovered on the ground, or what degree of blast damage each one sustained. It is absolutely certain that the investigators, and hence the Crown, had all that information. So did they know if the suitcase Bedford described could be shown to be a perfectly innocent piece of Heathrow interline luggage? If they did, wouldn't they have told us?

The question of whether the Heathrow interline luggage had been rearranged during the tarmac transfer from the feeder flight was of paramount significance, with the Crown now keen to propose that it had indeed been rearranged, although this was a complete reversal of the position taken at the time of the Fatal Accident Inquiry. It appears that the man who would be able to enlighten us as to whether such a rearrangement took place was the man who collected the container after its controversial forty-five-minute sojourn outside Walker's office and drove it on to the tarmac. The man, in fact, who completed the chain of custody between Bedford's evidence and Crabtree taking possession of it to load it on to *Maid of the Seas*. The man who would be the obvious witness to call to speak to that part of the narrative, even if there was no issue over the arrangement of the suitcases. But the Crown chose instead to bring a witness from India, who had been present only intermittently and was probably not in a position to know whether anything already in the container had been moved to a different position.

Is it fanciful, at this point, to wonder if someone is trying to hide something?

Nevertheless, this is the evidence the bench had to work with. A judgement has to be made on the basis of the evidence presented, not on the basis of evidence not presented. The primary onus is on the prosecution to present a case they believe stands up beyond reasonable doubt. The job of the defence is to introduce that reasonable doubt.

The defence clearly believed the case was already so riddled with entirely reasonable doubt that they were somewhat superfluous. Their challenge was notably half-hearted, and in particular the astonishing *volte face* by the Crown on the matter of the rearrangement of the Heathrow-loaded suitcases seems to have been accepted with grateful thanks. Indeed, the proposition that the baggage handlers were in the habit of moving suitcases around in a container was actively encouraged, as evidenced by Mr. Davidson's cross-examination of Terence Crabtree.

One can see why. The original FAI position that the suitcases had not been moved, and that the forensic evidence excluded the case in the position occupied by the Bedford bag from being the bomb, might have been a difficult point to counter if it was solidly founded. Now the Crown had handed the defence an escape clause on a silver platter. The suitcases *had* been moved, apparently. So the defence were free to argue the possibility that the Bedford bag had been replaced on top of the Coyle suitcase, and so was the bomb.

Timeo Danaos et dona ferentes.

★ ★ ★ ★ ★ ★ ★

In no other Scottish murder trial has the public been afforded the opportunity to discover the reasoning behind a verdict. Jury deliberations and decisions happen behind closed doors, and are supposed to remain there. Zeist was different. Because the trial was by judicial bench rather than by jury, the judgement was explained in an eighty-two-page 'Opinion of the Court'. As an exercise in circular reasoning, it has probably never been surpassed.

The reasoning behind the decision on the Malta evidence has already been discussed in chapter 2. The court acknowledged that "the absence of any explanation of the method by which the primary suitcase might have been placed on board KM180 is a major difficulty for the Crown case" and then simply left it at that. One is left to infer that the other strands of evidence demonstrating that the bomb had indeed been carried on that aircraft were so strong that this difficulty could simply be brushed aside.

The only evidence suggesting that the bomb had been carried on KM180, however, was the infamous tray 8849 in the Frankfurt computer printout. The judges summarised the defence submissions in relation to the transfer baggage, but remained unimpressed.

> The evidence in regard to what happened at Frankfurt Airport, although of crucial importance, is only part of the evidence in the case and has to be considered along with all the other evidence before a conclusion can be reached as to where the primary suitcase originated and how it reached PA103. It can, however, be said at this stage that if the Frankfurt evidence is considered entirely by itself and without reference to any other evidence, none of the points made by the defence seems to us to cast doubt on the inference from the documents and other evidence that an unaccompanied bag from KM180 was transferred to and loaded onto PA103A.

So what about tray 5620, the mystery tray matching the Warsaw flight on the printout? The judges explicitly noted the point – and then moved on without comment.

The fundamental problem is that the court was never made aware that there were considerably more than these two unidentified items on the computer printout. That the twenty-five transfer items in fact divided into two groups – the minority where the printout/worksheet reconciliation matched up to clearly-documented legitimate transfer baggage destined for PA103, and the majority where it did not – with tray 8849 being a part of the latter group.

The evidence as presented allowed the inference that since the Vienna and Kuwait luggage could be shown to tie up so neatly, it was quite reasonable to conclude that tray 8849 tied up equally neatly to something carried on KM180. If you don't know about all that luggage from LH241 and PA637 being entered into the system without the slightest trace of it appearing on a worksheet, or that at least four of these items, presumably legitimate luggage from the latter flight, had defied all attempts to work out what they were and how they got there, it might seem fair enough. If you then deliberately exclude all reference to the pretty strong evidence from Malta showing that there was no such thing on KM180, as the judges did in the above passage, it's a positive no-brainer.

So, we don't know how that suitcase got on board KM180. It's a difficulty. But if we ignore that (and a bunch of other stuff nobody actually told us about), then there *was* another case on that flight that was coded for PA103A. That's settled, then.

But what about Heathrow? Is it not the case that the Bedford bag at least introduces reasonable doubt? Nobody was able to describe the suitcase in tray 8849 – if it was a suitcase. Even if there was an unaccompanied and undocumented item carried on KM180, can we be sure it was the bomb? Particularly in view of the witness description of a brown Samsonite hardshell that appeared in mysterious circumstances in the interline shed before the feeder flight landed? We now know that the FAI findings were arrived at by way of a completely false assumption, that this suitcase had not been moved. If it was moved in order to put the Coyle case on the floor of the container, it could easily have been replaced on top of that case, in the location the forensic scientists were promoting as the position of the bomb suitcase. How can the bomb be determined to have come from Malta beyond reasonable doubt with that thing sitting there unexplained?

Like this, actually.

It was argued on behalf of the accused that the suitcase described by Mr. Bedford could well have been the primary suitcase, particularly as the evidence did not disclose that any fragments of a hard-shell Samsonite-type suitcase had been recovered, apart from those of the primary suitcase itself. It was accepted, for the purposes of this argument, that the effect of forensic evidence was that the suitcase could not have been directly in contact with the floor of the container. It was submitted that there was evidence that an American Tourister suitcase, which had travelled from Frankfurt, fragments of which had been recovered, had been very intimately involved in the explosion and could have been placed under the suitcase spoken to by Mr. Bedford. That would have required rearrangement of the items in the container, but such rearrangement could easily have occurred when the baggage from Frankfurt was being put into the container on the tarmac at Heathrow. It is true that such a rearrangement could have occurred, but if there was such a rearrangement, the suitcase described by Mr. Bedford might have been placed at some more remote corner of the container, and while the forensic evidence dealt with all the items recovered which showed direct explosive damage, twenty-five in total, there were many other items of baggage found which were not dealt with in detail in the evidence in the case.

Sorry, what? The judges accepted "for the purposes of this argument" (which itself doesn't sound like a ringing endorsement) that the bomb suitcase wasn't on the floor of the container. They also note that the suitcase which *was* on the floor of the container seems to have been the Coyle case, which was underneath the bomb. This means that the Bedford case must have been moved, which means it could have been put back on the second layer, on top of the Coyle case. Additionally, they note that the only brown Samsonite recovered from among the blast-damaged luggage was the bomb suitcase itself. So far so good.

But then, accepting that the Bedford case was moved, it *could* have been moved to "some more remote corner of the container", out of range of the blast. The only items of luggage described to the court were those which were damaged by the explosion. So it is possible Bedford's brown Samsonite was undamaged, and simply not among the items the Crown chose to present in evidence.

Paraphrased only slightly, the court judgement states that because the Bedford bag *might* have been moved much further than the defence suggested it had been moved, it has not been proved to have been the bomb. Thus, it may be assumed that it wasn't the bomb. And hang the concept of 'reasonable doubt', apparently.

It seems that the 'escape clause' provided by the Crown's surprising decision to introduce the idea that the Bedford bag had been moved didn't work out as expected. Instead of allowing for the possibility of that case being the second-level bomb suitcase, it allowed the judges to hand-wave it away to "some more remote corner of the container". What on earth was Sidhu doing with these suitcases that afternoon? Training for the shot put?

Then, the Crown's decision not to tell anyone what the legitimate passenger baggage interlined into Heathrow looked like, or to present a complete reconciliation of all the recovered luggage from AVE4041, allowed for the possibility that what Bedford saw was just a late-arriving item of normal luggage, which had been moved somewhere else.

In fact, moving the Bedford case turned out to be lethal for the defence. If that case had not been moved, then according to the forensic scientists' scenario it was right underneath the bomb suitcase when it exploded. It would have been in the group of blast-damaged luggage described in the Joint Forensic Report and presented in court. It would have been open to the defence to point out that lacking the remains of that suitcase, it was a compelling inference that it was indeed the bomb suitcase. *Just how certain was that conclusion that the bomb could not have been in the bottom layer of luggage, anyway?*

It is entirely clear that the judges' exclusion of the Bedford suitcase was spurious, even taking into account the severely limited information at their disposal. The evidence from Malta was indeed a "major difficulty", which the evidence from Frankfurt was by no stretch of the imagination conclusive enough to overcome. The defence submission that the Bedford case could well have been replaced on top of the Coyle case was absolutely unanswerable, representing the strongest possible degree of reasonable doubt, and categorically should not have been hand-waved away with nothing more than "well it might not have been", which is what the passage quoted above boils down to.

Of course, there was more to it than that.

The law as it relates to circumstantial evidence was laid out in more detail in the Appeal judgement, however it is quite simple. It is not necessary for every piece of circumstantial evidence to be proved beyond reasonable doubt, or indeed that any individual piece is proved to that standard, so long as the case viewed as a whole presents a compelling picture. In this way a number of less-than-certain pieces of evidence may be held to corroborate each other, in that they fit together to provide a coherent narrative pointing to guilt.

This is an entirely reasonable position and completely in accordance with natural justice. Nevertheless the exercise of building up this 'compelling picture' carries the risk of creating a self-fulfilling prophecy, where dubious points of evidence are held to reinforce each other in a never-ending circle that ends with the snake swallowing its own tail. In effect, A is held to be true because B is assumed to be true, but B is held to be true because A is assumed to be true. This logical fallacy is known as *petitio principii*, or circular reasoning.

The additional factor taken into consideration by the court was of course the presence of Abdelbaset al-Megrahi, the 'first accused', at Luqa airport when KM180 was checking in. However it wasn't quite as simple, or as blatant, as merely declaring that there was a suspicious person in the vicinity at the time of the alleged Malta introduction whereas no suspicious person had been shown to be present at Heathrow, therefore the former *modus operandi* was proved to have occurred and the suspicious person was therefore guilty.

There was a second, entirely separate piece of evidence against Megrahi, and that was his identification by Tony Gauci, the Maltese shopkeeper who sold at least some of the clothes found to have been packed in the suitcase with the bomb, as "resembling" the man who bought these clothes. If Megrahi really did buy the clothes then he was undoubtedly complicit in the Lockerbie atrocity whether or not he had a hand in actually putting the bomb on the plane. The court took the view that he had bought the clothes, and therefore the presence at Luqa airport that morning of someone who was complicit in the atrocity could be held to prove the Malta introduction theory over the Heathrow one.

The evidence and the reasoning behind the decision that Megrahi was indeed the clothes purchaser are explored in more detail in chapter 8. That, by itself, was in fact another example of *petitio principii*.

Evidence from Tony and his brother Paul, in conjunction with the date the Yorkie trousers were supplied by the manufacturer, narrowed the date of the purchase down to either 23rd November or 7th December 1988. Dispassionate examination of the weight of evidence supporting each date inevitably comes down pretty heavily in favour of the November day, with the December day being more of an outside possibility. The only problem for the prosecution was that while Megrahi was very definitely on Malta on 7th December, travelling openly on his own passport, there was no evidence he was anywhere near the place on 23rd November, under any name whatsoever.

The judges decided that the clothes had been purchased on 7th December, without giving any reason for that decision.

Then, when it came to examining the very questionable identification evidence, the judges decided that although the identification was "not absolute", the purchaser was indeed Megrahi because the purchase had occurred on a day when he was on the island and was in a position to have visited 'Mary's House'. In addition he had been present at the airport at the time when the bomb had been loaded on to the plane.

Tray 8849 on the computer printout was held to show the bomb transiting from KM180 to PA103A, despite the evidence from Malta showing that no unaccompanied luggage was carried on that flight, because the clothes packed in the bomb suitcase had been purchased only three miles from Luqa airport. Of course there was ample time between the purchase of the clothes and the actual bombing for the clothes to have been round the world and back, but then the man who bought the things was at the airport at the time…

And if you're looking for a reason for the judges picking the December date of purchase over the November one, then the only thing that really springs to mind is that the man who was at the airport on the 21st was also around on the 7th.

Round and round and round she goes, where she stops, nobody knows.

The judges themselves seemed to be aware of the potential criticisms of their reasoning.

> We are aware that in relation to certain aspects of the case there are a number of uncertainties and qualifications. We are also aware that there is a danger that by selecting parts of the evidence which seem to fit together and ignoring parts which might not fit, it is possible to read into a mass of conflicting evidence a pattern or conclusion which is not really justified.

Uh, yes. *Hello?* Are you even *listening* to yourselves?

> However, having considered the whole evidence in the case, including the uncertainties and qualifications, and the submissions of counsel, we are satisfied that the evidence as to the purchase of clothing in Malta, the presence of that clothing in the primary suitcase, the transmission of an item of baggage from Malta to London, the identification of the first accused (albeit not absolute), his movements under a false name at or around the material time, and the other background circumstances [...], does fit together to form a real and convincing pattern. There is nothing in the evidence which leaves us with any reasonable doubt as to the guilt of the first accused, and accordingly we find him guilty.

Evidently not.

★ ★ ★ ★ ★ ★ ★

Of course there was an appeal, which was also heard at Camp Zeist between 23rd January and 14th February 2002. Megrahi was by then residing alone in the attached prison, his friend Fhimah having been released to return to Libya after receiving a 'not guilty' verdict. The Crown had alleged that Fhimah was the person who had gone airside to engineer the introduction of the bomb suitcase on to KM180, but as they were unable even to prove that he had been at the airport that day, there was really no case against him. The conundrum of how Megrahi had accomplished the deed without having gone airside himself or having any other identified accomplice was simply left hanging.

The appeal proceedings have been much criticised, not least by the UN-appointed observer to the trial Prof. Hans Köchler, however to understand the problems it is necessary to understand the grounds of appeal lodged by the defence.

Where a verdict has been arrived at by faulty reasoning, the usual ground of appeal would be to the effect that no reasonable jury, properly directed, could have returned this verdict. Mr. Taylor, lead advocate for the defence, specifically disavowed reliance on this ground, apparently because the trial had not been heard by a jury but by a judicial bench who directed themselves and delivered a written judgement. He was therefore of the opinion that the "no reasonable jury" argument was inappropriate.

It seems that this was a misapprehension. Perusal of the 200-page "Opinion of the Court" delivered by the five appeal judges reveals numerous instances where the judges more or less explicitly state, well you didn't appeal on this ground so we don't have to consider it, but if you had, well...

Instead the appeal was mounted on more or less a repetition of the original defence case, at each point claiming that the judges had not given proper consideration or proper weight to certain items of evidence. This was a very bad mistake.

In their written judgement, the trial court judges repeatedly made reference to the defence submissions, or to obvious problems with their own reasoning, and then stated something along the lines of "having taken all that into consideration and having given due regard to these factors, we nevertheless find that..." and then chose the interpretation that favoured guilt, regardless of how much more probable the interpretation favouring innocence might be. You can't appeal against that by declaring that the judges haven't given due consideration to something they explicitly stated they *did* give due consideration to.

The decision as to how a matter of fact should be interpreted is for the trial court. Appeal judges are extraordinarily reluctant to substitute their opinion for the opinion of the trial court in this respect. Repeatedly, the appeal judges at Zeist pointed out that it simply wasn't the case that the trial judges hadn't given consideration or weight to a particular point; the fact was that they self-evidently had considered the point, but the defence disagreed with the interpretation the judges had chosen to favour. The appeal judges noted that it wasn't for them to override the opinion of the trial court in this way *unless* they were faced with a submission arguing that the conclusions were irrational. And the defence advocate had specifically disavowed this argument.

It is clear, nevertheless, that the appeal judges had their reservations about the reasoning of the trial of the first instance. As noted on page 18, Lord Osborne specifically observed that the decision that the bomb must have flown on KM180 "may not be a rational conclusion", in the light of the "considerable and quite convincing evidence" that there had been no breach of security in relation to the departure of that flight. Examination of the appeal transcripts reveals any number of similar examples.

However, when decision time came, the grounds of appeal were comprehensively rejected. It is probably not relevant to note in this context that the events of 11th September 2001 occurred between the trial and the appeal, and involved Arab Moslem suicide bombers using airliners to attack targets on the mainland of the USA. Nevertheless the point has been raised by some, including by Megrahi himself.

The Opinion of the Appeal Court goes into additional detail on a number of important points, with the treatment of "the provenance of the primary suitcase" running from pages 35 to 152 of the 200-page judgement. The section from pages 118 to 141 deals with the single piece of new evidence presented to the appeal court: the evidence of the break-in into the Heathrow Terminal 3 airside area during the night preceding the disaster.

This evidence came to light in an unusual way. In 2001 Mr. Raymond Manly, a retired security guard at Heathrow airport, heard about Megrahi's conviction through the media. He then contacted Megrahi's defence team to ask why they had not called him to give evidence. The defence team had no idea what he was talking about.

It transpired that Ray Manly had been on duty at Terminal 3 during the night of 20th to 21st December 1988. In the course of his security round, at about half past midnight, he had checked a particular door which gave access between the landside and airside areas at the terminal. He discovered that its padlock, which was secured on the landside aspect of the door, had been forcibly broken. The door had been locked at 22.05 and everything was secure at that time. He had informed his supervisor of the incident and submitted a written report.

Manly had been interviewed in the course of the original Lockerbie investigation in January 1989, and had given a signed statement describing his discovery of the broken padlock. He had however had no subsequent contact with the investigation, had not been re-interviewed, and had not been cited as a witness at the Fatal Accident Inquiry. His statement and other related statements had not been disclosed to the defence at the original trial.

The defence team was granted permission to call Manly and his supervisor Philip Radley to testify at the appeal. The story was generally confirmed, and was indeed recorded in contemporary airport documentation and witness statements. The Crown called several witnesses on its own behalf in an attempt to minimise the significance of the incident, painting it as no more than the work of late-working baggage handlers intent on taking a short-cut to the exit rather than making a detour to the door kept open overnight for that purpose.

There were two specific problems which bedevilled Manly's testimony. The first was the sheer difficulty of remembering the details of an incident that had happened more than thirteen years previously, and which he had not been required to recall subsequently. The baggage handlers and security guards at Heathrow each gave half a dozen or more statements to the police over a period of eighteen months, and appeared in the witness box in Dumfries in 1990 where they were taken through their recollections by an assortment of advocates representing the various interested parties. None of this happened to Manly, with the result that his memory, when tested, was confused and contradictory. He misremembered the layout of the area in question and the location of the door, and while his original report said merely that the padlock was "broken", he insisted in the witness box that it had been "cut like butter", as if by bolt cutters.

A second problem was highlighted by Prof. Köchler in his report on the appeal.

At the beginning of his testimony [Mr. Manly] told the court that, because of an accident, he was under medication and that he was afraid he might have to vomit in the course of his testimony. He looked very frail and behaved in a highly emotional, at times even aggressive manner. For the undersigned it was impossible to obtain any specific information about the factors which led to this deplorable state of health. In spite of the efforts promised by the Scottish Court Service, it was not possible to obtain any information on the kind of medication under the influence of which Mr. Manly may have acted in the way he did, or on the time and nature of the accident that made this medication necessary. In fact, Mr. Manly's testimony – seen in its entirety – may even have been counterproductive in regard to the defense strategy.

Manly reacted badly to pressure from prosecution counsel, which he interpreted as making a mockery of something he saw as a very serious matter. Shouting at advocates and criticising their line of questioning is not usually conducive to a witness being taken seriously in court.

Nevertheless the break-in happened. The correct door was identified in the contemporaneous records, and whether the padlock had been severed by bolt cutters or forced by some sort of crowbar or jemmy, it had been fastened on the landside side, and it had been broken. The inference that someone had broken *into* the airside space, into the very area where the luggage for PA103 was handled the following afternoon, was pretty clear.

The important question for the appeal judges was, if the trial judges had been aware of this extra evidence, would it have been sufficient to change their verdict? They decided not. It had never been part of the Crown case that the airside space at Terminal 3 was secure. On the contrary, it was a known fact that many hundreds of airside security passes were unaccounted for, and doubtless obtainable on the black market. Thus, evidence showing that an actual security breach had occurred more than twelve hours before baggage handling for the doomed flight commenced, would, they reasoned, have made no difference.

It's difficult to know what to make of the break-in. It's true that it happened many hours before the mysterious brown Samsonite appeared in AVE4041. It's true that there were other Pan Am transatlantic flights before PA103. It's true that the break-in happened closer to the baggage build-up shed than to the interline shed. It's true that simply walking in through security with a purloined pass and the right overalls would probably have been a piece of cake.

On the other hand, walking through a security check-point with a purloined pass *carrying a suitcase containing a Semtex IED* might be something a prudent terrorist would baulk at. As a means of getting the *suitcase* airside, the break-in has a certain rationality. There could be any number of reasons for not hitting an earlier flight, or the busy baggage build-up shed. The regular practice of an easily identifiable container sitting around all afternoon in the quiet interline shed, sometimes unattended, gathering occasional, piecemeal suitcases for PA103, might have been known to the terrorists. If it was, it was an absolute gift.

It comes back to that 'overall picture' thing. It's perfectly possible for the Bedford bag to have been the bomb, even without a break-in at midnight. It's perfectly possible the break-in was unrelated to the atrocity. However, if the Bedford bag was the bomb, it's a pretty fair inference that the two events are likely to be related.

More than its importance to the case as such, the Manly affair is interesting for what it tells us about the conduct of the inquiry in January/February 1989. The appeal judges noted that the Crown itself had been unaware of the existence of Manly's statement at the time of the original trial, therefore it was scarcely in a position to have disclosed it. No explanation was proffered as to how the Crown came to be unaware of a witness statement which might have been considered to be rather important to the investigation, particularly in its early stages.

This aspect remained unexplained until Dr. Jim Swire, the father of one of the Lockerbie victims, contacted the then Chief Constable of Dumfries and Galloway Constabulary in early 2012 to inquire about the matter. This is the reply he received.

email   executive@dg.pnn.police.uk   Our ref PS/NA
Phone   01387 242 201

Dear Dr Swire   2 April 2012

I refer to your recent correspondence headed 'Apparent Suppression of Evidence'. This letter seeks to fulfil the undertaking I gave you to provide you with an unambiguous response to concerns you raised regarding the handling of statements and evidence in connection with the insecurity detected at Heathrow.

I can confirm the following:

1. In January 1989 BAA security notified the Metropolitan police that an insecurity had been detected within terminal 3 at Heathrow during the early hours of 21 December 1988.
2. The Metropolitan police passed this evidence to the Police Incident Room at Lockerbie and Actions were raised to investigate this matter.
3. During the course of this investigation Mr Manly, the BAA Security Team Leader who discovered the insecurity, was interviewed by an officer from the Metropolitan Police and a

statement was obtained from him. The interview took place on 31 January 1989. A number of other witnesses were also traced and interviewed regarding the insecurity.

4. Mr Manly's statement was passed to the police incident room at Lockerbie and was registered on the HOLMES system on 2 February 1989. This statement and those from other witnesses identified at Heathrow were considered by enquiry officers at the time in the context of a range of emerging strands of evidence.

5. In 1991 the police report outlining the evidence against Mr Megrahi and Mr Fhima was submitted to the Crown Office. This report did not contain a reference to the insecurity at Heathrow and made no mention of Mr Manly's statement.

6. The surrender of Mr Megrahi and Mr Fhima for trial in the Netherlands prompted a massive preparation exercise during the course of which over 14,000 witness statements were provided to Crown Office in 1999. Mr Manly's statement was included in the material supplied to Crown though again the police made no reference to it.

7. In 2001, as a result of Mr Manly contacting defence representatives, the insecurity at Heathrow was subject to a fresh investigation, the Crown disclosed the relevant statements to the defence and as you know the matter was considered during Mr Megrahi's first appeal. The appeal judges, in rejecting the appeal, made it clear that their assessment of the significance of this additional evidence must be conducted in the context of the whole circumstantial evidence laid before the trial court and concluded that "it cannot be said that the verdict falls to be regarded as a miscarriage of justice on account of having been reached in ignorance of the additional evidence". As the Lord Advocate explained at the meeting in London it is not for the appeal court to look at the case "afresh", it has to consider the new evidence in the context of the whole case that the trial court had before it.

In summary I can categorically state that no suppression of evidence took place and I hope this information alleviates your concerns in that regard.

Signed: Patrick Shearer, Chief Constable.

This is a rather interesting narrative. The Lockerbie investigation itself didn't approach BAA (British Airports Authority, the company owning and running Heathrow airport which had been privatised by Margaret Thatcher in 1986) to ascertain whether there had been any security breaches prior to the departure of the doomed flight. In the absence of such an approach BAA itself recognised the potential significance of Manly's report to the fledgling investigation, and approached the Metropolitan Police with the information.

The Met were only peripherally involved in the Lockerbie investigation, which so far as the UK was concerned was a predominantly Scottish baby. Officers from London had indeed turned up in Dumfriesshire in the early stages, looking to take control, only to return to the metropolis soon afterwards following a round of political horse-trading which was won by the Scottish Lord Advocate, principally on account of his trump card, that Scottish citizens had been murdered in their own homes on Scottish soil.

Officers from the Met did however provide 'gopher' type assistance to the investigation due to their proximity to Heathrow, in the same way as officers in the north of England helped to gather wreckage and debris that had blown into England. The initial statements from baggage handlers and other airport staff were taken by Metropolitan Police detectives, most by DC Adrian Dixon. Mr. Shearer's email confirms how it worked. In this case, the first notification of a potential witness was received by the Met. The Met's initial response was simply to notify Lockerbie of what they had been told. Lockerbie's response was to request that a London-based officer should interview Manly and take a statement from him. This was done on 31st January, four weeks after Bedford's first interview, when he had described the mysterious appearance of a suitcase in more or less the position of the explosion. The Met, however, didn't do anything with Manly's statement beyond passing it straight back to Lockerbie.

This might be regarded as slightly odd, because in addition to low-level assistance with statement-taking and so on, New Scotland Yard did conduct its own investigation into the Heathrow aspect of the case, led by Superintendent Roger Pearce of the Metropolitan Police Anti-Terrorist Branch. However, London involvement appears to have faded into the background as the investigation became focussed on Malta, and it is difficult to know how this endeavour fits into the inquiry as a whole. No reports of its findings are in the public domain, and no reference was made to it at either the trial or the subsequent appeal. Whatever its scope, however, this does not appear to have extended to following up Ray Manly's evidence and establishing whether or not the midnight break-in was connected to the bombing.

So, Manly's statement and the other statements and evidence relating to the break-in were simply sent to Lockerbie, where they were registered in the computer system being used to keep track of the evidence. They were considered by the Scottish inquiry officers – and deemed to be of no importance whatsoever.

No follow-up statements were taken from the witnesses. The fact of the break-in did not become part of the narrative of the case as it existed in the first half of 1989. Neither Manly nor his colleagues were deemed to have anything relevant to contribute to the Fatal Accident Inquiry, and the FAI was never made aware that there had been a break-in at Heathrow. When the indictments were being prepared against Megrahi and Fhimah in 1991, the fact of the break-in did not form part of the report on the Heathrow evidence.

When the case was being prepared for trial, Manly's statement was included among the mountain of over 14,000 statements covering all aspects of the investigation. However, it was not mentioned in any summary material or lists of important or relevant statements.

It has been said, if you want to hide a tree, plant it in a forest.

Apparently the Crown itself didn't notice the statement, buried as it was among so much material. So it wasn't at fault as regards the statement not being disclosed to the defence. The statement wasn't knowingly or deliberately withheld. Mr. Shearer hopes Dr. Swire and the rest of us are OK about that.

Whether or not that's the case, it's not the main point, not any more. What does this narrative reveal about the first couple of months of the Lockerbie investigation? The period when the basic bones of the atrocity were still being reconstructed. The period when Thomas Hayes was guessing that the bomb suitcase might have been flat on the floor of the container. The period when the best estimate of the position of the explosion was the one drawn by the German police (figure 4). The period when the Scottish police were still completely unaware of the possibility that an unaccompanied suitcase had been transferred to the feeder flight from a flight from Malta.

What it reveals is that nobody had the slightest interest in following up the possibility that the bomb might have been introduced as an unaccompanied 'rogue' bag smuggled directly into the Heathrow baggage handling system. Despite their awareness of Bedford's testimony.

★　★　★　★　★　★　★

After the conclusion of the appeal Megrahi was sent to Scotland for the first time, to continue serving the twenty-year sentence imposed by the trial court (this was later increased to twenty-seven years on appeal). The following year he applied to the Scottish Criminal Cases Review Commission for leave to mount a second appeal.

This application saw the start of an investigation by the SCCRC which lasted close to four years and resulted in an 800-page report accompanied by thirteen volumes of appendices being submitted to the Crown Office. Leave to appeal was granted. The Commission had identified no less than six grounds on which they believed it was possible Megrahi might have suffered a miscarriage of justice.

While the full report was initially kept secret, on 28th June 2007 the SCCRC took the unusual step of issuing a press release outlining the situation. Four of the six grounds were described in that document.

The first was that "there is no reasonable basis in the trial court's judgment for its conclusion that the purchase of the items from Mary's House, took place on 7 December 1988."

The second was that "new evidence not heard at the trial [...] indicates that the purchase of the items took place prior to 6 December 1988. In other words, it indicates that the purchase took place at a time when there was no evidence at trial that the applicant was in Malta."

The third was that only four days before Tony Gauci picked Megrahi out of an identification parade, he had seen a magazine article with a photograph of Megrahi, clearly identifying him as the man on trial for Lockerbie.

The fourth wasn't spelled out in detail, but was understood to refer to the fact that after the appeal was concluded Tony Gauci had been paid a reward of at least $2 million with a further $1 million to his brother Paul, courtesy of the US Department of Justice 'Rewards for Justice' scheme. Although Paul himself didn't testify at Zeist, the reward was deemed appropriate for his "maintaining the resolve of his brother". Such 'rewards' are illegal under Scots law.

All four grounds relate to the identification of Megrahi as the man who bought the clothes packed in the bomb suitcase. The first ground relates to the conclusion that was the unsupported basis for the entire daisy-chain of circular reasoning on which the original conviction depended. If the purchase didn't occur on 7th December, Megrahi wasn't the purchaser. The others undermine the identification in different ways: additional positive evidence favouring 23rd November as the date of the purchase, evidence that the line-up identification was tainted, and evidence that the eye-witness had been, not to put too fine a point on it, bribed.

Basically, the SCCRC shot the idea that Megrahi even might have been the man who bought the clothes in the bomb suitcase, right between the eyes.

This development has clear knock-on ramifications in relation to the baggage transfer evidence. An important part of the original finding that the bomb must have travelled from Malta despite all the evidence that it really didn't, was the assumption that the man who bought the clothes was present at the airport when the flight in question departed.

Go figure.

Except, there's no evidence that anyone did go figure. In all the subsequent commentary, the point that the SCCRC had also by inference fatally undermined the Malta introduction theory, completely failed to register.

Megrahi's second appeal eventually made it to court in April 2009, but progress was slow and adjournments frequent. The timetable set by the court scheduled the hearings to continue into early 2010, which was beyond the appellant's then-estimated life expectancy. In September 2008 Megrahi had been diagnosed with aggressive prostate cancer, and at that time wasn't expected to live beyond the end of 2009. As everyone who hasn't been residing under a rock since the turn of the century knows, the appeal was abandoned as part of the deal that saw him return home to Libya on 20th August 2009, having been granted compassionate release as a result of the cancer diagnosis.

The full text of the SCCRC report (but not the appendices) was leaked by the press on 25th March 2012, less than two months before the cancer finally claimed Megrahi's life.

So, how did the SCCRC view the question of the route of introduction of the bomb? The answer is right there on the very first page of the introduction.

So far as the procedures at Heathrow, Frankfurt and Luqa airports are concerned, the application contained very limited submissions. Because of this and the substantial attention given to these matters at both trial and appeal, the Commission did not undertake specific enquiries into this aspect of the case. During the course of its review, the Commission came across nothing which might cast doubt on the evidence led by the Crown in this connection.

O... K...

If that demonstrates anything at all, it is this. Despite all the years the defence team spent examining the evidence, despite the extraordinarily wide range of allegations they threw at the SCCRC (including numerous allegations of tampering with or fabrication of evidence), they had absolutely no idea that they had in their possession, and had had all along, the evidence that conclusively proved the Bedford suitcase was the bomb.

6

THE ELUSIVE HEATHROW EVIDENCE

A number of documents which were in the possession of the defence from 1999 allow a complete analysis of the interline baggage handling at Heathrow, and enable a picture to be built up of where the blast-damaged items were loaded in the container and how they were positioned in relation to the bomb suitcase.

Not only did the defence have these documents, the all-important Joint Forensic Report was admitted in evidence at the trial. Much of the raw data in that report which allows the analysis of the way the luggage was packed was actually read out in court by Thomas Hayes, or contained in photographs which were referred to in court.

Statements from various Heathrow witnesses confirm the details of seventeen passengers who transferred to Pan Am 103 at Heathrow from twelve incoming flights, as detailed in table 3 overleaf.

Investigating the passengers who flew from Malta to Frankfurt is untroubling. These people came to Camp Zeist, alive and well, untouched by the tragedy. Their suitcases are just a nice intellectual puzzle. Moving on to the feeder flight is harder. We cry inwardly for Karen Noonan and Tricia Coyle, for Ken Gibson and Thomas Walker, for the Rattan family who disembarked from their booked flight because of a sick child, for Ibolya Gabor and her travelling companions who missed their original flight for no particularly good reason, and for the other names on the transfer passenger list we can see engraved on the memorial at Dryfesdale. At the same time, though, we're cheered by Adolf Weinacker's lucky escape and smile over Fiona Leckie's sprint for her connecting flight leaving her garden gnome behind.

Dealing with the transatlantic luggage is simply heartbreaking. Every single person on the list overleaf died at Lockerbie. These suitcases, which it's easy to

Passenger	Flight	From	Arrived	Checked-in luggage
Nicola Hall	SA234	Johannesburg	06.46	1 *
Bernt Carlsson	BA391	Brussels	11.06	1
Charles McKee	CY504	Larnaca	14.34	2
Matthew Gannon	CY504	Larnaca	14.34	1
Ronald LaRiviere	CY504	Larnaca	14.34	0
James Fuller	LH1628	Hannover	14.51	0
Louis Marengo	LH1628	Hannover	14.51	0
Gregory Kosmowski	BD777	Birmingham	15.07	0
Robert Fortune	BD108	Amsterdam	15.18	0
Elia Stratis	BD108	Amsterdam	15.18	0
Michael Bernstein	BA701	Vienna	15.35	2
Arnaud Rubin	BA395	Brussels	16.15	1
Joseph Curry	BA603	Pisa	16.21	2
Peter Peirce	BA603	Pisa	16.21	3 *
James Stow	BA729	Geneva	16.34	0
Daniel O'Connor	CY1364	Larnaca	16.43	1 *
Richard Cawley	BA941	Dusseldorf	16.57	0

Table 3: Passengers transferring to PA103 at Heathrow.

treat like a game of Tetris, belonged to real people; were packed by real people looking forward to Christmas. They never saw Christmas, but instead in their last moments saw their airliner coming to pieces around them at cruising altitude, in the dark of a Scottish winter.

Eight of these passengers were shown not to have checked in any hold luggage. The remaining nine checked in a total of fourteen items between them, and it is to these fourteen items we have to look for the luggage Bedford loaded into AVE4041 in the interline shed.

Three of the items, asterisked on the list opposite, were not loaded on to PA103.

Nicola Hall was a student at the same college as Jim Swire's daughter Flora, but it's unclear whether either of them knew that the other was on the plane. Nicola, who was Australian, was travelling from her home in Johannesburg to spend Christmas in the USA. Her flight landed very early in the morning, in fact so early that her luggage shouldn't have been booked for a direct transfer – Pan Am only permitted this when there was less than eight hours between the incoming and outgoing flights. Although her suitcase was tagged for PA103, it was discovered in New York the day after the disaster, having flown in on PA101 which left Heathrow at 11.00. It's possible this was a mistake, but it was also known that baggage handlers would sometimes put such cases on an earlier flight to get them out of the way, the thinking being that if they were going to New York anyway, it didn't really matter how they got there.

The morning after the disaster Daniel O'Connor's single suitcase and one of Peter Peirce's checked-in items were found still in the interline shed at Heathrow, having been accidentally left behind. The remaining eleven items were loaded on to *Maid of the Seas*.

That group of eleven is divided into two. Those which flew in on flights landing before 16.00 arrived in the interline shed while AVE40401 was still there, and were placed in the container. Those arriving on later flights didn't get to the shed until after Bedford had taken the container away, and were loose-loaded into a pallet in the rear of the aircraft along with a handful of items from the feeder flight which were left over when the container was full. It was during this rather hurried exercise that Mr. Peirce's and Mr. O'Connor's cases were overlooked.

This division is confirmed by the location and condition of the recovered luggage. The earlier group were found along with the rest of the items from AVE4041 in 'I' sector, the area around Newcastleton, twenty miles east of Lockerbie. All were confirmed to have been in contact with explosives, and most showed actual explosion damage. The later-arriving group in contrast were found in 'C' sector, the north part of Lockerbie town itself, where debris from the rear of the plane was recovered. A yellow duffle bag belonging to Mr.

Peirce was noted in the Henderson report as not recovered, but the bag was indeed returned to the victim's family some years later.

Thus we can see, and this was entirely agreed by the investigators, that only six items of legitimate transfer luggage were placed in the container in the interline shed (table 4).

	Flight	From	Arrived	Passenger	Luggage
1	BA391	Brussels	11.06	Bernt Carlsson	Grey Presikhaaf hardshell
2	CY504	Larnaca	14.34	Charles McKee	Grey Samsonite hardshell
3	CY504	Larnaca	14.34	Charles McKee	Grey American Tourister hardshell
4	CY504	Larnaca	14.34	Matthew Gannon	Navy blue soft-sided Samsonite
5	BA701	Vienna	15.35	Michael Bernstein	Maroon soft-sided Samsonite
6	BA701	Vienna	15.35	Michael Bernstein	Tan/brown patterned 'saddlebag'

Table 4: Heathrow transfer luggage placed in AVE4041.

These items, along with the rest of the transfer luggage, were painstakingly matched up to their owners by Derek Henderson. All were recovered at Lockerbie, and all but Major McKee's American Tourister featured among the group of blast-damaged items described in the Joint Forensic Report and spoken to in the witness box by Dr. Hayes. Although the grey American Tourister had suffered no appreciable blast damage, it was noted as testing positive for explosives contamination.

John Bedford's statements provide additional information about the arrangement of the luggage which was not heard at the trial. He stated that when he selected AVE4041 and labelled it up for the PA103 luggage, just after two o'clock, he noticed that "one or two" cases had already arrived for the flight and were sitting beside the x-ray machine, security stickers attached to indicate that they had been x-rayed. This was the first luggage to be placed in the container and it was placed to the extreme left of the flat part of the floor. As the afternoon wore on he remembered "four or five" more items arriving, which he placed beside the first, working across the container from left to right.

It's clear from the above that there was in fact only one early-arriving case, not two, and it belonged to Mr. Carlsson. His was therefore the case at the extreme left of the back row, immediately behind the explosion. The remaining five, one would expect, would make up the rest of the row, with the Larnaca luggage in the middle and Mr. Bernstein's cases to the right. The container was recorded as 62 inches wide on the outside measurement, and "3 to 7 inches less" on the inside measurement, which suggests that a row of six upright cases would fill the space without being jammed too tightly.

This raises the question of the two later arrivals, the cases that appeared mysteriously while Bedford was on his break. The obvious candidates are Mr. Bernstein's two items, but there are problems with this interpretation. First, although one of his cases was indeed a maroon Samsonite (though a soft-sided suit carrier rather than a hardshell), the other was a peculiar 'saddlebag' design, also soft-sided, tan in colour, and with a very distinctive maker's motif all over it. This is completely at variance with Bedford's description of either mystery item. Second, the two Bernstein items not having arrived until after Bedford went off on his break would mean that Bedford loaded only four cases in total, which is difficult to reconcile with his statements – he consistently indicated he had loaded more than that. Third, the lock of the bomb suitcase was blasted into the saddlebag, demonstrating that it was in the row at the back at the time of the explosion.

The statements from the three staff members in the shed build up a picture of the afternoon's work. Although nobody was able to say with certainty exactly how many items had been in the container, everybody was there or thereabouts, sometimes mentioning a number that included the late-arriving items. Although some 'memories' were obviously mistaken, such as Bedford's belief that one or two of the cases (possibly the early arrival) had a Lufthansa tag, much of what was said checked out against the known baggage movements.

Kamboj remembered that the luggage was a mixture of British Airways and Cyprus Airways baggage, and that there was no online Pan Am incoming luggage. He also remembered that one item was a large, heavy maroon suitcase which he collected from the conveyor himself and put through the x-ray machine. Although Mr. Bernstein's maroon case was a suit carrier rather than a suitcase, it was noted by BA as weighing 22 kg, so it would obviously have appeared as a large, heavy item. Kamboj consistently confirmed that he had not placed anything into the container that afternoon.

Parmar also remembered BA luggage and "something beginning with S", and again didn't recall any Pan Am incoming luggage which he said he would have remembered because he wouldn't have x-rayed it. He couldn't describe any of the items. He didn't remember putting anything in the container and he didn't think he would have done that as the shed was very quiet and Bedford didn't need any help.

The shed had clearly been busy in the morning, with a number of outgoing flights and up to six containers being filled simultaneously. The afternoon shift was by comparison extremely quiet, with only one flight and six suitcases to be handled over a period of several hours. What were these guys doing all that time?

Kamboj went for a lunch break about two o'clock, and when he returned Parmar took his break. Bedford, as we know, went off for half an hour at about quarter past four. There was another little vignette which was confirmed by all three men.

Kamboj, whose twenty-sixth birthday was the following day, had a girlfriend – well, a "good friend" as he himself put it – who was a Pan Am air hostess. This friend was one Susan Stone, but she didn't know Kamboj's real name – to her, he answered to 'Pinky'. Susan had told him that she would be flying on PA103 on 21st December, and Kamboj had a little surprise for her – he had bought a box of makeup which he planned to give to her as a Christmas present. Early in the afternoon he asked permission from Bedford to go out to the plane on the tarmac and give Susan the present. Bedford was agreeable so long as he waited until he himself had returned from his break, and was back in time to deal with any late-arriving luggage at about quarter or twenty past five.

Kamboj went out to the plane about five o'clock, but when he got on board and looked around he couldn't see any sign of Susan. He spoke to the air hostesses who were on duty and wished them a happy Christmas, then left, with the present in its Christmas wrapping still in his hand. He discovered later that Susan hadn't been on the doomed flight after all, and he was able to give her the present.

Nevertheless, this only accounts for a small proportion of the afternoon. How did they occupy the rest of it?

Strangely, in the light of Bedford's tale of the mysteriously-appearing suitcases, neither Kamboj nor Parmar was ever asked to recall what the pair of them were doing during the time Bedford was away from the shed, the time when the suitcases materialised. During the Fatal Accident Inquiry they were asked in general terms what they did when the work was very quiet, and the answer was that they might hang around by the x-ray machine or they might wait in the office, which was a small hut within the shed, not far from the work station.

The interline shed was open to the elements, and this was midwinter. It's probably not hard to guess where they were, especially if there was a heater. It's also worth remembering they were working twelve-hour shifts of physically demanding labour, regularly. Kamboj had been at work since 5.30 am, and

Parmar since 5.45. If they didn't catch the odd nap in the afternoon, they must have been superhuman.

One thing was perfectly clear from all the statements. Security airside was non-existent, they didn't keep the container under observation, and anyone could have interfered with it without a great deal of difficulty.

*   *   *   *   *   *   *

Although neither Kamboj nor Parmar could recall the arrangement of the luggage in the container (which again tends to support their contention that they didn't place the final two suitcases at the front), two other baggage handlers who saw it after Bedford went home were able to confirm his description.

Not long before the feeder flight was due to land, Tarlochan Sahota was asked by his supervisor to check the container to ensure there was sufficient space to allow it to be used for the Frankfurt transfer luggage. He again described a row of cases across the back, with two flat on the front, side by side. He stated that the entire floor of the container was covered, and all the suitcases were in contact with the floor with nothing on the second layer.

The third person to look inside was Amarjit Sidhu, who had been given what was usually Bedford's last job of the day, to take the container out to the tarmac and load the Frankfurt luggage. Sidhu also described the same arrangement, and confirmed what Bedford had said about the suitcases being loaded in such a way that they wouldn't slide around, with the two front cases wedging the back row in place.

Sidhu was also able to describe the two front cases. At first he said they were "large, black" cases, but in a later interview he revised that to "dark", as he said he hadn't really been aware of a specific colour. (It's likely he saw the cases in such poor lighting that he would have had little colour vision.) He thought they might have been soft-sided, but he wasn't sure.

Sidhu gave no less than eight police statements between the disaster itself and his appearance at the Fatal Accident Inquiry, and in three of them he made reference to how he had dealt with the existing luggage when he loaded the items from the feeder flight. He was also asked about it in some detail at the FAI. Here is what he said:

Police statement, 10th January 1989
I recall that the JFK baggage had to be unloaded very quickly as we only had about 15 minutes to get this baggage transferred to the 747. Sandy and I filled up the container on top of the baggage which was already there.

Police statement, 7th August 1989

Further to my previous statements. When I took the AVE from the baggage build up to the 727 I did not reposition any of the interline bags in that container. I did not see anyone else reposition the interline bags prior to the Frankfurt bags being loaded into the container.

Police statement, 13th February 1990

I took the container out to the 727 and positioned it at the bottom of the rocket so that bags could be put straight in. I undid the curtain and saw the same bags inside in the same position because they didn't have room to move about. I did not reposition any of these bags and didn't need to because of the position they were in already. Dave Sandhu didn't touch the bags either. Dave Sandhu and I loaded the bags from the rocket into the container and on top of the 5 or 6 or 7 bags already there.

Fatal Accident Inquiry, 29th October 1990

Q Did you rearrange the cases which had originally been in the container?

A No I did not.

Q Did you take any of them out and put them on a different level or anything like that?

A No, I didn't because I was quite satisfied they were loaded.

Q You were satisfied about the way they were loaded?

A Yes.

It's clear why the Fatal Accident Inquiry was able to decide with reasonable confidence that the Heathrow interline luggage wasn't moved after Bedford went home. Despite the concerns first expressed by the FAA and PCAST, it appears that nobody interfered with the container during the time when it was parked beside Walker's office, open and unattended.

It's also as clear as it can reasonably be that Sidhu didn't indulge in any 'suitcase-shuffle' out on the tarmac that afternoon, just as the FAI reasoning had assumed. The arrangement that Bedford, Sahota and Sidhu all described was preserved under the Frankfurt luggage when the container was loaded on to *Maid of the Seas*. And the Crown knew this very well, but chose not to tell the court about it.

Knowing this, it becomes possible to look at the six items transferred into the container in the interline shed, and establish whether the degree and distribution of the blast damage confirms the arrangement Bedford's evidence implies. Figure 15 shows the six cases.

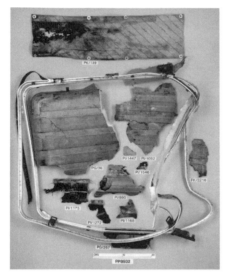

Carlsson (1)

McKee (2)

Gannon (4)

McKee (3)

Bernstein (6)

Bernstein (5)

Figure 15
The six items of passenger luggage loaded into container AVE4041 in the Heathrow interline shed.

The first thing to note is that none of these cases can possibly have been immediately below the bomb suitcase at the time of the explosion. Only the Carlsson case is showing catastrophic damage, and that damage is not consistent with its having been under the bomb. In fact the damage shows that it was exactly where Bedford said he put it, sitting handle-up immediately behind the IED. Close-up shots of the damaged frame illustrate this perfectly (suitcase handle to the left in the close-up images).

 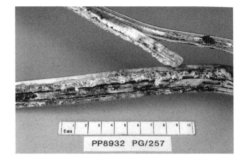

Figure 16
Blast damage to metal frame of Mr. Carlsson's case, with close-up on right.

The more severely damaged of the two McKee suitcases also shows clear evidence of having been upright behind the bomb suitcase, and fairly close to the explosion. As the only other case showing appreciable fracturing, it must have been the next one to the right of the Carlsson case, which is again consistent with Bedford's evidence.

Surprisingly, the next item in the row turns out to be the Bernstein saddlebag. Although the blast damage is not particularly clear in the photograph, the metal fragments seen at the bottom of the picture clinch the deal. These belong to the lock of the bomb suitcase, which was positioned near the corner of the case.

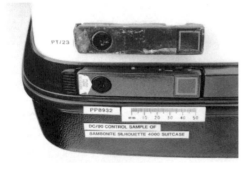

Figure 17
Samsonite suitcases have a snap lock on either side of the top of the case, in addition to a combination lock in the centre, under the handle.

The Gannon case was noted as having superficial explosion damage only, and appears to be the next in line. Finally, the other McKee case wasn't damaged at all by the explosion, merely testing positive for explosives contamination.

The real anomaly here is the condition of the Bernstein suit carrier, which is shown unfolded in the photograph with the detached handle below it. It does have blast damage, but not in a pattern consistent with its having been handle-up anywhere in the back row. The damage is evenly distributed along the top, the side from which the handle has been wrenched – and on the handle itself. There is only one possible position consistent with this pattern of damage, and that is flat on the floor of the container, to the right of the bomb suitcase, with the handle to the left. It seems that Mr. Bernstein's over-stuffed maroon Samsonite suit carrier was the second 'Bedford bag', on the right-hand side at the front.

The schematic below (figure 18) illustrates the arrangement of the suitcases as described by Bedford, identified according to the information laid out above. The identifying numbers relate to table 4 (page 102).

Lacking a legitimate suitcase which might have been positioned under the explosion, we must conclude that there were seven items in the container, not six.

At this point it seems almost superfluous to mention another piece of evidence demonstrating that more than six suitcases were loaded in the interline shed. In January 1989 Bedford, Sahota and Sidhu were all (separately) asked to load a container to resemble as closely as possible the arrangement of the luggage as they last saw it. All loaded either seven or eight items, and indeed it is impossible to make the row at the back appear complete, and cover the entire floor, by using only four suitcases.

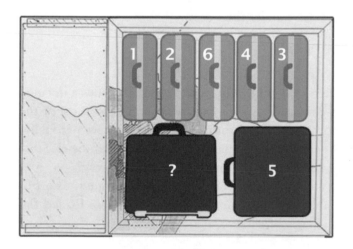

Figure 18
Top view of AVE4041 showing apparent arrangement of Heathrow-loaded luggage.

The anomalously-positioned cases in relation to Bedford's evidence are Mr. Bernstein's two items, the last two to arrive. Instead of being on the right-hand end of the row at the back, one is flat at the front and the other is in the middle of the back row.

So, is there any possible alternative candidate for the mystery item, something which might have shown up in the interline shed and been loaded in a position that in the end was underneath the bomb suitcase?

Unaccompanied baggage might be the answer, but in contrast to Frankfurt there is no rush-tag luggage recorded as heading for PA103 at Heathrow. The only outside possibility in this respect is Mr. Hubbard's misrouted suitcase, which was indeed a brown Samsonite. The route taken by his two cases from Berlin to Heathrow was never definitely established, and although they were believed to have gone via Frankfurt on PA637, there was a possibility they might have gone via Hamburg, or even Hannover (see page 33). In that case, they must have become separated in the interline shed, with one waiting safely overnight for the Seattle flight on Thursday and the other being mistakenly loaded into AVE4041. This possibility was raised by the plaintiffs in the US civil action, in response to the suggestion from Pan Am's defence that the stray Hubbard case might have been the thirteenth item x-rayed by Kurt Maier at Frankfurt.

However, the balance of probabilities is very much against the Hubbard cases having passed through the Heathrow interline shed. None of the staff in the shed reported seeing a rush-tagged case, and both Kamboj and Parmar explicitly stated that they didn't see anything with a Pan Am tag. The loading of the container in the shed was calm and unhurried, and it seems an unlikely way for the cases to have become separated compared to the semi-pandemonium of the unloading of the feeder flight. The bottom line though, is that whether or not Mr. Hubbard's lost case was routed through the interline shed, it wasn't the case Bedford saw. It was recovered with no evidence of any explosives involvement. It wasn't under the bomb.

★ ★ ★ ★ ★ ★ ★

Well, let's try something else. The Joint Forensic Report includes a detailed description of all the blast-damaged luggage, and photographs of most of the items. Most were little more than singed round the edges, but we're looking for something fairly comprehensively blown to bits. Is there anything else that might possibly have been under the bomb, and loaded at Heathrow?

Figure 19 shows the only items described which demonstrate the sort of damage that would inevitably have been sustained by a suitcase loaded flat against the bomb suitcase.

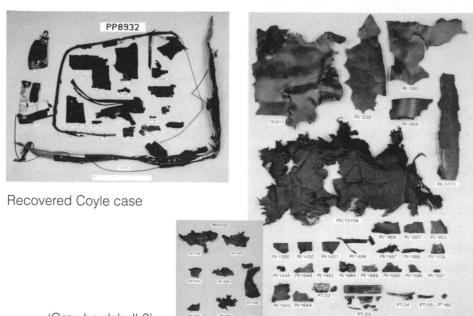

Recovered Coyle case

'Grey hardshell 2'

Recovered bomb suitcase

Figure 19
Fragments of the suitcases which were in very close proximity to the explosion.

The one on the left is the Coyle case, which came in on the Frankfurt flight. The one on the right is the bomb suitcase itself, with fragment PI/911 shown on the top left of the montage. The small insert is a bit of an oddity, showing a group of seven quite tiny fragments which were obviously very close indeed to the explosion, but which were never matched to any of the other explosion-damaged items, and simply labelled "grey hardshell 2".

This is yet another strange chapter in the baggage analysis saga. It appears that at an early stage Thomas Hayes may have compared these fragments to the damaged McKee Samsonite ("grey hardhell 1"), and concluded that they weren't from that case because the grain and pattern of the fake leather texture didn't match. In March 1992, just before the civil action against Pan Am came to court in the USA, Allen Feraday was asked to compare the fragments to another grey Samsonite hardshell belonging to Mr. George Williams, a Frankfurt boarder. While the texture of the fake leather appeared to be a reasonable match this time, the materials and construction of the Williams case were quite different from the mystery fragments. Furthermore, Mr. Williams's case was recovered intact and essentially undamaged. It wasn't close to the bomb, and it didn't have seven fragments missing from it.

One might think that 'grey hardshell 2' was potentially very significant indeed, even though only a few scraps were recovered. These fragments were obviously very close to the explosion. If the bomb suitcase was on the second layer of luggage as the investigators believed, there must have been *two* cases loaded flat against it. The Coyle case was one, and this, surely, was a prime (indeed the only) candidate for the other.

However, there is no sign whatsoever of the forensics officers arriving at this conclusion. 'Grey hardshell 2' was not presented in court as a potential candidate for the missing 'secondary case' which should have been on the other side of the bomb suitcase from the Coyle case, whichever way up you want to stack them, and it was certainly never presented as a possible candidate for the suitcase Bedford saw. The complete absence of any coherent thought about 'grey hardshell 2' is simply astonishing.

The fragments exist, though. Is it possible they represent all that remains of a stray, undocumented piece of lost luggage which happened to find its way to the interline shed about half past four, was loaded by Kamboj, and was perceived as brown by Bedford?

Actually, no. The fragments are perfectly simple to identify, from the descriptions in the examination notes and the high-resolution photographs in the Joint Forensic Report. Close inspection of these photographs reveals the texture of the mystery fragments to be identical to the grain of the fake leather finish of the bomb suitcase and its undamaged twin supplied by Samsonite (see plate 5). The 'antique copper' coating was only a thin skin over a shell of grey plastic, something which can be removed by sufficiently violent treatment – a process known as 'spalling'. It is quite obvious that 'grey hardshell 2' is nothing more than some additional bits of the bomb suitcase with the shiny finish cooked off. It doesn't exist as a separate entity.

It is an unfathomable mystery why the forensic scientists didn't realise this.

So, if the same people were right about the bomb suitcase not being on the floor of the container, do we have to go back to the Coyle case as being the one under the bomb? Must we after all follow the reasoning of the prosecution and assume Sidhu was mistaken in his repeated testimony that he didn't move that case?

Again, no. First, that doesn't really solve anything. As noted above, if the Coyle case was under the bomb, then we're still missing the other Frankfurt-origin case that must have been on top of the bomb. And second, the Coyle case was *not* under the bomb.

Patricia Coyle's case was made of navy-blue canvas, but it also had a maroon plastic trim and a blue plastic lining with a cross-hatched or diamond-shaped pattern, which was sometimes described as 'foamed'. Reading through the text of the Joint Forensic Report as it appears in the trial transcripts it is striking just how many other pieces of luggage have some of that case deposited on them. At least five suitcases are recorded as bearing traces of either the maroon trim or the same blue foamy material found on PI/911 – those belonging to Michael Bernstein, Charles McKee, Susan Costa, Thomas Walker and Willis Coursey. In contrast none of that material was recorded as adherent to the container floor or to the damaged airframe below it.

The circumstances of the recovery of the largest piece of the Coyle case, the part with the handle, are also interesting. It arrived at RARDE in association with the largest part of the Coursey case and the frame of another Frankfurt-origin case belonging to Lawanda Thomas. Hayes didn't draw, describe or photograph these in their original condition, but it seems they were tangled together. He originally assigned the same production number to all three items.

It is physically impossible for a case which was positioned below the bomb suitcase, and which was blasted down through the base of the container and away from the rest of the luggage, to have left traces of itself on so many suitcases. In particular, it is impossible to see how the handle and associated frame of the case could have become entangled with a side panel from one Frankfurt-origin case and the main frame from another.

If the Coyle case was blasted up, against the luggage stacked above it, might it then be possible to identify the case that was loaded on top of it? That case is actually quite obvious – it's the one belonging to Johannes Schäuble, another Frankfurt boarder, which is illustrated in plate 6 (it is essential to examine this photograph in colour).

The Schäuble case suffered significant blast damage. It contained a small fragment of the bomb suitcase, plus a screw, a magnet and a fragment of black plastic from the Toshiba radio-cassette player. The screw was driven head-first into the tan leatherette trim at the stitching line. A blue deposit can be seen covering a substantial area of the lid, and the lower left view shows that it lies on top of the weave of the canvas fabric. It's present on the trim as well as the canvas. (Surprisingly, in the Joint Forensic Report the deposit wasn't described as blue, but as black, and the case itself was described as green.) Part of the deposit was removed and examined in more detail, which revealed the diamond pattern characteristic of the Coyle suitcase lining. There were also larger, pale fibres on top of the deposit which could well originate from something packed inside Tricia's case.

The condition of the Schäuble case is irrefutable proof that it was on the other side of the Coyle case from the bomb. It contains fragments from the Samsonite and from the radio, lodged in such a way that they must have been blasted straight through another suitcase. It also has a substantial amount of the Coyle case plastered across its lid. Since the position of the explosion was much too low to have been in the third layer of luggage, the Coyle case was indisputably on top of the bomb suitcase.

Where does that leave PI/911? Hayes thought it had been blasted against a "relatively immoveable surface". It was also, obviously, blasted against the Coyle case. Which is likely to have provided the greater resistance to the blast, on the other side of the Coyle case? A single sheet of aluminium, or a stack of suitcases weighing around 150 kg?

The explosive blast caused catastrophic damage to a relatively small number of items of luggage: the bomb suitcase itself, the Coyle case above it, the Carlsson case behind it, and one of Karen Noonan's holdalls. Ample fragments of all of these items were recovered by the search teams. There isn't the slightest trace of another blown-to-bits item that might have been below the bomb suitcase.

★ ★ ★ ★ ★ ★ ★

Peter Claiden of the AAIB and any number of scientists at RARDE were convinced the bomb suitcase couldn't have been on the floor of the container. Allen Feraday told the FAI that he was "adamant" that wasn't the case. He produced the diagrams reproduced in figure 14, showing the two positions he believed the suitcase could have occupied, and asserted that it was "physically impossible" for it to have been in any other position.

As noted above, these illustrations showed the suitcases drawn badly out of scale, so that they are actively misleading as regards the packing of the luggage into the container. It is helpful at this stage to introduce correctly-scaled diagrams (figure 20).

The position of the explosion is shown at 5 cm (2 inches) to the left of the upright support of the container, and 25 cm (10 inches) from the flat part of the floor. This was the position unanimously agreed by the investigators until Peter Claiden suddenly changed his mind in the witness box at Camp Zeist and mentioned "13, 13 and a half inches", claiming to have spotted a mistake in the diagram he himself had drawn in April 1989 and which had since been reproduced in several official reports without alteration. Feraday nevertheless stuck with "25 to 28 cm" in his own evidence, despite the Coyle suitcase itself being close to 25 cm deep.

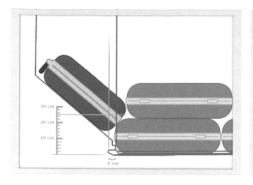 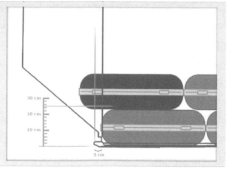

Position 1 ('first postulated position')   Position 2 ('second postulated position')

Figure 20
Correctly scaled versions of Feraday's two 'postulated positions' for the bomb suitcase.

The first description of these two "postulated positions" appears in an interim report dated June 1990, much of which was incorporated verbatim in the 1991 Joint Forensic Report.

> To account for the direction of blast, the likely orientation of the modified cassette recorder, and the standoff required to provide the various observed degrees of damage suffered by the specific parts of the luggage container, two positions of the primary suitcase can be considered. It is probable that the primary suitcase was placed in the angled overhang at the port side of the luggage container, supported in a near upright position by the container's angled wall panel on one side and a vertical stack of horizontally-lying suitcases on its other side. It is also possible that this suitcase lay horizontally in the second layer of the front row, with its port-facing end overhanging the corresponding end of the suitcase lying beneath it. In both cases the empty lower apex of the container's sidewall overhang would then provide the required obstruction free standoff from the longitudinal base strut for the relatively small charge of high performance explosive.

From this, it appears that Feraday's preferred position was actually the first one, the one where the suitcase was loaded in the overhang section of the container – the position that was ignored at Zeist in favour of the flat-loaded position.

This was fairly improbable from the start. The baggage handlers generally reserved the overhang section for holdalls, or, as Bedford said, "soft type zip-up bags or suitcases". It was quite unlikely that Sidhu would have put a full-size hardshell in there, though strangely enough that's another thing nobody thought of asking him about.

It's likely that Feraday's preference for the upright position was coloured by his assumption about how the Toshiba would have been packed within the suitcase. He packed the sample case provided by Samsonite with facsimiles of all the items believed to have been in the bomb suitcase, and photographed the result.

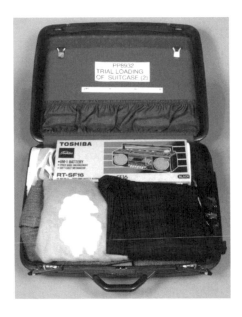

Figure 21

Trial loading (2) of the Samsonite Silhouette 4000, with the radio-cassette player, the clothing, and other articles believed to have been packed with the bomb.

Trial loading (1) merely shows the radio unboxed, in the same position in the suitcase.

This arrangement places the radio-cassette player in the position one would intuitively pack such an item into a suitcase, to balance its 3 to 3½ kg weight evenly across the case. If the case were packed in the manner shown, Feraday's 'first postulated position' is the only loading position that would allow the IED to reach the hot-spot of the explosion, given that the flat-loaded cases were normally placed either handle-in or handle-out.

However, *that* position is in fact physically impossible. Not only is it virtually impossible to see how the thing could have been blasted against the Coyle case to produce PI/911 in that position, the recovery of the lock blasted into Mr. Bernstein's saddlebag proves that the handle could not have been facing upwards. In addition, a fragment from the hinge end of the bomb suitcase was found in or in association with the only item of Heathrow check-in luggage to have sustained blast damage, a purple holdall belonging to Sophie Hudson. This indicates that the hinge end of the suitcase was facing the adjacent container AVN7511, which also suffered minor damage in the explosion.

Taken together, these findings show without any doubt whatsoever that the bomb suitcase was loaded flat, with the handle facing the back of the container. This also just happens to be exactly the loading orientation Bedford described for the mystery suitcase.

Position 2 of course was the scenario presented at Zeist in 2000, where Feraday's 'first position' was essentially ignored. However, the investigators had all the information necessary to arrive at the above conclusion well before the end of 1989. It is therefore beyond astonishing that Feraday presented his first position to the FAI in 1990, included it (with the above text indicating it as the favoured position) in the 1991 Joint Forensic Report, and continued to promote it in 1992 to the US hearings.

Given the loading position of the suitcase it can be seen that the packing was nothing like the arrangement proposed by Feraday. The Toshiba must in fact have been packed along one side – an arrangement which doesn't even rate a mention in any of the forensic reports.

It's actually quite a strange way to pack a case. The radio weighed over 3 kg. The entire suitcase weighed only 13 to 14 kg. It's very counterintuitive to put the radio down the side, where it would inevitably unbalance the case for carrying. It also means that *Maid of the Seas* was desperately unlucky twice over. The blast that destroyed the aircraft was in virtually the perfect position to do maximum damage. Not only was the lethal suitcase loaded in the right *position* to do this, one of the relatively few positions in the container close enough to the skin of the plane to inflict catastrophic damage, it was placed *the right way round*.

However, these arguments apply just as much to the Crown's preferred position, with the suitcase on the second layer, as to any arrangement with the bomb suitcase on the floor of the container. The real question is, how might the suitcase have been positioned in the latter configuration to get the centre of the IED, in the radio in its box, into the hot-spot of the explosion? As drawn (either version), the bottom-level case is slightly too low and too far to the right to be in the frame.

This is where the third position advanced at Camp Zeist by Richard Keen comes in. It was originally suggested by forensic scientists from Northern Ireland, who were consulted by the defence as independent experts. They didn't appear to have any serious problem with the idea that the bomb suitcase might have been the one on the bottom of the stack. They noted that the cases aren't necessarily regularly stacked in the containers, like bricks in a wall; the loading can be a bit haphazard, as the photograph below demonstrates. The photograph is of a similar container loaded randomly for a test explosion, shown in a BBC2 *Newsnight* feature on 6th January 2010. It wasn't packed with the intention of illustrating this point.

 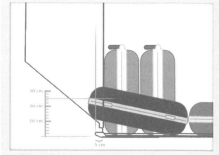

Position 3

Figure 22
Third possible position for the bomb suitcase (right), compared to a normally loaded container (left).

The attachment of the overhang section in these containers introduces a 3-inch (8 cm) step at the left-hand side of the flat floor, before the angled floor of the overhang begins (see figure 2). All that's needed is for the left-hand side of the suitcase to be elevated on to this step, either by being loaded there originally or shifting there during flight, to bring the side of the case into the right position. Whether the left-hand suitcase was flat or partly in the overhang when Bedford saw it was yet another question nobody thought of asking. However, there was a high wind blowing that night, and a lurch in flight or even banking can easily cause cargo to shift a few inches – especially if the bottom item is a shiny convex hardshell with rounded corners.

This 'third postulated position' shows that it was perfectly possible for the case on the floor of the container to have contained the bomb, based on the forensic investigators' own estimate of the position of the explosion. This is what Fhimah's advocate Richard Keen tried to explain to Feraday during the trial. Feraday affected to be unable to see how the left-hand side of the case could be elevated sufficiently to match his 25 to 28 cm estimated height of the explosion, although it is clear from the above images that this could be achieved with relative ease. He then admitted, "I have not specifically examined that

PLATE 1

Top: Empty aluminium AVE-type aircraft baggage container.

Bottom: Similar container loaded with suitcases.

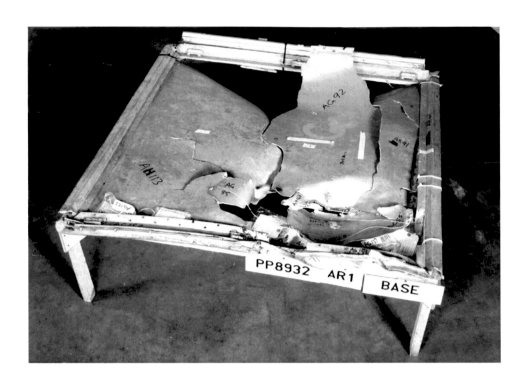

PLATE 2

Two views of the reconstructed base of baggage container AVE4041.

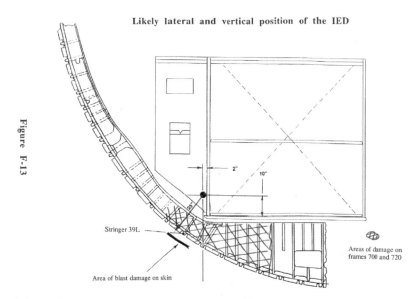

Likely lateral and vertical position of the IED

Figure F-13

Stringer 39L

Area of blast damage on skin

2"

10"

Areas of damage on frames 700 and 720

PLATE 3

Top: Colour version of the Claiden diagram, showing the position of the explosion agreed by the forensic scientists and the area of blast damage to the airframe highlighted in red.

Bottom: Reconstructed airframe, showing the area highlighted in the diagram.

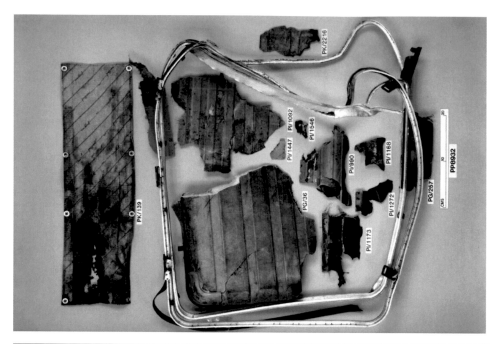

PLATE 4

Remains of the two suitcases sitting upright immediately behind the bomb suitcase. Top, Bernt Carlsson's Presikhaaf hardshell; bottom, Charles McKee's Samsonite hardshell.

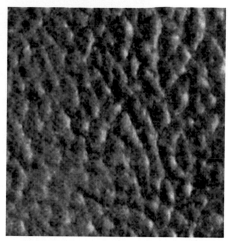
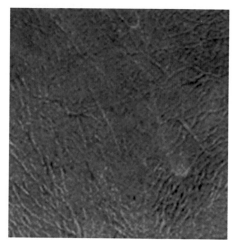

PLATE 5

Detail of surface texture of simulated leather hardshell suitcases

Top left: Sample 'Silhouette 4000' supplied by Samsonite in 'antique copper'.
Top right: Fragment of bomb suitcase, PI/911.
Bottom left: Badly damaged 'grey hardshell 2' fragment PI/1537.
Bottom right: Major McKee's grey Samsonite hardshell.

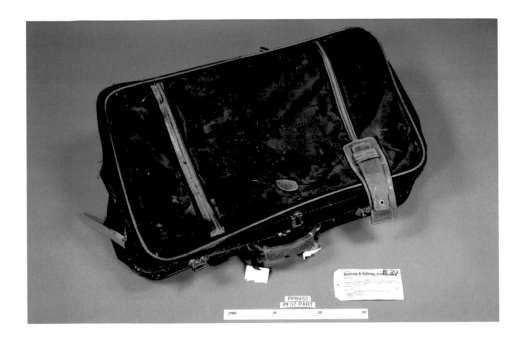

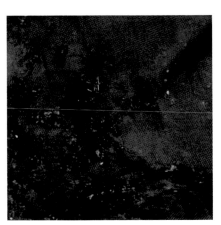

PP8932 PF37 PART

PLATE 6

Johannes Schäuble's canvas suitcase

Top: Entire case. The position of the screw can be seen as a black dot midway along the left-hand section of trim.
Bottom left: Detail of lid showing blue deposit lying on top of the canvas of the case, and larger white fibres on top of that.
Bottom right: Screw from the booby-trapped Toshiba radio-cassette recorder driven headfirst into the leatherette trim. Note blue fibres in foreground, and around the penetration hole of the screw.

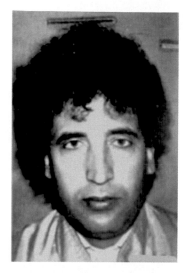 

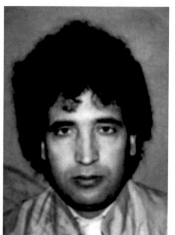 

PLATE 7

Photographs of Abdelbaset al-Megrahi

Top left: "Open-neck shirt" photo supplied by FBI special agent Phillip Reid to DCI Harry Bell in January 1991, apparently taken from an identity document in Megrahi's own name.

Top right: "Collar and tie" photo supplied at the same time, before the tie was cropped off. This was the photograph in Megrahi's own passport, issued in 1986.

Bottom left: Photograph in the coded passport issued to Megrahi in 1987 in the name of "Ahmed Khalifa Abdusamad".

Bottom right: Megrahi photographed in February 1992. The apparent 'hair extensions' are in fact the hair of a woman standing behind him.

PLATE 8

Fragment of green-backed circuit board found at Blinkbonny Farm

Top left: RARDE photograph dated September 1989, front view.
Top right: Matching photograph of the back view.
Bottom left: Fragment after sectioning, with the larger of the removed segments placed back in position.
Bottom right: Comparison MST-13 circuit board manufactured by Thüring AG.

scenario, to my way of thinking, because of the observed damage to the floor itself."

So, we're back to the reconstructed floor, again. Maybe we need another look at that. (See also additional images in plate 2.)

Figure 23
Various views of the damaged, reassembled floor of baggage container AVE4041.

There's no pitting on the floor, such as is present on the base strut – but bear in mind that the IED was very close to the base strut, while the other contents of the suitcase were between it and the floor of the container. As Mr. Keen pointed out, even sticky tape can be enough to protect surfaces close to a welding torch, for example. The floor seems dished, rather than completely punched out – but that point, made by Mr. Claiden who was not an expert in explosions, was predicated on the suitcase being "in contact with" the floor. In position 3, the suitcase is *not* "in contact with" the floor, except at the extreme right-hand side, the furthest from the explosion. Dr. Cullis purported to be able to see "an indent that looks like the imprint of a suitcase that has been impulsively driven into the base of the container" – presumably not the bomb suitcase itself.

It's palmistry. Frankly, you might as well ask Mystic Meg to read its fortune.

No experimental data were presented in court to back up any of these opinions. Data had been acquired of course, from a number of experiments conducted in the USA during 1989. The first series, in April, consisted of only five tests, all using different configurations of luggage arrangement and explosive charge. Only one of these had the bomb suitcase on the floor of the container, and in that one the whole thing caught fire with very little data being acquired. The test which seemed most successful was one with the bomb suitcase on the second layer, but in that example the container floor was merely bent, not fractured. Four further tests in July added little additional information, with the final two not even involving a baggage container. These tests were barely mentioned in court, perhaps not surprisingly, as any conclusion from that lot that the bomb suitcase couldn't possibly have been on the bottom layer was going to be on very shaky ground.

Nobody seemed to think of looking at the damage to the actual airframe, shown in the two illustrations below. (See also plate 3.)

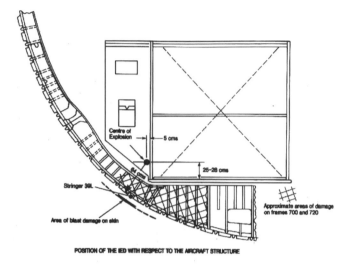

POSITION OF THE IED WITH RESPECT TO THE AIRCRAFT STRUCTURE

Figure 24
Joint Forensic Report version of the Claiden diagram (above, see also figure 12) which shows the distribution of the damage to the airframe, and the actual damage as photographed (left).

Look at the cross-hatched part of the airframe, which is the part which showed explosion damage. Very little of it to the left of the IED, but a lot to the right – the part of the airframe that was underneath the bomb suitcase. The lower photograph is the reconstructed airframe showing blast-damaged ribs which were described in court by Christopher Protheroe of the AAIB as showing pitting and sooting.

Bear in mind the relatively superficial damage to the Schäuble suitcase, shielded from the bomb only by the Coyle case. The canvas was barely ripped, the trim was undamaged and it still had all its contents inside when it was recovered. It's clear that the packed suitcases absorbed the explosive blast to a quite remarkable degree. Does that airframe really look like something that was shielded from the explosion by another suitcase below the bomb?

There are of course two other items which bear witness to the presence, or absence, of another case below the bomb suitcase – the two Heathrow interline cases sitting behind it in the back row, the cases belonging to Bernt Carlsson and Charles McKee.

The pattern of damage to the McKee case (figure 15) is extremely striking. The blast has clearly come at it very low down, and there's no question of the bottom of that case having been protected by another case sitting on the floor of the container, "jamming it in place" according to Bedford's description. Thomas Hayes almost seems to have realised this when he drew the suitcase on 20th January 1989, a drawing which was viewed and discussed in court.

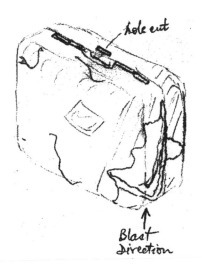

Figure 25
Sketch of Major McKee's Samsonite, from Dr. Hayes's notes. Paradoxically, much speculation has surrounded his indication of the 'hole cut' at the top, although that is nothing more sinister than a narrow slot where a combination lock has been fitted, then blasted free by the explosion.
The lower note indicating the 'blast direction' is altogether more interesting.

The height of the damage to the Carlsson case (figures 15 and 16, and plate 4) is more difficult to assess, however it doesn't appear to have been right on the bottom – not incompatible with a second-layer explosion, but also exactly as you'd expect with the bomb suitcase in position 3, with the left-hand side up on the 'step'.

More striking than the damage to the suitcase frame is the condition of the separate panel of lining fabric recovered, which appears to originate from the inside of the hinge end.

Figure 26
Lining panel PK/139, photograph rotated to match the orientation of the previous image.

The right-hand side of this panel has suffered severe, destructive charring. As with the damage to the bottom corner of the McKee case, such charring could not have occurred if the bottom corner of this case had been protected by another case lying below the bomb suitcase.

★ ★ ★ ★ ★ ★ ★

It is absolutely clear that the blanket assertion in court from AAIB and RARDE investigators that the bomb suitcase could not possibly have been on the bottom layer of the stacked luggage was not well-founded. It was based solely on examination of the container itself, and appears to consist of little more than unsupported opinion.

The forensic scientists from Northern Ireland didn't regard the condition of the container floor as an insuperable barrier to the bomb suitcase having been on the bottom layer. Other independent forensic experts agree, adding the opinion that Feraday's estimate of 25 to 28 cm (10 to 11 inches) for the height of the explosion is too high, with the pattern of damage to the horizontal strut suggesting 7 to 9 inches (17.5 to 22.5 cm). Even 25 to 28 cm would only allow for a fairly thin suitcase to have been under the bomb – something significantly thinner than Tricia Coyle's large case. A height of around 20 cm (8 inches) is a slam-dunk for the bottom layer, and position 3.

Uncounted man-hours were spent collecting the debris from the plane from the cold winter fields around Lockerbie and sorting it out into manageable categories. Thomas Hayes spent a great deal of time meticulously describing every one of the damaged suitcases, and drawing a fair number of them. The resulting database is an absolute gold-mine, which should have been strip-mined for every inference it was capable of supporting. It is perfectly simple to figure out how the suitcases closest to the bomb were arranged in the container, especially with access to Bedford's account of how he loaded it, Sidhu's statements that he did not disturb that arrangement, and the incoming passenger and flight records.

Despite Hayes's comment in the witness box about "assembling a picture" taking into account "the positioning of the fragments, the location, recovery of those fragments" and "other considerations", there's no evidence at all that he actually did this. If such an analysis was undertaken, it has certainly never seen the light of day. All that was presented in court was the raw dataset, and the sole attempt at analysing it, the conclusion that the Coyle case was below the bomb suitcase, was demonstrably wrong.

There is no item of luggage recorded as having been loaded in the interline shed which reconciles as the mysterious suitcase Bedford saw on the left of the container, the one he described as a brown or maroon Samsonite hardshell. There is no item of luggage recovered on the ground which could have been under the bomb suitcase. The Coyle case was definitely on top of the bomb suitcase. The condition of the container floor does not exclude the bomb suitcase having been on the bottom layer of luggage, and the condition of the two suitcases behind it, and the airframe under the container, confirm that that is exactly where it was.

The 'Bedford bag' was the bomb, beyond any reasonable doubt.

★ ★ ★ ★ ★ ★ ★

What then happened in the interline shed that afternoon? The possible narratives probably number as many as there are people thinking about it, but here's one suggestion.

Having seen the condition of the recovered suitcases, and noted the relatively light damage to all but the few which were in immediate contact with the bomb suitcase, one thing is perfectly clear. The packed suitcases absorbed the blast to a quite remarkable degree. If that case had been loaded anywhere but the bottom left-hand corner of the container, or even if it had been placed the other way round with the bomb at the right, *Maid of the Seas* would not have been fatally wounded. A suitcase loaded at random by Bedford or Sidhu (or even Kamboj) would have had only a small chance of ending up in that position.

The counterintuitive packing of the suitcase, with the heavy radio unbalancing it on one side, calls up a picture of someone filling it who knew very well he would have control over where it was placed in the container. That case was meant to be loaded flat, with the IED to the left, as close to the cutaway corner of the container side as possible. That rules out simply placing it on the conveyor belt outside the shed, as Whyte's did with the interline luggage, and letting it take its chances with Bedford's positioning.

Let's say the bomber knew about the routine for PA103 and the baggage handlers' habit of leaving a container lying around the interline shed all afternoon, gathering occasional pieces of transfer luggage. He knew there was a fair chance the single baggage handler would go off for a break at some point. He knew the x-ray operators didn't guard the container from unauthorised interference, and might even catch a nap if things were quiet.

Let's say he was wearing the overalls of one of the other airlines operating in the shed. If a baggage handler took something off the carousel by mistake, something intended for a different airline, he would usually just put it back on. However, what was to stop a helpful chap who had accidentally pulled off a Pan Am suitcase taking it over to the Pan Am station? Nothing at all. If he was seen, that's all he was doing. He hardly needed to be Caucasian to blend in, either.

Bear in mind that radio was x-ray proof, at least to an operator who hadn't been made aware of the Autumn Leaves warning. If push came to shove, and the container was never unguarded, Kamboj or Parmar could be allowed to x-ray it. The routine was that baggage handlers presented the cases for x-ray, then put them in the container. It's quite possible Kamboj or Parmar would have allowed someone from BA, for example, to do just that. In the unlikely event of them being suspicious of the radio, the helpful stranger could just slope off before security arrived. It wasn't his suitcase, after all.

That was probably plan B. Did it happen, and then Kamboj was too afraid for his £2.70 per hour job to say so? The thing that makes that unlikely is the rearrangement of the luggage. Only one additional suitcase was loaded, not two, but the other cases seem to have been rearranged, apparently to make the container appear "properly loaded" and minimise the chance of the bomb suitcase being 'rejigged' into a less lethal position, well enough that Bedford didn't notice anything had been moved. It's highly unlikely a terrorist would have risked doing this with Kamboj looking on.

Let's say plan A worked, and the terrorist found Bedford off having a natter with Walker and Kamboj and Parmar having a kip. He approached the container and was a bit thrown by the arrangement of the cases, sitting upright without an obvious place to put one flat. He put the bomb suitcase where he wanted it, flat on the floor with the IED to the left, then became concerned that it might be moved inboard. He hurriedly grabbed the last case in the row, Mr. Bernstein's saddlebag, to lay beside the bomb suitcase, then realised the tan patterned thing was the wrong shape and too conspicuous to do the job. Panicking slightly, he grabbed the next case, the suit carrier, and dragged that into position. That did it, but in his hurry the bomber didn't realise he'd loaded it handle to the side, which the baggage handlers seldom if ever did. He then had to spread the back row out a bit so that it still looked full with only five cases. In the course of that, the saddlebag ended up in the middle instead of on the end. He sauntered off nonchalantly, unnoticed by anyone.

It's very difficult to second-guess the thinking of a fanatical terrorist, probably in a high state of nervous tension and certainly in the process of committing mass murder, but that narrative seems to cover the evidence as it's known. It's certainly a good few light years better than any scenario suggested for Malta.

Finally, did Kamboj speak to Bedford about the extra cases? Maybe. Maybe 'plan B' above was actually what happened, but rather than go into the whole story of the other baggage handler, he just allowed Bedford to think the cases had arrived in the usual way and he'd loaded them himself. Then, after the disaster, he was afraid to explain what had actually happened. However, the rearrangement of the Bernstein luggage makes that scenario unlikely.

Otherwise, if Kamboj did speak to Bedford, it could suggest he was complicit in the plot. He put the bomb there himself, then mentioned the extra suitcases (in the plural, always) to forestall any curiosity on Bedford's part. Maybe the whole story about the girlfriend he thought was flying on the plane that night was a complete fabrication, to fool everyone into believing he wouldn't have wanted that flight to crash.

In 1989 there would have been no reason not to consider this. The cops should have been all over Sulkash Kumar Kamboj like a rash. They weren't, though. It doesn't even seem to have occurred to anyone.

Twenty-five years later, the knowledge of Kamboj's continuing modest and blameless life as a Heathrow security guard rather gives the lie to suspicions of that nature. So, did he speak to Bedford that afternoon?

Perhaps not.

Bedford had been told by Walker that he might as well go home, an hour before his usual knocking-off time. He'd had a long day too. He returned to the shed, prepared to take the container out ready for Sidhu to pick up, and clock off. He got there to see two cases that he didn't remember loading. But they had security stickers on them (the security stickers that were kept nearby in an unlocked drawer!), and they were probably fine. Kamboj probably put them there. So he just carried on, without asking any questions.

Then, later that evening when the news broke, Bedford remembered exactly which flight he'd been dealing with that afternoon, and the two extra cases, with a horrible sinking feeling. By the time the police got round to interviewing him, it was already public knowledge that there had been a bomb in the baggage container with the Frankfurt luggage.

Just maybe, John Bedford being a good citizen, wanting to do the best he could to help the police, he decided to tell them exactly what he'd seen that afternoon. Except, he added one little embellishment to forestall what he might anticipate would be the inevitable question. "Why didn't you *say* something?!"

This is of course just one person's take on it. Other hypotheses are available, or feel free to create your own.

It's not a perfect plan. Few plans are. Plenty of terrorist bombs have been intercepted by security or foiled in one way or another. That doesn't stop them trying. They only have to get lucky once.

7

HOW DID *THAT* HAPPEN?

Why did the Lockerbie investigators ignore the Bedford suitcase? The stock answer is, well, they were committed to the Malta theory and didn't want to look at anything that might call that into question. Or even, they were intent on getting a conviction against Megrahi, and to do that, they had to have the bomb coming from Malta.

To say that is to miss the point quite spectacularly. The investigators knew all about Bedford's evidence within three weeks of the bombing. He gave his first statement, in which he reported that two suitcases had appeared in the container in his absence, on 3rd January 1989. The Scottish investigators didn't know anything at all about tray 8849 and KM180 until August. The name Abdelbaset al-Megrahi didn't crop up in relation to the inquiry until January of 1991. This doesn't add up.

To some extent, the conundrum may be explained by the thinking of the investigators during the final days of 1988.

The first piece of the blast-damaged container was brought in from the fields on Christmas Eve. More pieces followed, including pieces with the serial number. By about 28th December it had been identified as the container with the luggage from the feeder flight.

Although *Maid of the Seas* was loaded from empty at Heathrow, and only forty-nine of the 243 passengers transferred from the feeder flight, the common flight number highlighted the Frankfurt origin from the outset. Bogomira Erac's evidence shows that some people at the German end originally believed the crashed plane had taken off from Frankfurt. The BKA were in Frankfurt airport by Christmas Day, interviewing baggage handlers.

The German police had a very good reason for jumping to the conclusion that the bomb might have originated in Frankfurt – the PFLP-GC, who had been making bombs clearly designed to attack airliners in flight. Although seventeen people had been arrested in the Autumn Leaves operation, all but two had been released shortly afterwards due to "lack of evidence". The BKA thought there was plenty of evidence. One bomb had been seized, but who knew how many others had been constructed?

This information, and the incomplete knowledge the German police had about the mechanism of the bombs, was immediately shared with the Scottish investigators. By the time AVE4041 was identified as the container holding the explosive device, nobody seems to have been terribly surprised. *The Times* told the world on Hogmanay. The bomb had started its journey at Frankfurt. What was not entirely understood at that time was that a bomb of the type seized from the PFLP-GC, as constructed by their bomb-maker Marwan Khreesat, would have exploded somewhere over Belgium if it had been loaded at Frankfurt.

There seems to have been general relief on the British side of the channel. It was known that the luggage from the feeder flight had been security-screened in Germany, and was not the responsibility of anyone at Heathrow. The prospect of being able to off-load the blame for this enormous tragedy to the German authorities was no doubt attractive.

It's unclear whether the investigators were aware at that time that there were a few cases already in that container before the Frankfurt luggage was added. The first baggage handler to mention them was Sidhu on 30th December, the very day the headlines were being prepared declaring that the bomb had come from Germany. Bedford's first statement, arriving into an investigation with a thousand and one things to think about and an awful lot of stuff to read, maybe wasn't exactly what anybody wanted to hear.

Nevertheless this was a very early stage of what was inevitably going to be a huge and protracted undertaking. Debris was still coming in from the countryside, and the forensic examination of the plane and its contents was only just beginning. This was not the time for closed minds, tunnel vision or pet theories. This was the time to cast the net wide, to avoid ruling anything out, and to leave no stone unturned.

As the evidence accumulated, and was presumably collated, surely some alarm bells should have started ringing.

Later in January, Hayes's notes reveal a belief that the blast had impacted on the McKee case at the level of the floor of the container, and a speculation that the side of the bomb suitcase might have been blasted directly down on to the floor.

About the same time, suspicions were mounting that the bomb might have been inside a brown plastic hardshell suitcase, suspicions articulated by Hayes in a memo dated 15th February. Within a fairly short time, it had been identified as a Samsonite make. Bedford had of course stated on 9th January that at least one of the cases he saw was a brown Samsonite hardshell.

Right in the middle of this, Ray Manly's report about the break-in was communicated to the Lockerbie investigators, followed a few days later by his police statement.

While it may have taken a little while to be certain that none of the later-arriving suitcases had found their way into the container, Bedford was fairly clear that he didn't believe anything that touched down after 16.00 would have got to the shed in time. Mr. Rubin's plane, the earliest of the late group, didn't land until 16.15. It shouldn't have been rocket science to figure out that the six items from Brussels, Larnaca and Vienna were probably the only interline ones in the container. Nevertheless, when the three baggage handlers were asked to load a container to demonstrate the arrangement of the luggage as they remembered it, everyone needed seven or eight cases to achieve the appearance as they recalled it from the afternoon of 21st December. Four items are simply not enough to fill the row at the back.

The investigators were certainly following up passengers on the feeder flight, especially Karen Noonan. The FAA knew about Maier's x-ray log and believed he had x-rayed one more interline item than was legitimately on the flight, which suggested an illegitimate item might be present, but it's very unclear if the Scottish police knew about that. They were focussed on Frankfurt, but they were frustrated by the lack of the computer data.

Of course all that was perfectly reasonable, but where was the investigation at Heathrow? Further statements were of course taken, but at a very leisurely pace. On 10th January Sidhu mentioned tossing the feeder flight luggage on top of what was already there, but it wasn't until 7th August that someone came back and asked him to confirm clearly and in words of one syllable that he hadn't moved the interline cases. Bedford said he hadn't seen anyone acting suspiciously in the interline shed in his very first interview, but it wasn't a topic that was pursued. Incredibly, nobody even asked him which of the two suitcases he was referring to as a brown Samsonite hardshell, and it wasn't until the FAI that he confirmed it was the left-hand one. Nobody asked Kamboj and Parmar where they were or what they were doing while Bedford was away from the shed. Kamboj was never questioned as a suspect. If anybody asked Susan Stone whether she'd changed her shift that evening and if so why, we don't know about it.

What was all that about? From the very earliest stages of the inquiry, that bottom front suitcase was in the frame. It was red hot. It was the clue of the century. You don't walk past something like that in the hope or expectation that a few weeks or months down the line the forensics chaps will helpfully confirm the explosion was too high. You gallop after it enthusiastically, spurred on by visions of promotion, the honours list, or even just the chance to get back to the wife and family in the evening. So what happened?

Nothing. Crickets and tumbleweed.

Some of the mood music coming from RARDE did suggest the explosion might have been too high. Despite his notes and drawings on 20th and 26th January clearly suggesting the exploding suitcase might have been on the bottom layer of luggage, and the BKA memo dated 7th January showing the blast almost at floor level, on 19th January Hayes sent a memo to Lockerbie stating that the explosion had been "approximately 18 inches" above the frame of the container base.

Bizarrely, the number one item on his appended list of "intended future progress" reads "Further luggage is being examined to (a) assist with the identification of all the container's contents *and their probable orientation relative to the centre of the explosion.*" There is of course no evidence that this exercise, in effect the exercise undertaken in chapter 6 of this book, ever took place.

Some of the contemporary press commentary also quoted a high position for the explosion – for example Emerson and Duffy, writing about the early months of the inquiry, stated that the Heathrow interline luggage could be ruled out because "further checking in Longtown showed that the bomb must have been eighteen to twenty-four inches above the floor of the container." Nevertheless by 5th May Hayes had revised his estimate to "approximately 35 cm" (14 inches), and the measurement decreased further after that.

Peter Claiden noticed at an early stage that a hole in the adjacent container AVN7511, which appeared to have been caused by "a relatively mild blast" from the explosion in AVE 4041, was centred 10 inches from the base of that container. It's difficult to know why this measurement was considered so critical in estimating the height of the explosion. The centre of the blast was nearly two feet from the face of AVN7511, the hole was eight inches square, and the blast was said to have come "at an angle". Nevertheless Claiden incorporated that measurement into his April 1989 preliminary report on the baggage containers, showing it as the height of the explosion from the base of AVE4041, and this estimate was maintained in the full AAIB report published the following year.

The scientists at RARDE concurred, and the Claiden diagram (see figures 12 and 24, and plate 3) was also incorporated by them into the Joint Forensic Report in 1991. However, although the measurement was the same, the justification was more detailed, incorporating "a careful consideration of the probable high explosive charge weight and the extent, severity and direction of the explosion damage to the light alloy base and supporting frame struts of luggage container AVE4041" as well as the location of the damage to AVN7511.

Also entering the equation was the forensic opinion that the bomb suitcase had not been on the floor of the container for other reasons. Claiden's April report included the passage quoted on page 46-47, speculating that the floor panel "had been protected by, presumably, a piece of luggage." This was repeated in the interim forensic report of June 1990 in rather more technical language, though oddly the passage was omitted from the final 1991 version in favour of relying on the two "postulated positions" of the bomb suitcase, neither of which was the case on the floor.

The scientists had been blowing things up, too. In total nine test explosions were carried out in April and July 1989, some at Indian Head, Maryland, and some in Atlantic City. Everyone was apparently quite happy that there had been another case between the bomb suitcase and the base of the container. And since nobody was even suggesting that the interline luggage had been moved, clearly the Bedford bag was out of the picture.

What is strangely missing from all this is any hint of conflict between the police investigation and the forensic scientists. One might imagine the police would be bitterly disappointed at having to rule out such a promising clue as Bedford's suitcase. They might even be challenging the forensic conclusions, declaring "how can that be, when we have a mysteriously-appearing suitcase answering to the description of the bomb suitcase, right there on the floor of the container?"

Not a bit of it. The police appeared entirely content to concentrate on the feeder flight and the luggage from Frankfurt, and go right on behaving as if Bedford's evidence didn't exist.

The conflict, as it happens, was elsewhere. Despite their initial attitude the German authorities had been protesting since New Year that the bomb had been introduced not in Frankfurt, but in London. The British team remained unimpressed. The prime suspects were the German cell of the PFLP-GC, so obviously the bomb had come from Germany.

This all blew up, literally, in April. Investigators had been aware for some time of intelligence reports that Marwan Khreesat, the bomb-maker of the PFLP-GC cell that had been busted the previous October, had made more than one bomb. In fact he was said to have made five, and it was likely the remainder were still in Neuss. Repeated searches by BKA officers had failed to uncover anything, until in April three more devices were found – two in hi-fi tuners and one in a computer monitor.

The events of 17th April would be funny in a Keystone Cops sort of way, if they weren't so tragic. One of the devices was accidentally triggered, and the resulting explosion killed the BKA explosives expert called in to examine it, Hans-Jürgen Sonntag. His assistant, Thomas Ettinger, was blinded and permanently disabled. No fifth device was ever found.

About a month later, and using some of the limited data that had been acquired from the Khreesat devices before the remaining ones were destroyed on safety grounds, the German police redoubled their efforts to explain to the British side of the inquiry why they believed the bomb must have been loaded at Heathrow.

Khreesat had been making a very particular type of bomb: his speciality, which operated on a dual trigger system incorporating a barometer to detect air pressure and hence altitude. Simplifying to some extent, it goes like this. When an airliner climbs after takeoff, pressure inside the skin at first falls with increasing height – this is the period during which ears pop and babies start to cry. Once the internal pressure reaches the equivalent of about 8,000 feet, the lowest that can reasonably sustain the comfort of the passengers and crew, the pressure is stabilised for the remainder of the flight. Khreesat's barometers were carefully set to detect this initial fall in pressure, an event that would not occur while the device remained on the ground at normal altitudes.

His early devices deployed in the 1970s had simply blown up at that point, but the resulting crashes weren't completely catastrophic. The aircraft were still too low for explosive decompression to occur, and close enough to the airport for it to be possible to turn back and effect an emergency landing. Not only that, airport security got wise to the plan, and started screening suspect luggage in pressure chambers which simulated the first ten minutes or so of flight, the time when the drop in pressure occurred. Both Frankfurt and Heathrow had such chambers in 1988, although none of the PA103 luggage was screened in that way. Presumably if Maier or Kamboj had reported suspicions about a radio-cassette player they saw in a suitcase, that would have been one approach to investigating it.

Khreesat had however modified the devices to stay one step ahead. Instead of the drop in pressure detonating the bomb directly, it triggered a capacitor to begin charging from an internal battery. That introduced an additional time delay of between twenty and forty-five minutes, depending on the capacitor. Only after it had fully charged, would it discharge and detonate the explosive. This would fool a pressure chamber, as luggage wasn't held in the chambers for that length of time, and once normal pressure returned the thing would simply reset itself ready to start again at the real takeoff. The modification also made the devices significantly more lethal. The extra delay allowed the aircraft to climb to cruising altitude and made catastrophic explosive decompression a real possibility.

The usual time taken for a flight to climb to the point where the barometer would trigger the capacitor to begin charging was about seven minutes. Some of Khreesat's capacitors were known to have a thirty-minute charging time. *Maid of the Seas* blew apart thirty-eight minutes after her wheels left the tarmac at Heathrow. The point about all this was that if a device of that nature had been loaded at Frankfurt, the Boeing 727 of the feeder flight would have blown up over Belgium. PA103A flew for about ninety minutes in its journey to London, and it had most certainly been pressurised down to the 8,000-feet trigger point in that journey.

Feraday, however, was having none of this. Rather than take on board what the German investigators were saying and take the possibility of a Heathrow loading seriously, he produced a list of about nine different ways in which, he maintained, a Khreesat device could be loaded at Frankfurt and yet not be triggered until the second time of asking.

These suggestions fell broadly into two categories. Maybe Khreesat had introduced yet another modification to count the take-offs. No doubt that would be possible, but no Khreesat device was ever recovered with such a modification, and when Khreesat himself was interviewed in Jordan by the FBI in November 1989, he wasn't even asked about the possibility. Alternatively, these devices weren't particularly robust. Maybe it had simply malfunctioned on the first leg, and being chucked into the container at Heathrow had shaken it back to life. Again, possible, but that would mean that the intended primary target was a humble 727 flying a European domestic route with only 121 passengers, only forty-nine of them headed for the transatlantic leg, and that the bombers had presciently equipped the suitcase with tags directing it to be transferred to the 747 for a second bite at the cherry if by some chance it reached Heathrow in one piece.

These suggestions certainly had merit as a demonstration of why Frankfurt couldn't be let off the hook completely. However, they seem subsequently to have been used to dismiss the possibility of a Heathrow loading entirely. That was ridiculous. The greatest probability still remained that a Khreesat device in the form they were known to exist had been loaded at Heathrow and had functioned as intended.

This spat happened in May. In July the second and third sets of controlled explosions was carried out in the USA, further reinforcing the mantra that there had been another suitcase between the floor of the container and the bomb.

In August, the investigators discovered that a number of items of clothing in the bomb suitcase had been manufactured in Malta, and shortly after that the BKA came clean about Bogomira Erac's souvenir printout and KM180. The rest, as they say, is history. The two warring factions buried their differences, quietly forgot about the huge security holes in both flagship international airports, and ganged up on little Malta with its guarded planes and double-counted luggage.

That wasn't quite the end of it, though. The Scottish investigators had supplied their German counterparts with copies of all the Heathrow witness statements. The BKA had had these statements translated, and a summary document produced noting the salient points of each witness's evidence. The summary included a concise report of what Bedford had told the police interviewer, right down to the left-to-right loading and the mysterious appearance of a brown Samsonite hardshell remarkably close to the eventual location of the explosion. In early November Helge Tepp of the BKA made some inquiries about this matter with the Scottish detectives. The reply he received from DI Brown was a bit strange.

> I have consulted DCI Bell in regard to this matter. Mr. Bell was referring to the statement made by the baggage handler John Bedford, who remembers two hard-sided suitcases, of 'Samsonite' type, one brown in colour and the other of similar colour. *These two suitcases were the last to be put into AVE4041 from the interline area.*

Then follows a list of Heathrow interline boarders who had luggage in the hold, including not just the four early passengers whose suitcases were actually in the container, but the three later ones whose cases were loose-loaded at the rear of the plane. The passengers were listed in random order with no information about their arrival times. No attempt was made to suggest which of these items might have been the two suitcases Bedford was referring to, but certainly none of them was a brown hardshell.

That memo is dated 23rd November 1989. It doesn't really sound as if the Bedford bag had ever been a big talking point in the investigation, does it?

No, it wasn't. In point of fact it seems that Ray Manly's evidence about the midnight break-in wasn't the only story from Heathrow that failed to become part of the general narrative of the case during 1989. Three books were written about the inquiry as it progressed by journalists with inside information: *Lockerbie, the real story* by David Johnston (June 1989), *The Fall of Pan Am 103* by Steven Emerson and Brian Duffy (February 1990), and *On the Trail of Terror* by David Leppard (May 1991). Speculation about how the bomb got on the plane is detailed and apparently well-informed in all three accounts. Nevertheless Leppard, writing after Bedford gave evidence at the FAI in October 1990, is the only one even to mention his evidence.

Leppard was getting his information from right inside the police inquiry. His is the only account of the mystery Samsonite published before the Zeist trial, and even he seems somewhat bemused by it. He notes Bedford's evidence and Kamboj's denial, and goes on to declare that the case was ruled out of contention by the Maryland explosives tests in April 1989. The question of what the investigators were doing about it *before* April is left hanging, because obviously in the midst of his detailed account of the interest in Karen Noonan's Jordanian acquaintance and Khaled Jaafar's checked-in luggage, there's nothing being said about a possible rogue bag at Heathrow, even in the earliest stages.

A number of internal police memos from the period have since escaped into the wild. While it was generally understood that there were some Heathrow interline bags in the container and how they were distributed, including that the bottom front left-hand case was one of these items, the information that it had appeared mysteriously when the container was unattended, that the three people manning the Pan Am interline station at the time all denied having put it there and that it had been described as a brown Samsonite hardshell, is never referenced. The impression among the police personnel seems to be that it was just an ordinary passenger bag.

The same is true of the forensic investigation. In all the memos and reports about the ruling-out of the suitcase on the floor of the container, its extraordinarily suspicious provenance is never mentioned. For all we can tell, Hayes and Feraday themselves didn't know about it.

★　★　★　★　★　★　★

The 'not the bag on the bottom' story held up during the Fatal Accident Inquiry and the civil hearings in the USA, precisely because there was nobody in either court with any interest in challenging it.

The FAI heard all about how the bag on the bottom had appeared mysteriously while the container was unattended, and that Bedford, Kamboj and Parmar denied having put it there, and that it had been described as a brown or maroon Samsonite hardshell. That court also heard that there was no legitimate passenger luggage matching the description of the bomb suitcase, that is, a brown Samsonite hardshell. (That last isn't strictly true, there were a couple on the feeder flight, but it's what the FAI findings state.)   Nevertheless the sheriff also heard that the case hadn't been moved, and that the forensic scientist was "adamant" that the case in that position was not the bomb. Should he have queried the point, and requested an independent review of the forensic opinion? Given the sensitive nature of the whole affair, and the fact that the police seem to have been telling him they had conclusive evidence they couldn't present in court that the bomb had flown in to Frankfurt as interline luggage, it would have taken a brave man to have done that. Sheriff Mowat took the line of least resistance and found in accordance with the case the Crown were keen to advance.

The same thing happened again in New York. It's unclear whether the Platt court even knew the details of Bedford's evidence, but the plaintiffs certainly presented the forensic opinion that the bomb must have been in the luggage transferred from the feeder flight. Just as in Dumfries, there was absolutely no advantage for Pan Am in asserting that the bomb had come from Heathrow. Frying pans and fires spring to mind.

And that's how things remained for several years. Indeed, without any knowledge of the detailed baggage reconciliation analysis, it's not entirely unreasonable. Lots of people have brown hardshell suitcases, and some of them are even Samsonites. Unless you know first that none of the Heathrow interline passengers was carrying such a case, and that all six cases they were carrying were recovered and had not been under the bomb, and then that none of the items of blast-damaged luggage recovered on the ground could be reconciled to the 'under the bomb' loading position, Bedford's evidence isn't a smoking gun.

Although the trial at Camp Zeist began in May 2000, preparation of the prosecution and defence cases began much earlier. Megrahi and Fhimah surrendered themselves for trial in April 1999, and after that, work was pretty incessant.

The legal players were not all entirely new to the game. Andrew Hardie, who had been lead advocate for the Crown at the FAI, was by this time Lord Advocate, and was expected to lead the prosecution case. It seemed at first that the case led would be very similar to the FAI case as regards the luggage in AVE4041 and the contention that the bomb suitcase had come from Frankfurt. As late as October 1999, prosecution counsel were talking about running an 'exclusion case', in other words that they would demonstrate exactly which items of luggage were in the container and show that each one of them didn't contain the bomb, leaving only the 'brown Samsonite from Malta'. This was to be based on DC Henderson's main report, although that was not to be produced at the trial as it contained some inaccuracies.

However, that couldn't fly, not like that. The baggage reconciliation evidence could show exactly what each passenger had checked in for the flight, and each known item of legitimate unaccompanied luggage (*viz.* Costa, Weinacker, Hubbard), and whether it had been recovered or not, and if not recovered whether its description matched the description of the bomb bag. DC Henderson's report does indeed document all that. However, that by itself can only confirm that the bomb was in an item of unaccompanied, undocumented luggage. It won't and can't reveal whether that item originated at Frankfurt or at Heathrow. It also won't and can't confirm that it was the item in tray 8849. There were five other trays on the printout with no idea at all what they were or whether they had been transferred to the transatlantic flight at Heathrow. Mr. Hubbard's case demonstrated that a misdirection there was possible, but any or all of the six mystery trays could have been tagged for New York. Tray 8849 could have been tagged for London. We have absolutely no idea.

The other little problem with the complete baggage reconciliation exercise is that it reveals no item of legitimate luggage, accompanied or unaccompanied, that can be reconciled to the left-hand of the two cases Bedford saw. All the legitimate Heathrow interline luggage was accounted for, and none of the items was either a brown hardshell or showing damage consistent with its having been under the bomb.

This must have been the real dilemma for the prosecution. As things stood, accepting Sidhu's assurance that the interline luggage wasn't moved, the Bedford case was a serious problem. Once the evidence was looked at as a whole, the story was undoubtedly getting a bit hard to swallow. It was necessary to propose that an unaccompanied and undocumented brown or maroon Samsonite hardshell (or a case that appeared to John Bedford to be a brown or maroon Samsonite hardshell) was somehow, innocently, loaded into AVE4041 that afternoon in circumstances which then became confused and forgotten about by whichever staff member was responsible. To propose that although this virtual lookalike for the bomb suitcase was placed and remained within a few inches of the centre of the subsequent explosion, it had nothing at all to do with it. To propose that another mysterious brown or maroon Samsonite hardshell which nobody had seen in all its travels, and nobody could explain how on earth it had supposedly got into a well-guarded plane at Malta, was coincidentally loaded right on top of this innocent suitcase. Then when the bomb suitcase exploded, despite ample quantities of it and everything else around it being recovered on the ground, all the fragments of the innocent unaccompanied suitcase from the interline shed somehow blew away and were never recovered.

Hmmmm. And the only evidence the Crown had to support this dubious narrative was the forensic opinion that although the explosion was pretty low down, there *must* have been something else between the bomb suitcase and the floor of the container. Was that going to be sufficient to hold it together?

Clearly, the Crown decided it wasn't. They didn't even try to lead the test results from April or July 1989, which at least avoided having to defend the methodology, and relied solely on the scientists' assertions. The whole thing was in danger of falling apart under the weight of its own improbability unless they could produce a blast-damaged suitcase that could be credibly represented as having been under the bomb. However, which one? The only real candidate was 'grey hardshell 2', with the suggestion that this handful of small fragments was all that was left of some unidentified piece of lost luggage Bedford had erroneously perceived as brown. However, that claim wasn't made, and in any case grey hardshell 2 doesn't actually exist. The fragments are only some more bits of the bomb suitcase with the 'antique copper' finish burned off, and it's likely the defence would have noticed this if the claim had been made. In the event Tricia Coyle's blue American Tourister was chosen, as the only identifiable suitcase showing damage consistent with its having been flat against the bomb suitcase.

It seems unlikely that anyone involved in the case had even considered the possibility that the blue Tourister might have been on the floor of the container before about November 1999. The narrative that the Heathrow interline luggage hadn't been moved had been more or less an article of faith from the earliest weeks of the inquiry. It was, after all, the original justification for excluding the Bedford bag from the investigation, so far as any justification can in fact be discerned. David Leppard, the journalist with the mole in the police inquiry in 1990, was quite clear that the Tourister had been on top of the bomb suitcase. Overturning that assumption was a huge gamble, and on the face of it potentially suicidal for the Crown case. Once one allows that the Bedford bag was moved during the tarmac transfer, and the Coyle case put in its place, the possibility is introduced that the mysteriously-appearing brown Samsonite from the interline shed was simply replaced on top, and was of course the bomb.

The other question one would imagine might arise is this. If the investigators knew that the interline luggage had been moved, and therefore that Bedford's mysterious brown Samsonite could have been replaced on the second layer, how was it ruled out of the inquiry, back in 1989? Where is the original investigation of this case? Let's face it, the date of the forensic examination now being used to support the theory that the interline luggage was moved was 26th January 1989.

Changing the scenario was a huge gamble, and potentially suicidal. Just less suicidal than the case as it originally stood, that's all.

If the interline luggage wasn't moved, the front left-hand case seen at Heathrow by three different people reconciles as the bomb, beyond any shadow of doubt. It would still reconcile as the bomb even if it had come in on the carousel and been loaded in the normal manner, based on the rest of the evidence. Conversely, if the case was moved, it could have been anything, because it no longer needs to have the catastrophic blast damage a case under the bomb would inevitably have sustained.

Even more starkly, don't move the interline luggage, and the Crown case is completely screwed. Allow it to have been moved, and while the case may still be lost on the grounds that the Bedford bag *might* have been the bomb, it's no longer *definitely* the bomb, and oh look a squirrel – I mean, all that other evidence from Frankfurt and Malta…

The Crown appears to have decided to jump out of the fire, back into the frying pan.

Curiously, it's unclear who actually took the decision to commit to the new scenario. In March 2000, just two months before the trial began, Andrew Hardie resigned as Lord Advocate, and passed the case over to his successor Colin Boyd, the former Solicitor General.

The revised scenario required a rather selective approach to the leading of evidence. Sidhu couldn't be called, obviously. The details of the Heathrow interline passengers and their luggage couldn't be admitted. No explicit theory of how the luggage was arranged was proposed to the court. The whole thing had to be left as vague as possible, to allow for maximum manoeuverability when delicately suggesting that this or that *might* have happened. It allowed the defence the same manoeuverability of course, but that couldn't really be helped.

To the observer, it all seems very strange. Why aren't we being told things that are obviously relevant, and must obviously have been known to the investigation? Why are we speculating about what a baggage handler *might* have done, rather than simply asking him?

The defence, regrettably, seem to have been too enchanted by the apparent get-out-of-jail-free card to remedy this.

★　★　★　★　★　★　★

And that, apparently, is how it happened. The investigators completely missed what should have been the clue of the century, in the very earliest weeks of the inquiry. A clue that was more or less festooned in fairy lights flashing "look at me!" In this they were enthusiastically abetted by pretty much everybody at the AAIB and RARDE, with a whole portfolio of reasons why the suitcase in that position wasn't even worth a second glance.

Then, eleven years later, when it became necessary to construct a plausible case against actual suspects on the basis of this scenario, the Crown prosecutors realised that according to all the pre-existing assumptions of the inquiry, the suitcase that inevitably reconciled to the bomb suitcase was the one that placed the scene of the crime a thousand miles away from where the accused men had been at the time.

To rescue this situation the Crown constructed an entirely new scenario, overturning the assumptions on which previous decisions in the case had been based, and losing a few rather central pieces of evidence down the back of the sofa in the process.

8

TONY GAUCI AND THE MYSTERY SHOPPER

One of the principal reasons for the judges accepting that the bomb suitcase had begun its journey on Malta despite the strength of the Luqa airport security was not simply that the clothes packed with the bomb had been sold on Malta, but that the man they had been persuaded was the purchaser of these clothes was at the airport when the flight to Frankfurt took off. That identification had its own problems though.

The tracing of these clothes to the shop where they had been sold was the big breakthrough of the investigation. The remains of a pair of trousers found burned as if by close proximity to the bomb still had their label, and the manufacturer's serial number stamped inside a pocket. Eventually the manufacturer was traced – the trousers had been made by a small firm on the island of Malta called Yorkie Clothing. Alexander Calleja, the owner, consulted his books and discovered that these trousers were almost unique. They were part of a small order that had been supplied to a local retailer on 18th November 1988.

The shop concerned was 'Mary's House' in Tower Road, Sliema, only about three miles from Luqa airport. It was owned and run by Edward Gauci and a number of his sons, in partnership. The investigators descended on the little clothes shop and talked to the two sons who were in charge at the time. During the conversation one of the Gauci brothers, Tony, suddenly remembered selling the trousers to a customer, some time before Christmas the previous year. Not only that, he remembered the man buying certain other items which also sounded remarkably like other items of clothing that had been found blast-damaged at Lockerbie.

Given that this conversation took place at the beginning of September 1989 it all sounds a bit too good to be true. The story has been questioned and some anomalies and inconsistencies highlighted, but realistically it's quite difficult to come to any other conclusion than that at least some of the items in the bomb suitcase were bought new from Tony Gauci not long before the disaster, and that Tony had some recollection of the transaction.

Two aspects assumed crucial importance. What was the date of the sale, and could Tony identify the customer?

Initial parameters for the date were easy to establish. No earlier than 18th November, the date the trousers had been supplied, and no later than 20th December, for obvious reasons. Tony remembered more. The customer had come to the shop in the evening, not long before closing time at seven o'clock. Tony was minding the shop alone, because his brother Paul had gone off to watch football on TV. Tony remembered that it had been midweek, which was agreed to have been a Wednesday, but which might actually have meant that he remembered the shop had been open both the day before and the day after. However, Paul thought the football match was one between Rome and Dynamo Dresden, and both possible matches had been played on Wednesdays – the first leg of a UEFA Cup tie at five o'clock on 23rd November and the return match at one o'clock on 7th December.

Tony remembered a couple of other things about the day. He thought the Christmas lights had not yet been put up, and he remembered that it had begun to rain while the man was in the shop. Because of this the customer had also bought an umbrella and opened it as he left. An umbrella similar to the ones Tony stocked was also found blast-damaged at Lockerbie.

No amount of discussion with the brothers was able to produce a definite decision one way or the other. In one statement Paul favoured the November date, but on another occasion he told one of the Scottish detectives he thought it had been the December date. Although the November match had been in the evening, the time the clothes sale took place, Paul might well not have bothered to return to work after the afternoon match in December.

Table 5 (opposite) shows the comparison reduced to its basics.

The holiday on 8th December, the Feast of the Immaculate Conception, wasn't a huge issue and it wasn't pressed at the trial. The time of day of the football match wasn't a huge issue either. Nevertheless, so far as they go, both points favour the earlier date.

The rain and the Christmas lights became the major issues. One of the three defence witnesses at Camp Zeist was Joseph Mifsud, who had been chief meteorologist at Luqa airport in 1988. Major Mifsud produced the weather charts for the period in question which showed that there had been light rain

Tony's memory	23rd November	7th December
Late November or early December	Late November	Early December
Midweek	Wednesday, normal midweek day	Wednesday, but 8th December was a public holiday
Paul was watching football on TV	Football match shown	Football match shown
Early evening	Match was in the evening	Match was in the afternoon
It was raining	Light rain in the evening	No rain recorded
Christmas lights were not yet up	Christmas lights not up	Christmas lights switched on the previous day

Table 5: The two possible dates of the clothes purchase

in the evening of 23rd November, whereas no rain was recorded at that time on 7th December. However, weather varies locally, even from street to street, does it not? Is it not possible there could have been a local shower in Sliema? Major Mifsud said he was 90% certain there had been no rain at all, but he couldn't completely exclude the possibility of a few drops of rain, though it wouldn't have been enough to wet the ground.

In court, the exact date of the Christmas lights being put up was all a bit uncertain. Was it before or after 7th December? Nobody seemed really sure. None of this was helped by Tony's evidence, which tended to drift closer and closer to what the police seemed to want with each statement he made. First, no lights. Then, the lights were actually being erected at the time. Then, they were on, weren't they?

It was the same with the rain. At first, it was "raining", certainly sufficiently wet for the customer to decide to buy an umbrella. Then, it wasn't much rain. Then, it was just "dripping".

The issue of the Christmas lights was in fact settled by the SCCRC, years later. They made their own inquiries on Malta and had little difficulty in putting the matter to bed. The then Minister for Tourism still had his official diary for 1988, and one of the engagements recorded was the ceremony of the switching on of the Christmas lights in Sliema. On 6th December. The Commission also took the view that Tony's earlier statements were to be preferred and that while the lights might have been in the process of being erected on the day in question, they weren't lit.

The Commission actually put its finger right on the heart of the problem with the trial court's reasoning, when it noted that there was "no reasonable basis" for the judgement that the date of the purchase had been 7th December. That decision was never explained and never justified, and yet it was the hook on which the entire daisy-chain was hung. The clothes were sold on 7th December, therefore Megrahi was the purchaser because he was in the neighbourhood that day, therefore the bomb was in tray 8849 because the man who bought the clothes was at the airport when KM180 departed, therefore Megrahi was the Lockerbie bomber because he was at the scene of the crime (and he bought the clothes).

Right from the beginning there was no reason to prefer 7th December over 23rd November, even if Joseph Mifsud was no more than 90% certain it had been dry all evening. Knowing that the Christmas lights were already up by that day simply clinched it.

There was of course no record of Megrahi having been on the island on 23rd November. His second appeal was hearing this evidence when the appeal was withdrawn in 2009.

★　★　★　★　★　★　★

Tony was able to give a surprisingly detailed description of his mysterious customer. However, it was a description from a man who sold clothes for a living. Quite a lot about the build and body size, but not so much about the facial features, although he did say that the man was clean-shaven and not wearing glasses.

Tony's customer	Abdelbaset al-Megrahi
Libyan accent	Libyan
About 50 years old	36 years old
Over 6 feet tall	5 feet 8 inches tall
Dark skinned	Light-skinned
Large build and big chest	Head and chest appear normal size
Heavily-built, 36-inch waist, 18-inch collar, the 42-inch jacket would have been too small	Normal to slight build in 1988

Tony volunteered the vital statistics. He had been sizing the man up for fit, and coming to the conclusion that he was buying clothes that didn't fit him. The description is of a burly man. Megrahi's vital statistics weren't referred to at the trial, but photographs reveal a man of average to slight build. While he was certainly taller than the diminutive Tony, he was at least four inches shorter than Tony's estimate of the purchaser.

Tony's estimate of the man's age was consistent, and maintained over a number of interviews. He himself was forty-four at the time. He estimated the customer as being at least five years older than himself. Megrahi was in fact eight years younger than Tony.

The skin colour is frustrating, because Tony was never asked to explain what he meant by "dark skin". His assessment of the customer as Libyan was based on his belief that the man was speaking Arabic with a Libyan accent (Tony himself was not fluent in Arabic), and Libyan people come in quite a wide range of skin tones. Megrahi was very much at the light-skinned end of that range. The photofit and artist's impression Tony helped create a few weeks later (figure 27) were in black and white, but suggest quite dark skin. It's possible Tony was describing a negro or mixed-race customer.

Tony said that both images were reasonable likenesses, but of the two, the artist's impression was better. He was concerned that the photofit image appeared about ten years too young to match the customer, however the police notes state that "an alteration to the picture to take this into account was not

Artist's impression   Photofit

Figure 27
Two forensic images produced by Tony Gauci on 13th September 1989.

possible without reducing the otherwise high quality." The two pictures are not particularly similar. Overall, it seems as if Tony remembered the man's body shape and size better than he remembered his face.

Despite all that, the police pretty much ignored Tony's vital statistics and proceeded to show him head-and-shoulders passport photos of men more or less (usually less) resembling his description of the clothes purchaser. Another thing they didn't pay much attention to was age, with many of the photos being of men considerably younger than fifty.

Tony obliged by picking out one or two photos he agreed "resembled" the purchaser, but unsurprisingly he invariably qualified his selections by stating that the man in the picture was too young. The only one of these picks in the public domain is the photograph of Mohamed Salam, but he also became quite enamoured by a picture of Abu Talb he saw in a newspaper, which identified him as the suspected bomber (as he was at that time). Mohamed Salam was only four years younger than Megrahi, but Gauci said his picture was too young "by about twenty years" to be the purchaser.

Figure 28
Two pictures identified by Tony Gauci as resembling the clothes purchaser.

Mohamed Salam   Abu Talb

At that time the main, and indeed only suspects were still the PFLP-GC, though with the focus shifted from Germany to a cell of the gang based on Malta. Megrahi didn't enter the equation until much later, after the focus had shifted yet again to Libya as the suspected prime mover. Although Megrahi's presence at the airport later became crucial to his conviction, this wasn't the reason for the cops homing in on him. This part of the case wasn't detected in the normal manner. Instead, in January 1991 two photographs of Megrahi were passed over to the Scottish police by the FBI, with the suggestion that he should be considered as a suspect.

The upshot of that was that another photospread was prepared to show to Tony, this time including one of these pictures. That photospread is reproduced on the following page, but first, it is helpful to have some idea of what Megrahi actually looked like. He was someone whose appearance didn't change a great deal over three decades, both before and after 1988.

| Wales, 1971-2 age about 19 | 1987 passport age when photo taken unknown | February 1992 age 39 | October 1998 age 46 |

Figure 29
Photographs of Abdelbaset al-Megrahi from his late teens to his mid forties.

The first picture is from his student identity card, from when he was studying marine engineering in Cardiff; the second is from the 'coded' passport in the name of 'Abdusamad' which was issued in 1987, but the appearance of the photo suggests it may have been several years old when it was used for that purpose; the third is a press photograph taken in Libya; and the fourth is a still from a documentary film again shot in Libya.

None of these, however, was the picture used in the photospread. Without reading further, can you spot Megrahi among the men pictured in Figure 30 overleaf? Conversely, does one of these pictures stand out as being noticeably different from the others? Perhaps, even, one of such poor quality that you might wonder why it had been included – unless, perhaps, it was the one they had to include?

Tony's first reaction was to state that all the photographs were "too young" to be his elusive customer, apparently including pictures 4 and 9, which appear to be of men in their forties. He declined to select any of them. The detectives then urged him to go back and pick someone, and at that point he selected the picture of Megrahi. However, once again he merely said that this image "resembled" the customer, and indeed he remarked at the time that the resemblance was less strong than the picture of Abu Talb.

Figure 30
Photospread shown by the Scottish police to Tony Gauci on 15th February 1991.

Much has been written about this exercise, and it has been criticised for not being tape-recorded or videoed. The image above was taken directly from the 'flip drive' as presented in court in 2000. If that is indeed what was shown to Tony in 1991, Megrahi's picture (middle row, extreme right) stood out to a quite remarkable degree. Not only is it smaller and of a very different quality to the others, it is peppered with white dots, sports a couple of horizontal lines, and has a very peculiar curved flash which is not present on the original passport photo. It also appears that only three or four of the twelve pictures bear much resemblance to the photofit or the artist's impression, and several of the men look extraordinarily youthful.

In addition, the pictures were sufficiently spread out for the police officers present, all of whom knew the identity of the suspect, to be aware of which picture

Tony was examining at any given time. This presents a clear danger of invoking something known as the 'Clever Hans effect', after a performing horse (*der kluge Hans*) from the early twentieth century who appeared to be able to count. After an investigation of the animal's remarkable powers, it was established that rather than being an arithmetical prodigy, Hans was skilled at picking up unconscious clues in his owner's body language, which he correctly interpreted as signalling when he should stop tapping with his hoof. In his autobiographical account of the inquiry DC John Crawford gives this account of the proceedings.

> When Tony began to look closely at each photograph in turn, I watched his eyes as he scanned each picture, his expressionless face moving from one to the other as he concentrated his thoughts on each. When he was finished he looked again at number eight and I thought, *he's gonna pick him!* He looked carefully at all of them in turn once again and then said solemnly, pointing to number eight, 'that is the man' or words to that effect.

Peter Fraser, who was Lord Advocate at the time of the original Lockerbie inquiry, once described Tony Gauci as "an apple short of a picnic". Nevertheless, if a horse can do it, so can Tony. Modern practice of course forbids anyone aware of the identity of the suspect from being present when photo-identity parades or identity parades are conducted.

The photograph is also a very poor likeness of its subject, who appears to be suffering from both mumps and a bad hair day. Of the better quality photographs of Megrahi, the one which most closely approximates to his appearance in December 1988 is probably the one from February 1992, which also matches Tony's description of the man as being smartly dressed in a blue suit. It's actually quite difficult to see this as the same person as the grainy, flawed, black-and-white image.

Figure 31
Photospread picture compared to Megrahi's actual appearance only three years after the date of the clothes purchase.

Passport photo   Megrahi aged 39

The provenance of that picture is unclear, but it seems to have been obtained from the authorities in Czechoslovakia. It is believed to be (presumably a photocopy of) the photograph in his own passport, held in his own name, and issued in 1986. This would suggest he was thirty-four in that picture, but Tony stated that the man, whom he estimated as being in his thirties, would need to be "ten or fifteen years older" before he would look like the purchaser. (There was some discussion of this point among the investigators, including the suggestion that the photograph might date from the late 1970s and so justify claiming that "ten years older" might describe the thirty-six-year-old Megrahi in 1988, but the fact remains that all Tony's statements concerning the age of the customer, including this one, were consistent in estimating around or even over fifty years.)

The FBI had however provided two photos of Megrahi: the one used in the photospread, which originally showed a collar and tie, and one with an "open neck shirt" (see also plate 7). The latter appears to be another print of the photo used in the Abdusamad passport, which seems to have formed part of another identity document in Megrahi's own name. Why they chose the blurry, smeared Czech image over this better-quality colour photograph is a complete mystery. Apart from everything else, the Czech picture had to be cropped to conceal the collar and tie, to match the other pictures in the photospread. Of course, it's possible someone had noticed that the Czech one bore a vague resemblance to Tony's 1989 photofit…

open-neck shirt image   collar-and-tie image   1989 photofit

Figure 32
The two photographs of Megrahi supplied to the Scottish police by the FBI, compared to Gauci's photofit image of the clothes purchaser.

Thus, in February 1991, over two years after the event, and after having been shown scores of photographs of men vaguely resembling his description (but all too young), the picture that Tony picked out as merely "resembling" his customer was a picture that didn't even look like Megrahi.

It's questionable whether Tony retained any real memory of the original customer by 1991, after so much prodding and hinting, poring over so many photospreads, and his fixation on the newspaper photograph of Abu Talb he kept referring to. However, if he did, and if the image he picked out then did indeed resemble the customer, then his selection of this image is surely one more thing that argues *against* the customer actually being Megrahi.

If the police had continued to show Tony photographs of clean-shaven middle-aged men with a full head of black hair, it seems perfectly probable that he would have continued to pick out pictures that resembled his memory of the customer, or that were at least the best fit of the group in front of him at the time. Nevertheless, matters were left there, and he was shown no more photographs. The suggestion that he might be shown a more recent image of Megrahi, a recognisable likeness, was rejected, "for fear of tainting what he has already provided." (Richard Marquise, head of the FBI Lockerbie investigation.) However, the investigators never again used the black-and-white Czech image to identify their suspect. When the official indictment was issued a few months later the colour photo was used, despite the basis for the indictment being Gauci's identification of the black-and-white picture. Later, the colour photo was again chosen for the 'wanted' posters, and thereafter it became somewhat iconic.

★ ★ ★ ★ ★ ★ ★

Eight years passed. Years during which Tony's memory of the original purchaser inevitably faded even more. Years during which Megrahi's age inexorably approached the age of the purchaser in 1988. Years during which many newspaper and magazine articles appeared containing newer and better photographs of him, including the 1992 photograph above and others from the same series. There was even a feature documentary, in 1994, and two other televised interviews, in 1991 and 1998. This was all of course completely improper in relation to a case which was officially *sub judice* and in which identification evidence was crucial, but nothing was done to prevent it.

In April of 1999, Tony was taken to Camp Zeist to face Megrahi in person in an identity parade. Four days before doing that, a copy of a magazine article with a good photograph of Megrahi was taken from him, apparently the 1992 picture. Tony had had this for several months, and others – apparently his brother had been saving press articles identifying Megrahi as the Lockerbie accused! Tony pointed to the magazine photograph and declared, "That's him!" Nobody seems to have enquired whether he meant "that's the man I saw in the shop," (unlikely, given the spectacular lack of resemblance between the 1992 picture and the image in the photospread) or "I know that's the man who is accused, whom I'm being taken to identify." Indeed, by the time of the identity parade the publicity had been such that anyone who had followed the case would have been able to recognise Megrahi in person, even if they had never seen him before.

Once again the problem of age reared its head. According to Tony's consistent estimate of the customer's age, by 1999 they should have been looking for a man in his early sixties. However, Megrahi at forty-seven was one of the oldest men in the line-up, with only one man slightly older than him included (and that man was only 5 feet 3 inches tall). Four of the seven stand-ins would have been in their twenties in 1988, one only twenty-one (and one of the men excluded after an objection by the defence was only fifteen at the time of the clothes purchase). By this time, of course, Megrahi was now close to the age the customer was said to have been in 1988. It is also said that he stood out by being visibly nervous, and that he was forced to wear brown leather shoes when the others all wore trainers.

Between September 1989 and February 1991 Tony was all over the place as regards the facial appearance of his customer, as evidenced by the variety of images he was prepared to identify as resembling the man. The fuzzy image he picked out over two years after the original encounter was only one of several in that category. Nevertheless, the investigators seized on this as the basis for issuing an indictment against Megrahi in November 1991. Then, over ten years after the original encounter, Gauci picked out Megrahi in person from the lineup. Yet again he only testified to a resemblance ("Not the man I saw in the shop, but..."), not to recognition, but this was enough for the prosecutors – and the judges.

Why? The peculiar picture Gauci picked out in 1991, as resembling his memory of the purchaser, bore no resemblance at all to the man he picked out of the identity parade in April 1999, as resembling his memory of the purchaser. Megrahi (in 1988 or 1999) also bore no resemblance to Gauci's original 1989 description as regards height, build, age or skin colour. He did, however, bear a close resemblance to the press photos Gauci had been perusing in the interim, photos illustrating articles clearly identifying Megrahi as the Libyan accused of the Lockerbie bombing...

Tony Gauci saw the clothes purchaser once, for less than half an hour, one wet evening in 1988. At the time he had no reason to imagine he would ever have cause to remember the man again, and indeed he had no such cause until nine months (and many hundreds of other customers) later. It was well over two years after the encounter before he was shown a picture of Megrahi, and that picture was virtually unrecognisable as its alleged subject. By the time of the identity parade, getting on for eleven years had passed. What is the accuracy rate for the identification of a complete stranger, of a different race, seen once, after that sort of time? Nobody knows, of course. The best available data suggest however that after only eleven *months*, witnesses perform no better than chance. Three separate expert witness reports prepared for the defence in 2008–09 examine this question in great detail and with copious references, and come to the same conclusion. The chances of Tony being able to make a reliable identification of his customer in either 1991 or 1999 are essentially negligible.

Eyewitness identifications have been shown to be false, conclusively, time and time again, under far more favourable circumstances than this exercise. In this case, the time elapsed was extraordinary. The witness never indicated a confident identification, and the accused's actual appearance was substantially different from his original description of the suspect. How did the judges manage to elevate that to support a conviction 'beyond reasonable doubt'?

What did appear to us to be clear was that Mr Gauci applied his mind carefully to the problem of identification whenever he was shown photographs, and did not just pick someone out at random. Unlike many witnesses who express confidence in their identification when there is little justification for it, he was always careful to express any reservations he had and gave reasons why he thought that there was a resemblance. There are situations where a careful witness who will not commit himself beyond saying that there is a close resemblance can be regarded as more reliable and convincing in his identification than a witness who maintains that his identification is 100% certain. From his general demeanour and his approach to the difficult problem of identification, we formed the view that when he picked out the first accused at the identification parade and in Court, he was doing so not just because it was comparatively easy to do so but because he genuinely felt that he was correct in picking him out as having a close resemblance to the purchaser, and we did regard him as a careful witness who would not commit himself to an absolutely positive identification when a substantial period had elapsed. We accept of course that he never made what could be described as an absolutely positive identification, but having regard to the lapse of time it would have been surprising if he had been able to do so. We have also not overlooked the difficulties in relation to his description of height and age. We are nevertheless satisfied that his identification so far as it went of the first accused as the purchaser was reliable and should be treated as a highly important element in this case. We should add that we have not made any attempt to compare for ourselves any resemblance between the first accused's passport photograph and the identikit or artist's impression, nor with the first accused's appearance in the video recordings of his interview with Pierre Salinger in November 1991.

The judges explicitly acknowledged that Megrahi was "comparatively easy" to pick out of the identity parade (and of course at the dock identification, where Tony said he was "not the dark one" compared to Fhimah's swarthy complexion). This sounds remarkably like an admission that the identity parade was fatally flawed. Nevertheless they decided that Tony was high-minded enough not to have identified Megrahi simply because he was the obvious pick, and only did so because he genuinely believed he resembled the clothes purchaser.

Their lordships didn't know about Tony's interest in the advertised $4 million reward, of course. Or that he seems to have believed that the police knew Megrahi was guilty and were relying on him to ensure that the "bad man" wasn't acquitted. Or about the article from the Maltese magazine It-Torca, which displayed not only a good photograph of Megrahi but a handy bulleted list detailing where his own statements conflicted with the Crown case, and which had been in his possession until only four days before the identity parade.

So they decided that he was an honest witness who appeared uncertain merely because of the length of time that had elapsed. Even though he had remembered a much older and taller and darker-skinned man, it had actually been Megrahi he had seen. And to prevent themselves from becoming confused, they didn't actually look at the pictures.

9

PT/35(b)

Why did *Maid of the Seas* crash over Lockerbie at 19.03? That's not quite as meaningless a question as it may seem.

Pan Am 103 was scheduled to be in the air for about seven hours *en route* to New York, arriving at 01.40 GMT on 22nd December (20.40 21st December, EST). The crash happened only thirty-eight minutes into the flight.

There are two reasons why that might be considered a little odd. First, the crash happened over land, and well-populated land at that, which allowed literally tons of evidence to be picked up by the police and search teams. Including, of course, the remains of the blast-damaged container and suitcases discussed in chapter 6. The entire broad expanse of the Atlantic was ahead, an ocean where most if not all of that debris could have been lost forever.

Second, thirty-eight minutes isn't a long time in the context of Heathrow airport, a stormy winter evening, and flight delays. Transatlantic flights miss their takeoff slots all the time, for all sorts of reasons. If the feeder flight had been just a bit later, or the wind a bit stronger, or if a no-show passenger had been taken as seriously as he ought to have been taken, exactly that would have happened to PA103 that evening. And if it had, a bomb set to explode at 19.03 would have gone off almost harmlessly on the tarmac. The 747 disintegrated due to overpressure and explosive decompression at 31,000 feet, not from the force of the initial blast. All that would have resulted from a tarmac detonation would have been a fairly small hole in the plane, a few passenger suitcases and a holdall shredded, and a bunch of people getting the fright of their lives. And if *that* had happened, the police wouldn't even have needed to organise a fingertip search of the countryside; all the evidence would have been right there.

Why would terrorists risk all that evidence being preserved? Why would they risk the entire plot going off at ground level like a damp squib?

Ah, but wasn't the plane late? Isn't that the answer to that objection? If only it hadn't been late, it would have disappeared over the Atlantic, but as it was, it only got as far as Lockerbie.

That's one of the enduring myths of Lockerbie, but it's wrong. The plane wasn't late.

The myth seems to have started on BBC breakfast time news on 22nd December, when John Stapleton reported that the flight had taken off twenty-five minutes late. That very early report was confused about several things, though. PA103 was certainly timetabled to depart at 18.00, however no aircraft magically levitates from the apron the minute the doors are closed.

At Heathrow, twenty-five minutes is simply par for the course for taxiing to the runway, getting in line, and getting airborne. The wheels left the runway at 18.25, which is absolutely on time for a flight with a nominal 18.00 departure time. In fact the flight pushed off from the gate at 18.04, delayed for just a couple of minutes because a passenger who had checked in, and who had two suitcases in the hold, failed to show up at the departure gate.

Jaswant Basuta, the luckiest man in known space, missed the plane. He was being seen off by a group of friends who took him to the bar in the departure lounge, where he became rather too well-lubricated and missed the last call. The Pan Am duty manager checked his background and found that he was a US citizen on his way home. At this point it was discovered that he was actually running for the gate, however the aircraft was already closed and about to push away. It was decided that as Mr. Basuta was officially low-risk the flight should simply leave rather than lose its departure slot and be delayed, possibly for an hour or more. When the police arrived a couple of hours later in response to the news of the disaster they found him still in the airport trying to book another flight to the USA.

This flight was so on time that it stranded a checked-in passenger who was minutes from the gate. Pan Am confirmed to journalists that it was on time, no official report has ever noted it as being delayed, and the Heathrow air traffic controller testified at Camp Zeist that it was not late. Nevertheless the myth persists.

So, did somebody set a timer to detonate that bomb at about seven o'clock, despite the virtual certainty the plane would still be over land when it was destroyed, and might well still be *on* land? The myth has an answer for that, too.

That wasn't the usual flight path. The plane took the northerly route that evening, unusually, because of the strong westerly gale and bad weather over Ireland. If it had taken the normal route, it *would* have been over the ocean!

Again, the myth is mistaken.

The left-hand image of figure 33 shows the actual flight path. Even if the plane had managed to take off ten or fifteen minutes earlier, it couldn't have got further than Glasgow. The right-hand image shows the usual route, close to the 'great circle' path. On that route there was a chance it might have gone into the Irish Sea, but it could just have easily have come down on Dublin. It also shows the wide expanse of Atlantic ahead, ready to swallow baggage container, suitcases, Yorkie trousers and radio-cassette player, forever.

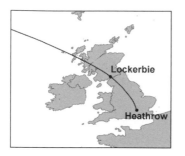 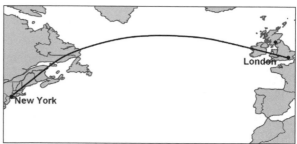

Figure 33

Transatlantic flight routes out of Heathrow. Left is the actual route of PA103 on 21st December 1988 and right is the more usual route over Ireland.

The original answer to all that, of course, was the Khreesat-type barometric timer device described in chapter 7. That type of trigger mechanism would wait patiently at ground level no matter how long the flight was delayed, and start its lethal countdown only when the altimeter sensed the pressure drop to the in-flight level.

Marwan Khreesat didn't seem to care if his devices exploded over land, or if he did, he didn't do anything about it. He didn't have any capacitors that ran for more than forty-five minutes, and most of them ran for a shorter time than that. The plane would be in the air, and have reached cruising altitude, and that appeared to be the objective. No Khreesat device was ever recovered with a longer delay time. The thirty-eight-minute explosion which destroyed Sherwood Crescent and so many lives on the ground makes complete sense in the context of a Khreesat IED with a thirty-minute capacitor.

During the first half of 1989 the Lockerbie investigators stuck firmly to the belief that the disaster had been caused by a Khreesat device loaded at Frankfurt, near where Khreesat had been manufacturing the things. Allen Feraday had his list of possible ways the device might have managed to travel on the feeder flight without blowing up, so that was all right then.

Exactly how they rationalised the concept of a Khreesat device making *two* preliminary hops before being loaded on to the target flight is not recorded, but throughout the first phase of the Malta inquiry, running into early 1990, that was still the assumed *modus operandi*. The PFLP-GC were still the prime suspects, a Maltese cell of the gang was being investigated, and Khreesat was still believed to be the bomb-maker.

Everything changed in the summer of 1990.

A US forensic investigator, Tom Thurman, with the help of an unnamed colleague from the CIA, succeeded in identifying a centimetre-square fragment of printed circuit board which had defied the detection skills of the Scottish police. It was part of a digital countdown timer. Specifically, it was part of a device known as an MST-13, which had been made for military use. Specifically, the MST-13 timer was a bespoke item made for the Libyan armed forces, and only twenty of them had been delivered to that country, in 1985 and 1986.

This put an entirely new complexion on the case, in more ways than one. First, it explained how the bomb suitcase had got from Malta to Frankfurt, then from Frankfurt to London, without blowing up. The MST-13 is a simple long-running timer, with no altimeter component. These things would run for however long they were set to run and detonate the device after the pre-determined delay, irrespective of whether the suitcase was in the air or on the ground.

Second, it perhaps explained why the investigation was getting nowhere in its pursuit of assorted Palestinians, Syrians and Jordanians. Libya was a terrorist state, definitely arming the IRA at the time, and quite capable of any atrocity in the eyes of the CIA. Time to turn the attention of the investigation towards Libya.

What it didn't explain, of course, was the thirty-eight-minute explosion. If the IED was detonated by a countdown timer, then all the objections detailed at the beginning of the chapter are back on the table, just as puzzling as before.

★ ★ ★ ★ ★ ★ ★

The late identification of the PCB fragment gave rise to another Lockerbie myth. During the 1990s, when much that was later revealed in court was still little more than rumour, it was said to have been found in the Kielder Forest in Northumberland a full eighteen months after the disaster, having lain out in the open through two winters. The finder was said to have been a CIA officer. If true, that would have been quite extraordinary.

The actual story is much more mundane, but in spite of that it still provides exceptional scope for speculation, suspicion and sundry allegations of fabrication and fraud.

The first recorded provenance relating to the fragment is Friday 13th January 1989, when a four-inch long scrap of shirt collar showing signs of blast damage was picked up from an open field beside Blinkbonny Farm, near the village of Newcastleton, about twenty miles east of Lockerbie. This was in 'I' sector, where most of the debris relating to AVE4041 was recovered. The rag of burned cotton was allocated the production number PI/995.

The second notable date is Friday 12th May 1989, when Thomas Hayes's hand-written notes detail his examination of the collar. It was an interesting item, in fact quite the treasure trove. The collar itself was later identified as part of a man's shirt which might or might not have been sold by Tony Gauci to his mysterious Libyan customer. That was one of the areas where Tony's conveniently malleable recollections tended to converge with the specifics the police seemed to want him to remember. Its contents were even more singular. Blasted into this little scrap of fabric were several fragments of the casing of the Toshiba radio-cassette player, a bit of the speaker mesh, a small wad of compacted paper that turned out to be from the radio's manual, and the infamous fragment of green printed circuit board. The wad of paper was dubbed PT/2, while the black plastic Toshiba fragments, the PCB chip and the piece of speaker mesh were lumped together as PT/35, (a) (b) and (c) respectively.

PT/35b then disappeared for a second four-month stretch. It reappeared on a memo dated Friday 15th September, sent by Allen Feraday to DI William Williamson at Lockerbie, enclosing some polaroid photographs of it and asking for the assistance of the Scottish "lads and lassies" in identifying its provenance.

Despite this appeal it nevertheless sank into obscurity for yet another four-month stretch. The real examination of the fragment didn't began until January 1990, when the physical object was finally passed back into the custody of the Scottish police. It would be extraordinarily neat if the date of this transfer was Friday 12th January, but it probably wasn't.

The circumstance that has fuelled the rumour mill since 2000 is that the paperwork attesting to each of these episodes is disturbingly flawed, as discussed in more detail in Appendix B. The original production label for PI/995 from January 1989 appears to have been altered, and the evidence of the police officer who signed it as having found the collar was described by the Zeist judges as "at best confusing, at worst evasive". The page on which Hayes recorded his examination of the item is at the centre of a confused muddle of inconsistent dates and over-written page numbers, which make it appear as if that page was a later interpolation into the notes. Feraday's need to rely on (undateable) polaroid pictures of an item that had been at RARDE for four months, coupled with the Scottish police apparently looking at a completely different PCB fragment at that time and making no mention of PT/35b, is also seen as suspicious. It has been suggested that a memo which was originally about the other fragment, PT/30, was re-written to refer to PT/35b in order to bolster a retrospective provenance for an item that had in fact only been introduced into the chain of evidence in early 1990. Finally, certain items of correspondence relating to the January 1990 upsurge of interest in the green fragment are capable of being interpreted as reporting an item which had only just been discovered.

All these allegations were submitted to the SCCRC by Megrahi's defence team and were investigated in some detail. While the Commission appears to have satisfied itself that the allegations were unfounded, it has to be said that some of the evidence presented to support that conclusion falls far short of compelling. Ultimately, endemic muddle and poor archiving practices at RARDE prevent provenance of the paperwork and photographs from being established beyond doubt, but at the same time prevent malpractice from being proven. It all depends on who you believe.

By early 1990 the potential importance of this tiny chip of fibreglass was beginning to be recognised. Richard Marquise, head of the FBI task force assigned to the Lockerbie inquiry, describes being told about the exciting new clue by DCS Stuart Henderson, then senior investigating officer, during a break in a case conference on 10th January. Despite the informality of the approach Marquise tried to muscle into the investigation on behalf of the FBI, only to be rebuffed by Henderson. The Scottish police were going to find out what it was.

A memo from DI Williamson to DCS Henderson dated 3rd September 1990 records the details of this impressively thorough investigation. Finally there is evidence of a real effort to identify the fragment, evidence which is strikingly absent throughout 1989. Inquiries in Germany and elsewhere failed to discover any circuit boards with a similar tracking pattern, and attention turned to the physical and chemical makeup of the chip. In the course of this examination the fragment was cut into three pieces, with the removal of a slice from the top and a larger square segment from the bottom right, as the item is usually photographed. Nevertheless comparison of various photographs demonstrates beyond doubt that it is the same item throughout the process, both before and after the sectioning.

The basic structure was nine-ply fibreglass, a common product in the electronics industry. Eight-ply is the more usual structure, but nine-ply is not particularly unusual and was "popular in Italy". The epoxy resin binding the fibreglass was unremarkable. The copper of the circuitry was traced to a manufacturer in Southampton, but the size of their world-wide market was such that "this fact can be only one of interest". The green two-pack epoxy solder mask applied to the reverse of the fragment was the most commonly-used type in the industry. A blob of tin-lead solder which still remained on the 'relay pad' element was also unremarkable.

By far the most interesting finding was discovered during testing carried out on 2nd March 1990 by Dr. Rosemary Wilkinson of Strathclyde University. This related to the thin coating overlying the copper circuitry, applied to facilitate the application of solder to the tracks, a coating usually referred to as 'tinning'.

> Without exception it is the view of all experts involved in the PCB Industry who have assisted with this enquiry that the tin application on the tracks of the circuit was by far the most interesting feature. The fact that pure tin rather than a tin/lead mixture has been used is very unusual. [...] Enquiry has been made with numerous companies throughout the United Kingdom involved in the printed circuit board manufacture, in an effort to learn more on the use of tin and the reason for its application to the tracks but these enquiries have so far proved negative, there being no companies known in the United Kingdom involved in the manufacture of printed circuit boards who continue to use pure tin in the manner that tin has been applied to Production PT 35.

Another expert report quoted in the Williamson memo describes this feature as "pure tin, probably from an electroless tin solution, presumably to aid solderability." This aspect is not explored further in the memo, however electroless plating (where the item to be plated is simply immersed in a chelated solution of the plating metal) is not popular with manufacturers primarily because PCBs produced in this manner must be populated within a few weeks of plating, otherwise the tin becomes very difficult to solder. The usual 'tinning' material employed in commercially-produced electronic components is an alloy of 70% tin 30% lead. Pure tin is however commonly used by amateur hobbyists making only a few items on a non-commercial basis, because the 'liquid tin' product used in the electroless process is very easy to apply.

It is clear nevertheless that at this stage in the inquiry the composition of the 'tinning' layer was recognised both as a very unusual feature which could be of value in identifying the fragment, and as something which was an inherent property of the PCB itself. Investigation seems to have continued throughout the spring of 1990, with the latest date mentioned in the Williamson memo being 23rd May. The Scottish police team were however unsuccessful in tracing the manufacturer or identifying the device the PCB had originally been a part of.

The big breakthrough came in June 1990, in the USA. Another international case conference had been called for 11th June in Virginia, and this time Stuart Henderson decided to share the still-mysterious clue with the Americans. FBI agent Tom Thurman, who had been at Lockerbie in the early weeks of the investigation and had been part of the team which had interviewed the PFLP-GC bomb-maker Marwan Khreesat in Jordan the previous November, requested photographs of the fragment so that he could attempt to identify it. Thurman took the photographs to a CIA agent usually referred to by the name 'Orkin', and between them they very quickly matched the pattern of the circuitry to a circuit board in a timer in the CIA's archive which had been seized several years previously in Togo, West Africa.

A strange anomaly surrounds this event. Thurman himself has confirmed several times that he made the identification on 15th June. He trots out the date at every available opportunity, as if it was his birthday or something. That is only four days after the Virginia conference. Richard Marquise, in his *Scotbom* memoirs, notes that "what Thurman did would yield fruit within two days", and that the Scottish and RARDE delegates pretty much had to turn round at Heathrow and get themselves back to the USA as a result. Clearly, Thurman went straight to the timer in question, and indeed Marquise confirms "he knew where to look". Nevertheless Thurman's own well-rehearsed story is different, describing "literally months" of searching through FBI files in his tireless attempt to solve the mystery. Very peculiar.

The identification was made purely on a visual comparison, with no reference to the analytical results detailed above. The pattern of the circuitry, even on the tiny surviving fragment, was distinctive (figure 34).

In fact, the comparison was closer than Thurman and 'Orkin' may have realised at the time. Not only is the major element of circuitry visible, the relay pad, a perfect match, the match is confirmed by the pattern of the copper tracking at the point where the narrow lines turn down at an oblique angle, at the bottom right of the fragment. (This corner of the tracking was lost when the fragment was sectioned.) The SCCRC report refers to the 'blob' of copper, which is most obvious on the upper track, as a "tracking inaccuracy", and notes that it is perfectly replicated on both the PT/35b fragment and the undamaged control PCB. In the witness box at Camp Zeist Feraday referred to the same feature as an "overrun of the line". These items are not merely similar, they almost certainly originate from the same template (figure 35).

Having identified the PCB fragment as a part of one of the circuit boards of the electronic timing device in the CIA archive, the next task was to find out

| Blinkbonny fragment | After sectioning | Comparison PCB |

Figure 34
Comparison of PT/35b with a corner of an MST-13 circuit board made by Swiss firm MEBO AG.

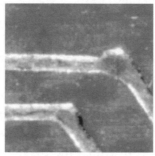
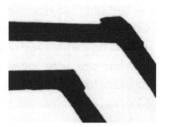

| Blinkbonny fragment | Comparison PCB | MST-13 template |

Figure 35
Area of the lower right-hand corner of the fragment, compared to the same area of the MST-13 timer board, and the original MST-13 template.

more about that item. The device was a fairly small, cuboidal instrument in a light grey plastic case with a digital readout on the front. Countdown time was variable depending on the setting, but it was capable of running for up to ninety hours. Inside were two green-lacquered circuit boards, the one which matched the PT/35b fragment and another, which had a maker's identification mark on it.

The mark had been partially obliterated at some time, but it was still possible to make a stab at reading the letters. ME8Q? Again, Thurman's account of the process is peculiar. He admits that "we knew what it was, really, but we didn't want to go there directly, we wanted to make sure we'd ruled out other possibilities." Apparently they knew immediately that the printed name was really that of the Swiss electronics firm MEBO, but spent some time looking at other possibilities before they followed up the right one.

The timescale of what happened next is quite confusing. The Williamson memo was written at the beginning of September 1990, well over two months after the Thurman/'Orkin' visual identification, but the identification isn't mentioned in the memo. It appears that the US authorities didn't put their Scottish counterparts in touch with MEBO until later that month. Nevertheless there are records of the FBI visiting MEBO's offices in Zurich in August. Indeed, there is a record of a Swiss police officer visiting the company in connection with the Lockerbie investigation in June *1989*. Make of that what you will.

That, however, still wasn't the earliest connection between MEBO and the Lockerbie case. One of the two founders and directors of MEBO AG, the colourful Edwin Bollier, surfaces as early as 20th January 1989. On that date Bollier hand-delivered a letter to the US embassy in Vienna, in which he stated that he had evidence linking Libya to the atrocity. Bollier is currently a highly vocal, though utterly bonkers, advocate of Libya's innocence. His January 1989 'catch-letter' has never been satisfactorily explained, other than Bollier's own assertion that a mysterious stranger asked him to write such a letter using a Spanish typewriter and deliver it to the embassy. He was to cast blame on Libya in whatever way occurred to him, simply by making up something incriminating. This one is right up there with the Interfor report in the annals of Lockerbie weirdness, and indeed probably surpasses it.

Nevertheless the PCB from which the mysterious PT/35b fragment had originated really did appear to have been part of a MEBO-manufactured MST-13 timer unit. The original template even showed the "over-run of the line" (figure 35). It got even better. The MST-13 timers were a bespoke order from the Libyan armed forces, and the PCBs in them had been designed and acquired to order for these units by MEBO. Even better, only twenty items had ever been supplied to Libya, some in 1985 and some in 1986, and apart from a couple of prototype models which had been handed over to the East German STASI, they had been supplied to nobody else.

There was only one little problem. While the Khreesat barometric devices were small and improvised, consisting of only an aneroid barometer, a capacitor and a few wires which could be quite easily squirrelled inside the Toshiba between its own components, the MST-13 timers were boxed and relatively bulky. There was no way one of these could be hidden inside a radio. The conundrum was solved by assuming that the innards of the timer had been removed from the case and tucked piecemeal into the radio beside the Semtex, in much the same way Khreesat had secreted his own trigger mechanisms.

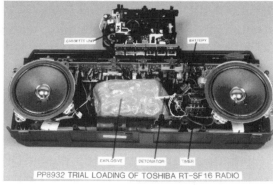

PP8932 TRIAL LOADING OF TOSHIBA RT-SF16 RADIO

Complete MST-13 timer   Trial loading of Toshiba radio-cassette player

Figure 36
Boxed timer (left), and Feraday's suggested method of fitting its components inside the Toshiba radio.

This new discovery galvanised the inquiry in much the same way as the discovery of the KM180 connection had done a year previously. No wonder the police were getting nowhere with their investigation of various dodgy Palestinians on Malta. They were looking for the wrong suspects. They should be looking for Libyans!

The cutting edge of the investigation changed direction and advanced towards Libya. In January 1991 the name Abdelbaset al-Megrahi was suggested to the Scottish police as a possible suspect, in February Tony Gauci picked out Megrahi's fuzzy black-and-white image from the photospread, and from then on things were looking up for the inquiry. Eventually the backroom boffins at RARDE did what they should have done in 1989 and analysed the composition of the PT/35b fragment.

MEBO itself was not in fact the manufacturer of the printed circuit boards incorporated in the timers. The PCBs were designed by MEBO's technician Ulrich Lumpert, who also made a few prototype boards for testing purposes, but manufacture of the finished boards was outsourced to another Swiss firm, Thüring AG. Thüring made the boards to Lumpert's design then delivered them to MEBO, where they were populated by soldering on the necessary electronic components and then fitted into their boxes.

MEBO supplied the Lockerbie investigation with a number of control samples of circuit board, all of which were left over from the original batch supplied by Thüring. This included one which was made up into a complete boxed timer instrument, designated DP/111. These items were examined in detail at RARDE during July and August of 1991, where Allen Feraday oversaw a range of comparative metallurgical tests with a Thüring-produced PCB designated DP/347a serving as the control. In December 1991 he produced a written report based on the findings of these tests, which he read into the court transcript at Camp Zeist.

> The particular tracking pattern of the fragment has been extensively compared with the control samples of the 'MST-13' timers and circuit boards (items DP/111, DP/84, DP/100 and DP/347 (a)), and it has been conclusively established that the fragment materials and tracking pattern are similar in all respects to the area around the connection pad for the output relay of the 'MST-13' timer.
> [...]
> A direct comparison between the fragment PT/35 (b) and the control sample circuit board (DP/347 (a)) is shown in photograph 336, wherein the section DP/31, which was removed from the fragment for investigational purposes, is included. The conducting pad and tracks present on the fragment PT/35 (b) are of copper covered by a layer of pure tin.

So that's fine then. It was all a complete match. Feraday's analyses had confirmed what Wilkinson had reported the previous year, that the Blinkbonny fragment's copper circuitry was coated in pure tin. And *mirabile dictu*, despite the Scottish investigators having comprehensively failed to find any commercial manufacturer of PCBs who used a pure tin tinning process, it seems the Thüring-produced boards had turned out to be exactly that! Not only the tracking pattern but the materials were "similar in all respects" to the control samples of genuine MST-13 components. The production manager of Thüring AG, Urs Bonfadelli, seemed to confirm this when he gave evidence at Camp Zeist, and also said "the trackings were in tin".

Not so fast.

The 1991 tests at RARDE weren't the only ones carried out on the investigation's new PCB collection. In the spring of 1992 a battery of further comparative tests was commissioned from academic and industry experts. These tests included further investigation of the 'tinning' component by Dr. Wilkinson, who had examined the fragment in 1990, and Dr. David Johnson of the University of Manchester Institute of Science and Technology. Once again the control PCB used was the one designated DP/347a. Independent analyses conducted by the two scientists demonstrated that the coating on

DP/347a had a fairly high lead content consistent with the usual 70% tin 30% lead alloy, while that of PT/35b was, as had been noted in 1990, more or less pure tin. This was the only discrepancy between the fragment and the genuine Thüring-produced boards.

How do we explain this? Feraday clearly reported that the tests in 1991 had shown the Thüring boards to be the same as the mystery fragment, in all respects – didn't he? Well, that's what he said in his December report, but that's not what he recorded in the notes he took at the time the tests were actually done. One note dated 1st August 1991 reported that the coating of PT/35b's tracks "is of pure tin" and another that the equivalent coating of DP/347a "is of [approximately] 70/30 Sn/Pb". That is exactly the same result as Wilkinson and Johnson reported.

Indeed, not only did Feraday appreciate that there was a difference between the two items, he recognised this was significant enough to require an explanation. In his August notes he speculated that the alloy coating of DP/347a may have been applied over a layer of pure tin, by a process of dipping or rolling, with the surface layer subsequently being stripped off by the explosion. This was simply surmise however, with no factual basis, and the hypothesised process is not something actually employed within the PCB industry. The train of thought appears to have stopped there and none of this made its way into his December fair-copy report, although otherwise that was to a large extent a verbatim transcription of his August notes.

Dr. Wilkinson also recognised the significance of the discrepancy, and also speculated about a possible explanation. Her idea was similar to Feraday's hypothesis, but more realistic. She suggested that the heat of the explosion had simply vaporised the lead component of the alloy, leaving only the tin behind on the recovered fragment. However, aware that this was really just a guess and this wasn't her area of expertise, she recommended that the suggestion should be tested by experiment. That was not done.

So, how did the Zeist court rationalise the discrepancy between Feraday's formal report stating (or at least implying) that the tinning on the Thüring boards was pure tin, like the fragment, while the Wilkinson/Johnson report stated that it was alloy?

It didn't. It didn't arise.

Despite Drs Wilkinson and Johnson having been commissioned by the police to provide expert reports, and indeed Dr. Wilkinson having been involved twice in that capacity, neither expert was called to give evidence. Just as the court was never told how many interline suitcases had arrived at Heathrow that afternoon, or that Sidhu had consistently denied moving these cases when he added the luggage from the feeder flight, it was not made aware that repeated analysis had shown the Thüring boards to have an alloy coating, or indeed that alloy 'tinning' was standard in the PCB industry. Although the Crown must have known there was a material difference between the fragment recovered at Newcastleton and the Thüring-manufactured MST-13 boards, thanks to Feraday having omitted this information from his report on the 1991 RARDE tests, it was able to keep this crucial information from the bench. The court accepted that the fragment had been part of one of the MST-13 units supplied to Libya by MEBO.

At this point we have to ask, what on earth were the defence doing? Mainly, they were hampered by non-disclosure of significant pieces of evidence. Although they had sight of the Wilkinson/Johnson findings, these scientists were metallurgists, not electronics experts, and their reports did not explain the significance of their results in relation to the manufacturing process. The experts consulted by the defence in their turn also failed to appreciate the point. As a result the defence failed to ask the electronics experts the right questions, and indeed failed even to ask Mr. Bonfadelli what he meant when he said "the trackings were in tin". The 1990 Williamson memo, which made the issue abundantly clear, was not disclosed. Neither were the results of the 1991 tests at RARDE or Feraday's contemporaneous notes, meaning that the defence were unaware that what Feraday had said in the witness box did not correspond with his experimental findings.

No additional material had been disclosed by the time of the SCCRC investigation, with the result that the issue remained unclear. The Commission appear to have misunderstood the evidence, concluding that the Thüring-produced boards were coated in pure tin, as Mr Bonfadelli's evidence seemed to indicate, and accepting that there was nothing in the results to suggest that PT/35b and DP/347a were not the same.

The issue was revisited by the defence team during their preparations for the second appeal. Two independent experts were instructed: Dr. Chris McArdle, a former UK government advisor on microelectronics and nanotechnology, and Dr. Jess Cawley, a metallurgist formerly of Sheffield Hallam University. These scientists immediately noticed the blob of solder on the relay pad, which still bore the imprint of a wire that had been soldered on to the pad. They realised that the solder could never have been hot enough to melt. Plastic explosives such as Semtex cause a momentary flash of intense heat, but the flash doesn't last long enough to melt lead. If the explosion hadn't even softened a blob of lead solder sufficiently to obliterate the imprint of a wire, it couldn't possibly have caused the lead component of an alloy to evaporate.

The defence experts decided to do what Rosemary Wilkinson had recommended more than ten years earlier. They designed a series of experiments with boards which were close replicas of Thüring's original specifications, however while some had the standard alloy coating, some had a pure tin coating. The results were clear. Heat exposure sufficient to melt solder blobs, which must have been greater heat than the Blinkbonny fragment had been exposed to, didn't change a tin/lead alloy coating to pure tin. Both scientists concurred. The PT/35b fragment had originally been manufactured with a tin coating, exactly as had been assumed by the investigation DI Williamson conducted in 1990.

In October 2008 the defence legal team asked the question which apparently nobody had thought of asking since 1991. Was the circuitry of the MST-13 PCB components coated with pure tin or with a tin/lead alloy at manufacturing? Mr. Bonfadelli was contacted and gave a clear and conclusive answer. All the MST-13 boards were coated with an alloy of 70% tin and 30% lead. There could be no mistaking this, he said, because this was the only production process employed by his company. The use of pure tin required a completely different process which had never been used by Thüring, and which they were not equipped to perform. His original statement had been misunderstood – in electronics shorthand, the tin/lead alloy used for tinning is commonly referred to as 'tin'.

The conclusion is inescapable. The PCB from which PT/35b originated was manufactured with a pure tin coating. Thüring AG only manufactured PCBs with alloy coating, and lacked the capability to produce boards with a pure tin coating. All the MST-13 boards supplied by MEBO to the Libyan armed forces contained Thüring-manufactured PCBs. Therefore, whatever PT/35b was, it was not a part of one of the MST-13 timers supplied by MEBO to Libya.

Sadly, by the time all this evidence had been uncovered and assembled, Megrahi had come to the conclusion that abandoning his ongoing appeal was necessary to improve his chances of being granted compassionate release. Desperate to return to his wife and family before he died, on 11th August 2009 he instructed his solicitors to withdraw the appeal.

★ ★ ★ ★ ★ ★ ★

So, if that fragment wasn't what the prosecution said it was, what was it?

It's rather a strange item. The irregularity in the tracking pattern shows that the visual resemblance to the MST-13 boards isn't just a coincidence. The Blinkbonny fragment almost certainly originates from the same template as the Thüring boards. That doesn't, however, mean that it must have been made directly from that template. Printed circuit boards are easy to copy by photo-graphing them, and any such second-generation copy would reproduce the tracking irregularities from the original. Anyone who had an original timer or even just a circuit board could make such a copy.

The mystery fragment is unusual in another way. It seems to be an odd mixture of professional and amateur construction. The curved edge, which has been trimmed away to allow the board to be mounted inside the plastic timer box, is smoothly cut as if by a machine rather than being hand-sawn. The green solder resist coating on the reverse is not something usually applied to amateur boards. The pure tin coating on the circuitry, however, is very suggestive of an amateur using an electroless plating technique, all the more so because the thickness of the coating is uneven and in places quite thin.

It's not just a bit of somebody's pocket calculator, obviously. It's an actual timer board, or a facsimile of one, and there seem to be only two possible reasons for making it. One is to use it as a timer, and the other is to pretend it's a timer.

Libya was running out of timers in late 1988, and inquired with MEBO about purchasing more. MEBO couldn't supply the quantity being talked about in the time available, and Bollier tried to fob them off with an alternative. The deal fell through when the Libyans informed MEBO that they now had what they required. Had they made a few cheap knock-offs using one of the original timers as a template? Alternatively, had some other group who had got hold of one of the original models decided to copy this nifty little number for themselves?

The incongruity in that respect is the green solder resist, which is an odd feature of the original MST-13 boards in any case. Solder resist is usually applied to the business side of a PCB, on the parts of the board not covered by the circuitry, to make it easier to solder on the various components. This requires another photographic template and is a relatively complicated procedure, which is why it's not usually seen on amateur-produced boards. However, the Blinkbonny fragment has the solder resist on the plain reverse side, not the side with the circuitry. Thüring's records showed that half the MST-13 boards supplied to the Libyan military had been made like that, while the other half had the green coating on both sides. Applying solder resist to the back only is unusual, and really just cosmetic. It would be less difficult to apply it to the reverse side, indeed it could simply be brushed on. However, it's unlikely someone copying one of the boards to make a few more timer units would bother, whether they were the Libyan military or another group who just wanted the instruments for use.

The same feature rules out the prototype boards made in-house by Lumpert for testing during the design process. These didn't have the green coating at all, on either side, and despite some of Edwin Bollier's more colourful interventions in the debate, the Blinkbonny fragment is most definitely green on the reverse, and always has been.

The possibility that someone made that fragment specifically to be planted in the Lockerbie chain of evidence is one that has been talked about since its existence first became public in 1991. The fact that the pointless green coating has been carefully applied to the reverse side certainly makes it far more likely to have been made for that purpose than merely to construct another timer unit. Indeed, apart from the tinning, the copy is perfect, nine-ply fibreglass and all.

But who would have done such a thing? The usual suspect in all the conspiracy theories is the CIA, generally supposed to be harbouring a desire to implicate Libya rather than the Syrian-based PFLP-GC in the atrocity, and/or to bolster the theory that the bomb made a triple-hop flight from Malta which the PFLP-GC's devices were not designed to do. Thurman's startlingly rapid identification of the fragment (with CIA assistance) and the anomalies in his later accounts of the exercise are often cited in support, as is his presence at Lockerbie during January 1989 and occasionally later. It's also pointed out that of all the centimetre-square segments of the PCBs in these timers, the fragment found at Newcastleton is probably the only one that's distinctive enough to be matched on a visual identification. Very convenient.

However, why would the CIA need a 'fake' board for that purpose? There were several timers in captivity, and if they were in touch with Bollier then he still had the leftover ones from the original order. If they didn't dare take a real one out of circulation and so decided to create a copy, that still leaves the problem of the tinning. Apart from the tinning it seems to be a perfect job, right down to the ply of the fibreglass. Get all that right, then just dip the thing in liquid tin? When it's likely, indeed intended, that it's going to be taken apart by a bunch of forensic scientists?

There's an answer somewhere. That fragment either fell from the sky, or it didn't. As things stand, though, it's not at all obvious what it is.

★ ★ ★ ★ ★ ★ ★

In the end the argument comes full circle. *Maid of the Seas* blew apart after having been flying for only thirty-eight minutes. That fact makes complete and perfect sense in the context of a barometric timer of the Khreesat type, loaded at London. The evidence of the suitcase positioning shows without question that the bomb was indeed loaded at London. And yet what was found in the debris was a part of a countdown timer, which doesn't make any sense at all.

No matter who planted that bomb, if he had an MST-13 timer unit, the time to set it for was eleven o'clock or midnight, not seven o'clock. Even if it was used in conjunction with an altimeter, what would be the point of switching the thirty-minute capacitor for a long-running timer, if not to ensure that the plane got as far as the deep ocean before coming down?

There isn't a perfect explanation that covers all the known facts in this puzzle. Perhaps more facts will emerge. But until they do, mysterious PT/35b remains mysterious.

10

ADEQUATELY EXPLAINED
BY STUPIDITY?

Lockerbie has attracted its fair share of conspiracy theories, perhaps more than its fair share. Some of them are simply tinfoil hat territory, and most of the others fall apart on closer examination of the evidence. A very persistent and plausible one however, is the tale of the investigation that was successfully building a case against the Syrian suspects, who were believed to be in the pay of the Ayatollah Khomeini of Iran, when the sleuths were suddenly called off and told to go chase Libyans instead. And the reason for this is said to be the involvement of the USA in the first Gulf War against Saddam Hussain, and the need to keep Iran onside as an ally. Gaddafi's Libya, of course, was in the outer darkness and always would be. Gaddafi was a handy scapegoat, and if Lockerbie could be used to bring him to heel and cut off the supply of Semtex and other munitions to the IRA, so much the better.

It's a nice idea, but the timing doesn't work. As noted in the previous chapter, the reason for the sudden change of tack in the autumn of 1990 was the identification of PT/35b as having originated from a countdown timer that was part of a bespoke batch of items ordered by and supplied to Libya. However, PT/35b was actually identified in June 1990. Not only that, the fragment was definitely present in the chain of evidence, in the hands of the Scottish police, by January 1990 at the very latest. It's far from impossible that the provenance does in fact go right back at least to May 1989.

Saddam Hussain invaded Kuwait, rather unexpectedly, on 2nd August 1990. Operation Desert Storm didn't begin until 17th January 1991. To have prepared and planted a crucial piece of evidence in the Lockerbie forensic investigation many months, even a year earlier, in anticipation of this development, implies a positively supernatural prescience. While it's perfectly likely that the change in focus suited the politicians very well indeed, it seems to be down to serendipity, not skullduggery.

However, all this is to a large extent missing the point. George Bush Snr. and Margaret Thatcher weren't investigating Lockerbie. Even the FBI weren't really investigating Lockerbie. The Dumfries and Galloway Constabulary were investigating Lockerbie, with assistance from other police forces in Scotland and (to some extent) in England, the investigators of the AAIB and the forensic scientists in the explosives laboratory at RARDE, and with the co-operation of the authorities in Germany and the USA.

It's not the politicians who need to be scrutinised, it's the investigators. And the period of the inquiry that needs to be looked at isn't 1990–91, it's the first half of 1989. This inquiry went catastrophically off the rails in January/February 1989, long before the events in the Middle East commonly held to have influenced its course, and indeed even before the March 1989 date given by the late Paul Foot (*Lockerbie: the Flight from Justice*) for his postulated agreement between Bush and Thatcher to "play down the truth" for political reasons. And it seems to have been derailed by the investigators themselves, rather than by outside influences.

A disturbing feature of the investigation is the sheer number of apparently unrelated errors and omissions which combined together to create the eventual case against Megrahi.

The grooming of Tony Gauci to identify him as the clothes purchaser was, sadly, nothing out of the ordinary – apart from the multi-million dollar bribe, sorry reward, of course. The police approach wasn't geared to figuring out whether it was really likely that Megrahi was the man who had bought the clothes. Instead the entire exercise was aimed at securing statements from Tony that could be used to support the assertion that he was. Nobody appeared to be thinking, "is it likely that this light-skinned medium-build thirty-six-year-old is Gauci's tall, burly, dark-skinned fifty-year-old?" What they were thinking was "he's gonna pick him!" Later, when video footage from Libya revealed just how bad a likeness the old passport photo that Tony had been shown really was, the decision was taken not to run another photo-identity parade with an up-to-date image for fear that Tony wouldn't recognise the good likeness. However, it seems that this is perfectly normal police practice, or at least it was in 1991. The policemen involved aren't even slightly coy about it.

If PT/35b really was a fabrication intended to implicate Libya and/or support the theory of a three-flight hop from Malta, that would be indescribably shocking. However there is no proof at present that it was. It's a genuine mystery, and nobody's interests are served by jumping to unsupportable conclusions. The concern in this respect is not so much the disorganised paperwork of 1989–90, but the burying of the metallurgy results in 1991–92. The forensic investigators, and Feraday in particular, knew very well there was a discrepancy in the analysis of the tinning layer, nevertheless this was omitted from the final report on the analytical results, which was worded in such a way as to suggest that the Thüring-produced PCB components had also been manufactured with a pure tin coating, just like the mystery fragment.

These things happened in 1991 or later, though. The primary and fundamental error was surely the all-pervasive conviction that the bomb must have been on the feeder flight, the overplaying of tentative guesswork evidence that pointed in that direction, and the utter imperviousness of the investigators to any evidence that ran counter to this. It is particularly striking that this occurred in the very earliest weeks and months of the investigation, long before the police even became interested in Malta, never mind Abdelbaset al-Megrahi.

The apparent conviction in late December 1988 that the bomb had probably flown in on the feeder flight was ridiculously premature, but it could quite easily have been reconsidered when evidence to the contrary appeared. And evidence to the contrary most certainly did appear. During January a steady stream of witness statements and forensic results poured into Lockerbie indicating that the bomb had been inside a brown hardshell suitcase in the bottom front left-hand corner of AVE4041, and that a brown hardshell suitcase had been placed in that corner of that container by an unauthorised person in the interline shed at Heathrow.

At this time, Mr. Shearer tells us, the Lockerbie inquiry was considering "a range of emerging strands of evidence". The problem is that this does not seem to have been one of them. Manly's statement was immediately buried without trace, apparently being deemed to be of no importance whatsoever. Nobody was sent to re-interview him, and nobody involved in the inquiry as it progressed appears to have been aware that a break-in had taken place at Heathrow the previous night. The remaining Heathrow staff were of course re-interviewed several times, but in none of the statements is there any sense of a line of inquiry being pursued in relation to the mysterious appearance of the two front-loaded suitcases.

January/February 1989 was of course too early for forensics to be able to state with any degree of certainty whether or not the case on the floor of the container could be ruled out. Empirically, the explosion could be seen to have been there or thereabouts. Even without Bedford's remarkable statement, normal police procedure should surely have dictated a serious look at Heathrow as the possible scene of the crime. However, not only was the possibility of a security breach in the interline shed simply not on the radar, investigators were already playing down the possibility that the bomb was in one of the legitimate interline suitcases.

Contemporary accounts cite a number of reasons for this. At the most basic, there was the view that since the vast majority of the luggage in the container was transferred from the feeder flight, then the bomb suitcase was probably among that group. A particularly egregious line of reasoning was presented to the first formal Lockerbie case conference on 28th March by DCS John Orr, the first senior investigating officer assigned to the inquiry.

> Evidence from witnesses is to the effect that the first seven pieces of luggage in this container belonged to interline passengers and the remainder was Frankfurt luggage, this being an amalgam of luggage relative to passengers travelling through Frankfurt and passengers boarding direct at Frankfurt.

> To date 14 pieces of explosive-damaged baggage have been recovered, and inquiries to date suggest that *on the balance of probability* [italics original] the explosive device was likely to be amongst the Frankfurt baggage items.

> Of all the currently-identified explosion-damaged baggage all but one item originated at Frankfurt.

It is unclear where Orr got his "first seven pieces of luggage" idea from. It's certainly true that reconstructions carried out by the baggage handlers in January showed that seven or eight items were necessary to achieve the layout within the container that all had described, but the evidence relating to the incoming passengers should have made it perfectly clear that only six legitimate pieces of interline luggage had been placed in AVE4041 in the interline shed. Mr. Rubin's flight arrived too late for his suitcase to have been in this group.

A moment's thought reveals the illogic of the "balance of probabilities" argument. The explosion was known to have occurred at about the level where the single layer of Heathrow items ended and the many-layered heap of Frankfurt items began. The layout was well established from the evidence of the three baggage handlers, with Frankfurt-origin items easily outnumbering Heathrow-origin items in that corner of the container. In this context, the relative prevalence of Frankfurt versus Heathrow items among the recovered blast-damaged fragments is not helpful in establishing the origin of the explosive device. Indeed, if any inference can be drawn, it is surely the converse. If the bomb suitcase was one loaded at Heathrow, then that actually *explains* a relative dearth of legitimate Heathrow items among the recovered blast-damaged luggage – exactly as was observed.

The argument is however more specific than that. Taking into account the geometry and the known packing arrangement of that corner of the container, there are only three possible positions for the bomb suitcase. Feraday more or less realised that at a later stage, but it is something that should have been quite obvious from the beginning. Either of the two lowest cases in the front left-hand stack, or a case (or holdall) dropped into the angle of the overhang section. Two of the items in these positions arrived on the feeder flight, but the third was loaded in the interline shed. A "balance of probabilities" argument simply cannot justify failing to follow up this suitcase, even if it had been a better argument than the one advanced.

Regardless of the provenance of the case on the floor of the container, there was only one way to eliminate it from the inquiry. Reconcile it to a known item of legitimate luggage loaded in the interline shed, and find it on the ground at Lockerbie as a distinct item from the bomb suitcase. There's no sign of any attempt to do that. The break-in, and the front left-hand case having been described as a brown Samsonite hardshell and not having been placed in the container by any of the Heathrow staff, weren't even part of the narrative.

Conspiracy or cock-up? The thing about conspiracies is that they usually have a motive, and in this case the motive would surely have had to be extraordinarily compelling. If the Bedford bag was indeed the bomb (as in fact it was), and the police failed to mount a serious investigation at Heathrow, they risked leaving the worst terrorist attack in British history unsolved, and the perpetrators unpunished. What could possibly induce anyone involved in the inquiry to take that risk, on purpose?

A number of suggestions have been put forward. Perhaps the senior Scottish police officers were determined to keep control of the case and not be forced to hand it over to the Metropolitan police, as would almost certainly have happened if Heathrow had been shown to be the scene of the crime. Perhaps the officers of the Met themselves discouraged the idea that the bomb had been introduced on their patch, because their anti-terrorism branch was already up to its collective eyeballs dealing with the IRA. Perhaps the UK government took fright at the prospect of a failure of BAA's security being blamed for the atrocity, in particular because BAA had been one of the flagship privatisations of the Thatcher era, only a couple of years previously. Perhaps the US authorities were concerned that attention should not fall on the luggage belonging to their two intelligence agents Charles McKee and Matthew Gannon, who were returning from a mission to Beirut in connection with the then-ongoing hostage crisis.

However, does any of that sound like a good enough reason to knock the nascent Lockerbie investigation off course in its earliest days and weeks? In particular, as regards the possibility of political interference, is there any senior investigating officer who would hold still for that sort of thing for five seconds?

There is another possibility. Perhaps the senior detectives were so convinced of the involvement of the German-based cell of the PFLP-GC that they couldn't seriously conceive of the bomb *not* having come from Germany. In other words, perhaps those in charge of this investigation were as dumb as a bag of hammers that failed hammer school.

★ ★ ★ ★ ★ ★ ★

Quite soon, though, the "not the bag on the bottom" school of thought attracted independent support. The forensic investigators eagerly espoused the position that there must have been another case between the bomb suitcase and the floor of the container.

It seems this was a joint decision involving both RARDE and AAIB personnel. The first documented opinion to this effect is Peter Claiden's, in his April report where he stated that the condition of the recovered floor "would seem to indicate that this had been protected by, presumably, a piece of luggage." However, Claiden was an air accident investigator, not an explosives expert, and it is likely he was articulating the opinions of the RARDE scientists with whom he was working closely. As the case progressed a number of these scientists joined in the chorus, all giving slightly different reasons for holding the same opinion. Lack of "pitting" on the metal, the dishing of the damaged portion of the floor and even the alleged imprint of another case on the battered aluminium sheet were all cited at various times.

It seems that a large part of the reason for the controlled explosions in the USA was to gather objective evidence to support this position, but given the small number of tests, the variety of configurations employed, the variable results and the problems that arose along the way, it's very difficult to understand how the investigators thought they could justify the complete exclusion of the suitcase on the bottom layer on the basis of these results. In the end, of course, the prosecution chose not to rely on these findings in court.

Another consideration was the estimated position of the centre of the explosion within the container. Although many commentaries make a big deal about the height of the blast above the container floor, it seems this wasn't the main issue. It's also quite a confusing narrative.

Claiden's April report placed this height at 10 inches, based on the position of a hole in the side of container AVN7511 that had been loaded cheek-by-jowl with AVE4041. Although in January Hayes had estimated a height of 18 inches (without giving a reason), by 5th May he was apparently singing from the same hymn sheet as Claiden and basing his estimate on the same hole. The oddity is that although Claiden had said 10 inches, Hayes quoted 35 cm (14 inches) for the same figure. Eleven years later, in the witness box at Camp Zeist, Claiden suddenly decided he had made a mistake and revised his estimate in line with Hayes's May 1989 figure to "nearer 13 inches", which then became "13, 13 and a half inches".

As already noted, it's extremely difficult to understand how an eight inch square hole in an object nearly two feet from the explosion caused by something impinging on it "at an angle" can possibly be relied on to derive an accurate height for the centre of the blast, to within an inch or so. When Hayes and Feraday put their heads together though, their forensic conclusions agreed with Claiden's original ten inch estimate, and Hayes abandoned his 35 cm position.

In an interim Joint Forensic Report prepared for the Fatal Accident Inquiry and dated 14th June 1990, the forensic scientists went even lower, down to 20 cm (8 inches), but as this measurement was related to the 5 cm high horizontal strut rather than the floor of the container, it may come to much the same thing – 25 cm or 10 inches from the floor. This figure wasn't merely derived from the hole in AVN7511, it was justified with reference to the precise nature of the explosion damage seen on AVE4041 itself. In the final Joint Report submitted in December 1991, the RARDE group co-opted Claiden's April 1989 diagram essentially unmodified, merely relabelling it in metric units and marginally tweaking the height to "25 to 28 cm" or 10 to 11 inches. The 25 to 28 cm figure was also quoted within the text, and appeared on the label of a separate diagram. Nevertheless in the list of conclusions at the end, this figure suddenly and inexplicably transmogrifies to "28 to 30 cm".

One additional measurement was taken into account by the RARDE team. However, the less said about Professor Christopher Peel's 'Mach stem effect' calculations of the stand-off distance of the explosion from the skin of the plane the better. Professor Peel's algebra and computer simulations were comprehensively shredded by Richard Keen in cross-examination at Camp Zeist, and he was left looking ever so slightly foolish.

The judges were given several figures to choose from for the height of the explosion, without being offered any unifying explanation. Claiden spoke to his 1989 diagram with the "10 inches" label and declared that the figure should really have been 13 or 13½ inches, even though it had been reproduced in several official reports in the intervening eleven years without correction. Feraday first read out the conclusions from the Joint Forensic Report including the 28 to 30 cm figure, but then under cross-examination consistently referred to "25 to 28 cm". In their written judgement the judges chose to quote the highest measurement of them all, Claiden's on-the-hoof 'correction'.

Reading through this lot is deeply depressing, evoking an impression of 'experts' who haven't really made up their minds despite all the guesses, experiments, time expended and the seriousness of the case. Estimates are transferred from one report to another without anyone really quite knowing how they were arrived at in the first place. Nobody seems to understand why earlier estimates have been revised. Differences of opinion go unreconciled. Can a military explosives laboratory and professional air accident investigators not turn in a more convincing and coherent performance than this?

This debate, however, begs an important question. Is it actually possible to prove which suitcase exploded simply by refining this measurement? Obviously it isn't. This is an exercise in playing in the cracks. The explosion was somewhere around the 10-inch mark, and the idea that the exact height can be established so precisely as to eliminate the bottom-layer case is fanciful. It's in the frame, and if it is to be eliminated with certainty that really has to be achieved in some other way.

Feraday's party-piece was in fact his 'two postulated positions' argument, which was first documented in the June 1990 interim forensic report. Once he came up with that idea, he appears never to have re-thought it. He was "adamant" at the Fatal Accident Inquiry (October 1990) that the bomb suitcase must have been in one of these two positions. During his examination-in-chief it was pointed out to him by the then Lord Advocate Peter Fraser that the finding of the lock of the bomb suitcase inside the Bernstein saddlebag essentially disproved the first position and heavily favoured the second position – intriguingly, Lord Fraser seems to have been aware that the saddlebag was sitting on the floor of the container. Feraday appeared to concede the point, but there is no sign that he took it on board or altered his thinking as a result. The text of the December 1991 final joint report was essentially unchanged from the 1990 draft. In early 1992 he swore an affidavit for the US civil action stating that it was "physically impossible" for the case to have been in any other than the two positions he described.

The problem with this isn't just the absence of consideration of the third position, the one with the left-hand side of the case elevated on to the 3-inch step, it's the physical impossibility of the *first* position, just as Peter Fraser noted. Long before June 1990 there was ample evidence available to demonstrate that this couldn't be right. Hayes's January 1989 description of PI/911 indicated that one side of the bomb suitcase had been blasted against a blue item which offered "a relatively immoveable surface" – an item that turned out to be the large American Tourister suitcase. It's very hard to see how the Tourister could have got itself alongside the bomb suitcase in the angle of the container so as to produce PI/911. The recovery of the lock from the saddlebag should have been a big pointer to the fact that the bomb suitcase had not been loaded handle up. And finally, Claiden's ubiquitous diagram which made its first appearance in April 1989 shows pretty clearly that the damage to the airframe was *under the floor of the container*, not next to the angled section (see plate 3).

It seems that Feraday favoured the impossible 'first position' simply because of his assumption that the radio had been packed across the hinge end of the case. He didn't even *try* packing it down one side, although that would inevitably have been the packing arrangement if his 'second position' had been the actual orientation, and he didn't relate this line of thinking to any of the other forensic evidence that had been assembled.

Again, the irresistible impression is of confusion, woolly thinking, ill-founded assumptions, and the absence of any attempt at a comprehensive analysis taking all the available information into account. Although the first position should have been easily and swiftly eliminated, Feraday continued to favour it while at the same time (according to his cross-examination at Camp Zeist) he gave no thought at all to the third position because of his assumptions about the condition of the container floor.

However, the elephant in the room is this. Why spend so much time and thought and effort, including computer simulations and even test explosions, all to try to prove exactly which position the exploding suitcase had occupied? It was self-evident that the blast had been inside a case in container AVE4041 in the bottom front left-hand corner. Why was it so important for the forensic investigation to refine this further?

Although none of the RARDE or AAIB reports mentions the point at all, the reason is clear. Because one of the suitcases 'in the frame' had a different provenance from the others.

The sheer single-minded dogmatism of the "no no it can't have been the one on the floor" chorus is fairly strange, even in isolation. In the context of the one on the floor being the one with the Heathrow provenance and the description matching the description of the bomb bag, it's downright peculiar. Nevertheless, consider this. The exercise is only relevant at all if it is known that the Heathrow suitcases weren't moved. If these suitcases were shifted, 'the one on the floor' could easily have become the one in the 'second postulated position' or even the 'first postulated position'. The whole thing becomes pointless.

Nothing better demonstrates the certainty of the investigators that the suitcases weren't moved than the concerted effort to rule out the one on the bottom. An effort that commenced *after* PI/911 was described, with the bits of blue foamed Tourister lining adherent to its cracked and compacted surface.

★ ★ ★ ★ ★ ★ ★

In contrast to the obsessive and repeated revisiting of the container floor, analysis of the container's contents is conspicuous by its absence. On 19th January 1989 Hayes explicitly declared his intention to work out the probable orientation of all the container's contents relative to the centre of the explosion. There is however nothing at all in the forensic records to suggest he actually carried out this intention.

The only hints that some minimal analysis may have been carried out come from Lord Advocate Peter Fraser, who apparently knew at the time of the FAI that the Bernstein saddlebag was positioned on the floor of the container, and from David Leppard. As already noted, Leppard twice makes reference to the fact that the blue American Tourister had been loaded *on top of* the bomb suitcase, presumably getting his information from his mole inside the police inquiry. However, Leppard's version places the Tourister on the third layer with the bomb suitcase on the second, apparently itself on top of the mysterious Bedford suitcase which he doesn't quite know how to deal with.

Again, we see indications that in 1989–90 the forensic scientists understood the real message of the blue deposit on PI/911 and the compacted state of the plastic; that is that the fragment was part of the upper aspect of the bomb suitcase which was blasted against the bottom case in the 150 kg stack of luggage above it. It also suggests that some faction within the investigation also understood that the 'first postulated position' wasn't really a runner, with the flat-loaded orientation being the only game in town. This was of course all concurrent with the writing and co-signing of reports worded so as to favour the former position, and entirely neglecting to consider the implications of the latter position as regards the packing of the radio into the suitcase.

However, this is as far as it seems to have gone. Even that rudimentary level of analysis is absent from the forensic reports disclosed to the defence. As to the identity of the cases to the right of the bomb suitcase, or in the row behind it, *or the one under it*, forget it.

In fact working out which case goes where in relation to the bomb suitcase is perfectly simple, particularly if one has the incoming passenger records showing which six cases were placed in the container in the interline shed and their order of arrival, knows which suitcase actually belonged to which passenger, has Bedford's evidence detailing the order in which he loaded the cases, and knows that Sidhu stated that he didn't disturb the arrangement. One would imagine that information would have been provided to RARDE as a matter of course, but it seems this was not the case. At the Fatal Accident Inquiry, Feraday stated that he was *not* "party to" the number of items of luggage that were in the container.

In the witness box in 2000 Hayes indicated that some such analysis was at least something he'd thought about. This is his cross-examination, again by Mr. Keen.

Q Well, let's look at your note, Dr. Hayes. You examined this fragment of suitcase, and your contemporaneously recorded opinion is that it exhibits evidence suggesting it was in contact with the luggage pallet's base. Do you see that?

A Yes, I do, sir.

Q And that was your contemporaneous opinion when you examined this fragment?

A Yes, it was.

Q What scientific basis did you have for changing that opinion, if any?

A I'm not sure I would use, in this context, the term 'scientific'.

Q Well, you are a forensic scientist, Dr. Hayes.

A I agree science is applied where appropriate. But in the examination of these very many items, a growing feeling, as I mentioned earlier, the question of assembling a jigsaw, which is hardly scientific, is applicable to the reaching of certain opinions and conclusions; and as further evidence -- some physical, some chemical, where appropriate -- assembles, opinions can be focussed and possibly even changed.

Q But looking to this fragment of the suitcase, Dr. Hayes, what scientific basis do you have for altering your impression as recorded on 26th January 1989, when you examined it?

A The reason for the change of opinion, scientific or otherwise, was clearly the further examination of items, and the assembling of a larger picture.

Q But you hadn't returned to make any annotation on this note, as you have on the subscription on page 19?

A That's quite correct.

Q And what is it now about that piece of suitcase that suggests to you that while you originally thought it was possibly in contact with the luggage pallet's base, it might now have been lying on top of another suitcase?

A I'm not sure that it necessarily follows that an exclusive examination of this piece caused me to arrive at a different opinion; only that in conjunction with other fragments, which clearly were at one time in association with this, has my opinion been adjusted.

Q Can you tell us what it is about the other fragments which causes you to alter the opinion which you've expressed here at page 25?

A Well, I used the word 'fragments'. Perhaps I was too narrow in my choice of words --

Q Well, that was your choice, Dr. Hayes. You referred to the other fragments of the suitcase, which is believed to have contained the IED. Now, what is it about those other fragments that would lead you to alter the opinion expressed at page 25 of your notes?

A Well, if we are looking exclusively at the fragments, and as I attempted to explain clearly, there were other considerations, then the positioning of the fragments, the location, recovery of those fragments, would help to assemble a perhaps rather different picture.

Q Do you record any such picture anywhere in your notes, Dr. Hayes?

A No. I can't help you with that.

That, frankly, is as clear as mud. Virtually all Hayes's evidence is like this. One wonders if he'd had training.

As discussed in chapter 6, it is *blindingly obvious* that Bernt Carlsson's case was immediately behind the bomb suitcase, to the left, that Charles McKee's grey Samsonite was next in line and that Michael Bernstein's saddlebag had to be next because of the lock of the bomb suitcase being found inside it. It's equally obvious that the blue Tourister was blasted upwards, among the other luggage, not downwards away from it, and that the case on top of it was Johannes Schäuble's olive-green canvas soft-shell. Hayes even notes that the contents of that case were "very densely packed", and the reason is not hard to figure out. Once one has got that far, positions can be worked out for at least another half-a-dozen items.

Of course, once the exercise is carried out, it becomes clear that there is no blast-damaged suitcase that reconciles to the "underneath the bomb" position, and that none of the Heathrow interline suitcases was either a brown hardshell or loaded under the bomb. It also becomes clear that the nature of the damage to the Carlsson and McKee suitcases is such as to exclude the presence of another suitcase below the bomb suitcase, jamming them in position (as both Bedford and Sidhu described the loading of the two front suitcases) and protecting their lower front aspects. It also becomes clear that even a single packed suitcase absorbed the blast remarkably efficiently, and that whatever one thinks about the condition of the floor of AVE4041, the airframe under it does not appear to have been protected by such a suitcase.

This could easily have been figured out in the first half of 1989.

★　★　★　★　★　★　★

"No one in this world, so far as I know – and I have searched the record for years, and employed agents to help me – has ever lost money by underestimating the intelligence of the great masses of the plain people," declared Henry Louis Mencken. He may have understated his case. Perhaps he should have included PhD-level scientists and maybe a professor or two.

Observing the dismal level of competence in relation to the examination of the baggage container and its contents makes it a lot easier to believe that the same people might have overlooked PT/35b for many months in 1989, even though it was right there in front of them. This wasn't a crack team of penetrating analysts, this was a bunch of chronically overworked guys muddling along, not thinking too deeply, not joining the dots, and not challenging their own or anyone else's opinions. Lockerbie isn't the only case where their expertise has been questioned, either – the May Inquiry into the wrongful conviction of the Maguire Seven had some very hard things to say about the RARDE scientific team, including Dr. Thomas Hayes.

The suspicion that the exclusion of the bottom-level suitcase was perhaps more than simple incompetence is however fuelled by the observation that all three instances of extreme tunnel vision were necessary for the inquiry to have been derailed quite so comprehensively. The police inquiry ignored Bedford's evidence, the forensic scientists went completely overboard insisting that the bomb suitcase was not on the floor of the container, and Hayes omitted to carry out an elementary analysis of the data he had so meticulously recorded and drawn which would have shown that the "not the bag on the bottom" mantra must be spurious.

If any one of these elements hadn't happened, attention would have been drawn to Bedford's evidence and that suitcase would have been properly followed up. Instead though, both sets of players seem to have separately and independently made three different crass errors, with these errors combining synchronously to catastrophic effect.

The police error appears to have been the earliest of the three. Were the scientific mistakes and misdirections entirely independent occurrences, or did the police indicate in any way to the forensic officers that a report allowing that the bottom front suitcase might have contained the bomb would be unwelcome? There is really no way of knowing.

However, the combined error gained extremely strong support in August/September of 1989, when the trail of the blast-damaged clothing led to the island of Malta, and almost simultaneously the BKA revealed their evidence suggesting that an unaccompanied item of luggage had been transferred to the PA103 feeder flight from a flight from Malta. After that time it was probably impossible for the thinking on the luggage positioning to be seriously reconsidered. Everyone now *knew* that the bomb suitcase had come from Malta. Nobody was even going to investigate Warsaw or Berlin or Bombay, the other airports from which unidentified transfer luggage loaded on to the feeder flight at Frankfurt appeared to originate. Certainly, nobody was going to suggest having another serious look at the Heathrow interline luggage, and anyone who did would have been laughed out of court.

The conviction that Malta was the answer survived the discovery of the rigorous Luqa security system, and the complete failure of the inquiry to find either any way the bomb could have been put on board KM180 or anyone present at the airport who might have done such a thing. Thus in early 1991 the investigators were very ready indeed to accept the revised scenario that they should really be looking for Libyans, not Palestinians, and when a Libyan suspect was handed to them on a plate, nobody was looking a gift horse in the mouth. The later discovery that this particular gift horse had actually been checking in at Luqa airport for a different flight at the very time KM180 was open for boarding, and that he had been travelling on a false passport, probably seemed like a divine revelation.

One thing is quite clear from reading the accounts of various police personnel involved in the investigation, on both sides of the Atlantic, and that is their genuine belief that Megrahi was indeed 'the Lockerbie bomber'. Realising how they arrived at that conviction, it's easy to understand why. Eight months of belief that the bomb was carried on the feeder flight, vindicated by the revelation of the printout and tray 8849. Nearly a year of fruitless investigation of Palestinians on Malta, followed by the revelation that the culprits were believed to be Libyan. Interminable follow-up of passengers and airport staff involved with flight KM180 to Frankfurt, followed by the discovery that the man who had been fingered as the clothes purchaser was checking in for flight LN147 to Tripoli at the same time, and that he had a mate with an airside pass who could also have been at the airport that morning. Megrahi was believed to be a Libyan spook, he had a business connection with Edwin Bollier, the manufacturer of the MST- 13 timers, he bought the clothes in the bomb suitcase and he was at the scene of the crime, incognito. Case closed, really.

The investigators didn't seem to realise quite what an odd plot they were proposing. On one hand Megrahi was a criminal mastermind, capable of engineering the smuggling of the bomb on to KM180 not only successfully, but so cunningly that even after the event there was no evidence that it had been done at all. On the other hand he was an idiot who had chosen to fill the suitcase with brand new, locally manufactured, easily traceable clothes he bought himself in a small owner-run boutique only three miles from the airport where this undetectable crime was planned, doing this on a visit to the island when he was travelling openly on his own passport and without even having the foresight to don a false beard. He then set a digital timer to detonate the bomb at such an early stage in the flight that there was a good chance the plane would still be over land when it exploded, and if the departure was delayed by as little as three-quarters of an hour, it would simply go off harmlessly on the tarmac. He used such a small charge of explosive that the case had to be loaded in a very particular corner of the container *and the right way round*, but trusted to the random actions of a baggage handler to get it in that position. And after personally buying the clothes, he showed up again at the airport while Fhimah was smuggling the suitcase on to KM180, for no readily apparent reason. Still, just like police officers and forensic scientists, terrorists sometimes do extraordinarily silly things.

Megrahi's presence at the other end of the blind alley the police had been obsessing over for eighteen months, looking remarkably shifty and fitting the requirement for a Libyan suspect extraordinarily well, is a fairly stunning coincidence. Indeed, the presence of tray 8849 on the printout, the most inexplicable of all the six mystery trays, pointing right at the island where the clothes were purchased, is a *very* stunning coincidence. Nevertheless, it would hardly be the first time an innocent suspect has looked as guilty as hell, because of a string of coincidences. To the investigators and the prosecutors however, this was no coincidence. The bomb suitcase had been introduced at Luqa airport, and they'd obviously given up on Saviour Mallia (who actually *did* check in a suspicious suitcase for KM180), so who else?

The investigators assembled all this evidence, plus a little bit more handily provided by the CIA and the US Department of Justice, and secured indictments against Megrahi and Fhimah. They were genuinely convinced they had their men, and there is nothing quite so lethal as a policeman, or a prosecutor, or indeed a forensic scientist, who is absolutely and sincerely convinced of a suspect's guilt.

★ ★ ★ ★ ★ ★ ★

The case then entered an eight-year hiatus, with Megrahi and Fhimah remaining holed up in Libya beyond reach of extradition, and vehemently protesting their innocence. The prolonged saga of Gaddafi's refusal to force Libyan citizens to submit to a foreign trial, the ensuing punitive UN sanctions that crippled the entire country, followed by the accused men agreeing to surrender themselves for a trial under Scots law in the specially-built court in the Netherlands, has been well-rehearsed elsewhere.

During that period various books, articles and documentaries were published expressing doubts about the Libyans' guilt, and about the reliability of the evidence against them. Tony Gauci's very tentative identification of Megrahi's old passport photo as "resembling" the heavily-built six-foot-tall dark-skinned fifty-year-old clothes purchaser was questioned. The stringent security regime at Luqa airport was highlighted, particularly in the light of Air Malta's victory in two sets of libel proceedings on the basis of their secure flight records. The suspicions over Khaled Jaafar's connections and luggage arrangements were dusted down and taken for a run, several times. However, nobody raised the question of how the suitcases loaded into AVE4041 in the interline shed had been eliminated from the inquiry, or whose the brown Samsonite hardshell Bedford had seen on the floor of the container had turned out to be.

Well, not quite nobody.

Some time in 1996 one private citizen read David Leppard's book, and spotted both the utter illogicality of John Orr's reasoning as regards the interline cases and Leppard's rather orphaned and unresolved account of the suitcase Bedford saw and Kamboj denied loading. He realised this was far far better evidence for the introduction of a bomb packed in a brown Samsonite hardshell than anything that seemed to have been discovered at either Frankfurt or Malta. Most importantly, he realised that this suitcase had not been eliminated from the investigation. The grounds presented for its elimination were essentially spurious.

He wrote to the MP for Southend-on-Sea, Sir Teddy Taylor, who at the time was interested in the case, and explained what he had read and his reasoning in respect of Bedford's brown Samsonite. Sir Teddy passed the letter to the Metropolitan police, and in due course the following reply dated 12th June was received from an officer in their anti-terrorist branch.

Dear Sir,

Thank you for your letter to the Commissioner, dated 5th June 1996 concerning a letter from your constituent Mr. B. Walker and his concerns about the conduct of the investigation into the "Lockerbie Bombing" and, in particular where, and by whom, the bomb was put onto the ill-fated flight, Pan Am 103.

Although the investigation into the tragedy was conducted by the Chief Constable of Dumfries and Galloway, the investigation into the allegation that the bomb was put on the aircraft at Heathrow was thoroughly investigated, on his behalf, by the Metropolitan Police Anti-Terrorist Branch. The allegation was proved beyond question to be without foundation.

I do hope this is of some assistance to you in allaying your constituent's fears.

Yours faithfully,

W J EMERTON
Detective Superintendent

This is a very peculiar letter. What "allegation" is DS Emerton referring to? A clue or a line of inquiry aren't allegations. What thorough investigation is he referring to? There is no evidence at all of the Anti-Terrorist Branch having conducted an investigation into the provenance of the Bedford suitcase, and certainly no evidence that they were able to rule it out as being the bomb.

Angry about being fobbed off in such a cavalier manner, Mr. Walker didn't take the matter further. He may in fact have been the only commentator to realise the significance of this issue before Bedford gave evidence at Camp Zeist, when pennies started dropping for quite a few people.

* * * * * * *

It seems likely that the prosecutors assigned to the Lockerbie trial at Camp Zeist initially assumed they would be repeating their performance from the Fatal Accident Inquiry, so far as the elimination of the Heathrow interline luggage was concerned. That story went like this. The suitcase loaded in the interline shed in the corner where the explosion happened was on the floor of the container, and there wasn't one on top of it at that stage. That suitcase wasn't moved thereafter. Allen Feraday and the rest of the forensics team were "adamant" that the bomb suitcase had not been on the floor of the container, which had been protected by another piece of luggage. Therefore, the bomb must have been in one of the cases transferred from the feeder flight.

The Crown's original stated intention was to lead evidence about all the legitimate cases known to have been loaded into AVE4041 and show that each of them could be excluded as being the bomb suitcase. Then, presumably, the above reasoning would demonstrate that the bomb suitcase had been flown in from Frankfurt. Then, the court would be invited to conclude that it must have been the item in tray 8849 and to have been transferred from KM180.

The trial was a very different animal from the FAI, however. For a start, all the evidence from Malta and Frankfurt would have to be led – unlike John Mowat, the Zeist bench was not going to be satisfied with "trust us, we know the bomb was loaded at Malta, never mind how we know but you don't need to pay any attention to the Heathrow evidence." This trial was going to hear all about the double-counting security system at Luqa and the absence of any evidence of an unaccompanied suitcase on KM180. It was also likely to hear about the shambles of the Frankfurt paper trail and the multiple unidentified transfer baggage trays – even if the prosecution skated past this, the defence would be free to tell the court all about it. And unlike Pan Am, the Libyan accused would have no reason whatsoever to refrain from implicating the airline's Heathrow operation in the atrocity.

Given the weakness of the evidence supporting the Malta transfer and the strikingly suspicious sighting of a suitcase fitting the description of the bomb bag in the right place in the container at Heathrow before the feeder flight landed, everything hinged on two particular points. Was it possible to reconcile the case seen at Heathrow to a legitimate (and non-exploding) item of interline luggage, and was the evidence of there having been another suitcase below the bomb suitcase absolutely incontrovertible – bomb-proof, even?

The first of these points was obviously a lost cause. The prosecution was thus facing the unenviable prospect of explaining away the case Bedford saw as some undocumented piece of lost luggage that just happened to match the description of the bomb suitcase, and whose fragments had all miraculously blown away even though plenty pieces of the bomb suitcase itself and the other cases surrounding it had been recovered on the ground. The only way this fairy-story would have any hope of standing up in court would be for the evidence that the bomb suitcase must have been on the second layer to be utterly rock-solid and unchallengeable.

Clearly, the prosecution team realised that it wasn't.

One can only imagine the discussions that must have taken place. Was it as blatant as, "Oh shit, the cops were looking for the bomb at Malta and there it was at Heathrow all along! What the hell do we do now?" Maybe not.

Court cases aren't usually discussed in an atmosphere of pure intellectual inquiry. The matter at issue isn't so much figuring out what actually happened, as figuring out which points can be spun as favourable to one side of the case or the other. Perusal of the defence briefing notes demonstrates the same thing. Nobody is asking, "What was that suitcase?" They're all asking, "Would it be to our advantage to suggest this – or that? But what if the other side suggest something else?" So it was probably all a bit more nuanced and oblique.

The central plank of the new scenario that emerged in late 1999 or early 2000 was Hayes's willingness to testify that PI/911, in his opinion, originated from the lower aspect of the bomb suitcase, with the blue Tourister thus having been underneath it. Fortuitously, his original notes included a speculation that the fragment had been blasted down on to the floor of the container, and although he must have reconsidered this almost immediately on noticing the blue foamed material adherent to the outer surface, he hadn't made any note of how he had revised his thinking.

What possessed Hayes, in 2000, to declare that PI/911 had been part of the lower aspect of the bomb suitcase? In the midst of all his obfuscatory waffle about assembling a jigsaw and a larger picture and "other considerations", did it not even occur to him that a good half-dozen of the other cases in the container had bits of the Tourister plastered across them, revealing without a doubt that it had been blasted upwards, among the rest of the luggage? Had it not occurred to him in 1989?

He must, surely, have realised then that PI/911 was in fact from the upper aspect of the suitcase. The Tourister had been transferred from the feeder flight, therefore according to the received wisdom of the time, it could not have been on the floor of the container. There is absolutely no necessity for the "relatively immoveable surface" to have been *under* the bomb suitcase. Spherical propagation, remember? If a single soft-sided suitcase lying on a thin sheet of aluminium could provide sufficient resistance to compact the grey plastic sheet, how much more effective in that respect would be the 150 kg stack of luggage on top?

The entire justification for the Bedford case being ruled out of the inquiry in the first place was that it had not been moved. This assumption of necessity remained an article of faith right through the entire investigation. It was absolutely essential to the Fatal Accident Inquiry's conclusion that the bomb had been transferred from the feeder flight. David Leppard specifically recorded that the police scenario in 1990 was that the Tourister had been on top of the bomb suitcase. It's inconceivable that Hayes thought the Tourister was under the bomb, back in '89.

Then, in 2000, it was. Did it occur to anyone that by turning this fundamental assumption on its head they were negating the basic premise on which all the forensic thinking had been built for more than ten years?

Once the Tourister had been suggested as the case on the floor of the container, it became necessary to lose Sidhu's testimony that he hadn't moved the interline luggage. A comprehensive rearrangement of the suitcases could then be implied, with the result that the case Bedford saw was no longer defined by having been under the bomb and inevitably having sustained catastrophic damage, therefore it could have been anything.

Then, lose all the information about the interline passengers who flew into Heathrow that afternoon, and the luggage they were carrying, and even the exact number of cases Bedford placed in the container. Now that case could be anybody's legitimate luggage, especially if you don't know that none of these passengers had a brown or maroon Samsonite hardshell, or you can imply that Bedford was mistaken about the colour anyway.

It shouldn't have worked, but it did. The defence mounted a half-hearted challenge, more interested in demonstrating doubt and uncertainty than in tackling the evidence head-on, and the judges bought the prosecution version. No wonder there was some high-fiving going on in the prosecution camp when Megrahi was handed a life sentence for murder in January 2001.

Hayes's evidence in relation to the examination of PI/995 (the fully-loaded shirt collar) and the renumbered pages has been criticised as evasive and shifty. The criticism he attracted from the May Inquiry and his subsequent career history have also been commented on in this context. Nevertheless his willingness to flip longstanding received wisdom concerning the orientation of PI/911 on its head was arguably the real game-changer in the Lockerbie case. Hayes was a PhD forensic scientist who should have had no difficulty in figuring out where the damaged suitcases had been positioned in relation to the bomb suitcase, in realising that none of them had been under the bomb, and in realising that the front lower corners of the two cases immediately behind the bomb suitcase showed no sign of having been protected by another case on the floor of the container. He appears to have given this rather obvious exercise a body-swerve. He then reinterpreted his analysis of a single isolated fragment in exactly the way that would get the prosecution out of a very serious hole, and avoided mentioning that his new interpretation was entirely at odds with the rest of the examination notes he had just read out.

Was it just an exercise in gamesmanship? Was there any real awareness among the prosecution or the forensics officers that the two men in the dock were a thousand miles away when the Lockerbie bomb was loaded into that luggage container, and what's more, the ordinary people of Libya had been made to suffer for eight years because of a complete misunderstanding of the evidence?

It's very difficult to know. Many have spoken of a 'canteen culture' in the forensic science service at that time, where scientists saw themselves as being in effect part of the prosecution team. 'Groupthink' is one word for it. Nobody was thinking outside the box – especially not thoughts that might undermine the favoured police theory, or latterly the Crown case. On the legal side, prosecution counsel prosecute their cases to the best of their ability, making the most of the material at their disposal. Is exculpatory evidence ever really recognised as such, or just regarded as an awkwardly-placed chess piece to be neutralised?

Consider also – the defence didn't spot it either. Not then, and not even during the very prolonged preparations for the second appeal.

Megrahi and Fhimah had a perfect alibi for the crime. An alibi far better than that of anyone who was in London or the Home Counties on the afternoon of 21st December 1988.

* * * * * * *

Can this atrocious debacle really be "adequately explained by stupidity"? There's no easy answer to that.

Stupidity is there, in abundance. So many aspects of the case that seem suspicious when first encountered turn out to be due to nothing more. The handling of the Frankfurt luggage records by the German police is a case in point. But at the same time, just because someone is incompetent doesn't mean they're not also trying to obfuscate and mislead. In the end, only the people who were actually involved in the inquiry know what they themselves were thinking when they did certain things or reached certain conclusions.

There have been calls for a public inquiry into Lockerbie since early in 1989. Reasons for refusing one have been as many as there have been Prime Ministers and First Ministers over the past twenty-five years. Public petition PE1370 calling for such an inquiry has been before the Justice Committee of the Scottish parliament since June 2011, but appears to be getting nowhere against the settled will of the Crown Office.

But what would one inquire into? The blatant railroading of a suspect, and a guilty verdict based on evidence that shouldn't have been sufficient to support the issuing of a parking ticket? How so? The official position is that Abdelbaset al-Megrahi *is* the Lockerbie bomber, and the First Minister and the Scottish government do not doubt the safety of the conviction. Far from questioning the verdict, Scottish police and legal officials have been junketing off to Tripoli to try to find Megrahi's supposed accomplices, and talking up the possibility of re-trying Lamin Fhimah now that the prohibition on double jeopardy has been abolished.

An inquiry is indeed required – an inquiry into how the Scottish police managed to overlook a shed-load of evidence showing that the bomb had been introduced at Heathrow, how the forensic scientists and even the AAIB inspectors compounded this error by misinterpreting and failing to interpret the evidence from the recovered debris, and why the Crown prosecution at Camp Zeist chose to conceal so much important information from the court and present a contrived scenario that was entirely at odds with fundamental forensic thinking about the case since 1989. But first, it is necessary to understand that that is what actually happened.

Twenty-five years have now passed since that midwinter evening when 270 people lost their lives. Do another twenty-five years have to pass before they, and the other victims who have accumulated along the way, are finally accorded justice?

Appendix A

FRANKFURT FOR ANORAKS

In total, 136 items of luggage are recorded in the baggage records as heading for PA013A at Frankfurt on 21st December 1988. 111 items were listed on Bogomira Erac's computer printout as being transferred through the automated system (figure 37), and in addition there were three Passenger Transfer Message telexes notifying the delivery of luggage being transferred directly across the tarmac from incoming Pan Am shuttle flights from Berlin Tegel airport.

PA643	on block 13.02	1 passenger	1 item of luggage
PA647	on block 15.25	18 passengers	21 items of luggage
PA649	on block 16.20	2 passengers	4 items of luggage

The total number of items on the PTA telexes is twenty-six, however as explained in chapter 3, the single suitcase from PA643 which belonged to Wiebke Wagenführ was entered into the central system rather than being sent straight to the departure gate because of its early arrival time. It is therefore included as one of the 111 items on the computer printout.

Little information is available about the tarmac-transfer items except that none of the passengers on these shuttle flights transferred to *Maid of the Seas* at Heathrow. It seems to have been assumed by the investigation that there was nothing questionable about any of these suitcases. It is the analysis of the computer printout that presents the intellectual challenge.

The key to the printout is the identification of the coding stations, which do not appear in clear on the printout. Paradoxically the numbering order is reversed between the computer codes and the actual numbering of the physical stations. Stations designated S05xx were those in the arrivals hall, where the

FUNIKI

KIK,SORT,TADD,8B1221,+FLN,PA   ,0103,+_G,008,895,DOKU

1932   DATEI VON:8B1221
 PA 0103 -1042 VZ:HS#0 ZN:B041 ZA:B044 BF:1512 EF:1165
 B 0033 F1042 S0539+Z1237--HS13+Z1513--B044+Z1519
 B 0103 F1042 S0539+Z1452--HS14+Z1525--B044+Z1531
 B 0568 F1042 S0543+Z1342--HS23+Z1513--B044+Z1519
 B 0622 F1042 S0072+Z1159--BP--HS13+Z1513--B044+Z1519
 B 0776 F1042 S0541+Z1510--HV30+Z1514--B044+Z1517
 B 0902 F1042 S0541+Z1510--HV30+Z1512--B044+Z1515
 B 0959 F1042 S0541+Z1611--HV30+Z1613--B044+Z1616
 B 1268 F1042 S0539+Z1238--HS33+Z1513--B044+Z1519
 B 1298 F1042 S0541+Z1556--HV20+Z1558--B044+Z1601
 B 1711 F1042 S0539+Z1238--HS23+Z1514--B044+Z1529
 B 1797 F1042 S0541+Z1515--HV20+Z1526--B044+Z1529
 B 1898 F1042 S0072+Z1159--BP--HS13+Z1513--B044+Z1519
 B 2083 F1042 S0539+Z1607--HV20+Z1609--B044+Z1612
 B 2088 F1042 S0541+Z1604--HV10+Z1605--B044+Z1608
 B 2208 F1042 S0539+Z1239--HS13+Z1529--B044+Z1535
 B 2377 F1042 S0072+Z1200--BP--HS32+Z1512--B044+Z1518
 B 2385 F1042 S0541+Z1609--HV20+Z1610--B044+Z1613
 B 2718 F1042 S0541+Z1600--HV20+Z1601--B044+Z1604
 B 2823 F1042 S0538+Z1505--HS13+Z1525--B044+Z1531
 B 3135 F1042 S0539+Z1239--HS13+Z1529--B044+Z1535
 B 3148 F1042 S0076+Z1131--HS32+Z1517--B044+Z1523
 B 3546 F1042 S0012+Z1241--TO--HS33+Z1514--B044+Z1520
 B 3593 F1042 S0541+Z1530--HV20+Z1532--B044+Z1535
 B 3698 F1042 S0543+Z1236--HS13+Z1524--B044+Z1530
 B 3834 F1042 S0541+Z1608--HV20+Z1610--B044+Z1613
 B 3849 F1042 S0552+Z1353--HS33+Z1513--B044+Z1520
 B 4120 F1042 S0541+Z1530--HV30+Z1532--B044+Z1535
 B 4362 F1042 S0547+Z1308--HS33+Z1518--B044+Z1524
 B 4367 F1042 S0541+Z1513--HV20+Z1515--B044+Z1518
 B 4573 F1042 S0076+Z1131--HS34+Z1523--B044+Z1530
 B 4606 F1042 S0541+Z1524--HV10+Z1526--B044+Z1529
 B 4759 F1042 S0544+Z1458--HS34+Z1524--B044+Z1530
 B 4809 F1042 S0074+Z1444--BP--HS33+Z1514--B044+Z1521
 B 4907 F1042 S0541+Z1513--HV20+Z1515--B044+Z1518
 B 4971 F1042 S0072+Z1159--BP--HS13+Z1513--B044+Z1519
 B 5070 F1042 S0074+Z1320--BP--HS23+Z1529--B044+Z1535
 B 5077 F1042 S0541+Z1535--HV20+Z1536--B044+Z1539
 B 5191 F1042 S0541+Z1518--HV30+Z1520--B044+Z1523
 B 5203 F1042 S0011+Z1241--TO--HS23+Z1515--B044+Z1531
 B 5246 F1042 S0539+Z1434--HS33+Z1518--B044+Z1524
 B 5336 F1042 S0543+Z1354--HS33+Z1514--B044+Z1520
 B 5559 F1042 S0539+Z1601--HV30+Z1603--B044+Z1606
 B 5567 F1042 S0543+Z1056--HS22+Z1514--B044+Z1529
 B 5586 F1042 S0541+Z1515--HV10+Z1517--B044+Z1520
 B 5620 F1042 S0074+Z1544--HV20+Z1546--B044+Z1549
 B 5766 F1042 S0541+Z1534--HV20+Z1536--B044+Z1539
 B 5936 F1042 S0011+Z1240--TO--HS33+Z1514--B044+Z1520
 B 6001 F1042 S0074+Z1445--BP--HS33+Z1515--B044+Z1522
 B 6080 F1042 S0541+Z1609--HV20+Z1610--B044+Z1613
 B 6239 F1042 S0539+Z1236--HS24+Z1518--B044+Z1532
 B 6338 F1042 S0539+Z1515--HV10+Z1517--B044+Z1520
 B 6364 F1042 S0541+Z1604--HV10+Z1605--B044+Z1608
 B 6391 F1042 S0072+Z1200--BP--HS13+Z1513--B044+Z1520
 B 6559 F1042 S0072+Z1200--BP--HS32+Z1512--B044+Z1519
 B 6696 F1042 S0072+Z1200--BP--HS32+Z1512--B044+Z1518
 B 6726 F1042 S0539+Z1237--HS24+Z1512--B044+Z1519
 B 6788 F1042 S0547+Z1308--HS33+Z1518--B044+Z1524
 B 6949 F1042 S0544+Z1411--HS23+Z1515--B044+Z1530
 B 6976 F1042 S0541+Z1556--HV20+Z1557--B044+Z1601
 B 7056 F1042 S0539+Z1557--HV10+Z1559--B044+Z1602
 B 7281 F1042 S0539+Z1238--HS24+Z1513--B044+Z1528
 B 7418 F1042 S0074+Z1446--BP--HS13+Z1514--B044+Z1521
 B 7576 F1042 S0543+Z1354--HS33+Z1514--B044+Z1520
 B 7619 F1042 S0539+Z1601--HV30+Z1603--B044+Z1608
 B 7724 F1042 S0541+Z1457--HS34+Z1517--B044+Z1523
 B 7730 F1042 S0552+Z1500--HS23+Z1512--B044+Z1519
 B 7738 F1042 S0539+Z1559--HV20+Z1601--B044+Z1604
 B 7832 F1042 S0539+Z1238--HS23+Z1514--B044+Z1530
 B 7848 F1042 S0539+Z1607--HV20+Z1609--B044+Z1612
 B 7951 F1042 S0539+Z1104--HS13+Z1525--B044+Z1531
 B 8004 F1042 S0539+Z1410--HS23+Z1515--B044+Z1530
 B 8042 F1042 S0070+Z1317--BP--HS13+Z1513--B044+Z1519
 B 8238 F1042 S0072+Z1159--BP--HS22+Z1513--B044+Z1519
 B 8374 F1042 S0544+Z1104--HS23+Z1524--B044+Z1537
 B 8415 F1042 S0541+Z1558--HV30+Z1559--B044+Z1602
 B 8673 F1042 S0539+Z1237--HS33+Z1513--B044+Z1519
 B 8734 F1042 S0543+Z1342--HS23+Z1512--B044+Z1518
 B 8831 F1042 S0541+Z1627--HV20+Z1629--B041+Z1631
 B 8849 F1042 S0009+Z1307--TO--HS33+Z1517--B044+Z1523
 B 9992 F1042 S0541+Z1628--HV20+Z1630--B041+Z1631
 B 9002 F1042 S0552+Z1238--HS33+Z1513--B044+Z1519
 B 9007 F1042 S0552+Z1100--HS32+Z1513--B044+Z1520
 B 9172 F1042 S0547+Z1305--HS13+Z1529--B044+Z1535
 B 9237 F1042 S0539+Z1544--HV20+Z1546--B044+Z1549
 B 9402 F1042 S0539+Z1608--HV20+Z1610--B044+Z1613
 B 9495 F1042 S0541+Z1524--HV10+Z1525--B044+Z1528
 B 9531 F1042 S0539+Z1557--HV30+Z1559--B044+Z1602
 B 9807 F1042 S0547+Z1323--HS23+Z1512--B044+Z1518
 B 9882 F1042 S0539+Z1532--HV20+Z1535--B044+Z1538
 B10073 F1042 S0552+Z1505--HS23+Z1523--B044+Z1536
 B10257 F1042 S0539+Z1239--HS13+Z1511--B044+Z1521
 B10461 F1042 S0541+Z1058--HS23+Z1511--B044+Z1536
 B10467 F1042 S0012+Z1239--TO--HS33+Z1512--B044+Z1519
 B10559 F1042 S0539+Z1448--HS23+Z1514--B044+Z1530
 B10576 F1042 S0541+Z1602--HV30+Z1604--B044+Z1607
 B10743 F1042 S0539+Z1238--HS23+Z1514--B044+Z1530
 B10773 F1042 S0012+Z1240--TO--HS33+Z1514--B044+Z1521
 B10797 F1042 S0539+Z1517--HV30+Z1519--B044+Z1522
 B10852 F1042 S0072+Z1200--BP--HS23+Z1512--B044+Z1519
 B11092 F1042 S0539+Z1458--HS23+Z1518--B044+Z1537
 B11289 F1042 S0539+Z1527--HV30+Z1529--B044+Z1532
 B11366 F1042 S0539+Z1557--HV30+Z1559--B044+Z1602
 B11435 F1042 S0072+Z1200--BP--HS13+Z1514--B044+Z1520
 B11442 F1042 S0544+Z1410--HS23+Z1514--B044+Z1530
 B11511 F1042 S0541+Z1530--HV20+Z1532--B044+Z1535
 B11621 F1042 S0539+Z1607--HV30+Z1609--B044+Z1612
 B11822 F1042 S0541+Z1524--HV10+Z1526--B044+Z1529
 B12014 F1042 S0541+Z1556--HV30+Z1559--B044+Z1602
 B12068 F1042 S0543+Z1354--HS35+Z1523--B044+Z1529
 B12116 F1042 S0541+Z1558--HV30+Z1600--B044+Z1603
 B12244 F1042 S0072+Z1159--BP--HS13+Z1513--B044+Z1519
TEILSUMME: 0111
GES.SUMME: 0111
1936SORT-ERF

Figure 37
The original database query as printed out from her KIK computer by Bogomira Erac at 19.32 on 22nd December 1988. For further explanation of the various computer codes, see page 24.

luggage from the Frankfurt-origin passengers was checked in. Stations designated S00xx were those in the two interline halls, where luggage transferred from incoming flights was coded.

INTERLINE STATIONS numbering of the counters:

S0078	HM1	S0014	V3 201
S0076	HM2	S0013	V3 202
S0074	HM3	S0012	V3 203
S0072	HM4	S0011	V3 204
S0070	HM5	S0010	V3 205
		S0009	V3 206
		S0008	V3 207

Examination of the printout reveals twenty-five items coded at the above stations; nineteen in the central hall (HM) and six on the apron (Vorfeld, V3). All the V3 items have the extra code "TO" in their data line, recording transit through the east tunnel ('Tunnel Ost') which connected the V3 hall to the main part of the transit system. All but three of the HM items have the code "BP", signifying a 'bypass' route taken by most of the luggage entered into the system in the central hall.

The table overleaf extracts these twenty-five lines of code and sorts them by time of coding (rather than by tray number, as Bogomira originally arranged the information).

This arrangement immediately starts to make sense of the data. Items coded within a few minutes of each other at the same coding station have probably come in the same wagon from the same flight, and are likely to belong to the same passenger or to passengers travelling together. The key above allows the coding stations to be identified. It's then a simple matter to look up the appropriate worksheets and check which flights were being dealt with at the relevant time.

The table on page 199 is the result, with the worksheets confirming that the five items coded at the V3 location between 12.39 and 12.41 were from the same flight; two wagons from Vienna being handled simultaneously at adjacent coding stations.

Flights C, E, F and G are completely uncontentious and are dealt with in chapter 3. The four flights identified as worksheet matches for the coding of these items were all carrying legitimate passenger luggage for the Heathrow flight, and indeed were carrying the right number of items. That was how it was supposed to work. Jürgen Fuhl and Kurt Berg got these four straight out

	Tray number	Coding station	Time of coding		Gate	Time of exit
A	3148	S0076	11.31		B044	15.23
	4573	S0076	11.31		B044	15.30
B	0622	S0072	11.59	BP	B044	15.19
	1898	S0072	11.59	BP	B044	15.19
	4971	S0072	11.59	BP	B044	15.19
	8238	S0072	11.59	BP	B044	15.19
	12244	S0072	11.59	BP	B044	15.19
	2377	S0072	12.00	BP	B044	15.18
	6391	S0072	12.00	BP	B044	15.20
	6559	S0072	12.00	BP	B044	15.19
	6696	S0072	12.00	BP	B044	15.18
	10852	S0072	12.00	BP	B044	15.19
	11435	S0072	12.00	BP	B044	15.20
C	10467	S0012	12.39	TO	B044	15.19
	5936	S0011	12.40	TO	B044	15.20
	10773	S0012	12.40	TO	B044	15.21
	3546	S0012	12.41	TO	B044	15.20
	5203	S0011	12.41	TO	B044	15.31
D	8849	S0009	13.07	TO	B044	15.23
E	8042	S0070	13.17	BP	B044	15.19
F	5070	S0074	13.20	BP	B044	15.35
G	4869	S0074	14.44	BP	B044	15.21
	6001	S0074	14.45	BP	B044	15.22
	7418	S0074	14.46	BP	B044	15.21
H	5620	S0074	15.44		B044	15.49

of the box without any trouble at all. Even flight F, which had no actual passengers booked to transfer to PA103A, was easily solved when Alitalia provided documentation to show that a legitimate rush tag item destined for New York had been on that flight and had been expected to transfer to the Heathrow flight at Frankfurt.

	Coding Station		Time coded	Number of items	Flight number	From	Coding window
A	S0076	HM2	11.31	2	AI465	?	11.31-11.35
B	S0072	HM4	11.59-12.00	11	no flight	–	–
C	S0012	V3 203	12.39-12.41	3	LH1453	Vienna	12.39-12.44
	S0011	V3 204	12.40-12.41	2	LH1453	Vienna	12.37-12.45
D	S0009	V3 206	13.07	1	KM180	Luqa	13.04-13.10
E	S0070	HM5	13.17	1	PA643	Berlin	13.16-?
F	S0074	HM3	13.20	1	AZ422	Rome	13.18-13.20
G	S0074	HM3	14.44-14.46	3	LH631	Kuwait	14.44-14.49
H	S0074	HM3	15.44	1	LH1071	Warsaw	15.41-15.45

Ten items down, fifteen to go.

Fuhl's initial February 1989 analysis is reproduced on pages 25-26. If the four uncontentious flights are removed, the following five remain.

AI (Air India) 465	Sydney – Singapore – Bombay	2 items
AI 165	Bombay – Delhi – Frankfurt	5 items
LH 177	Nürnberg – Frankfurt	6 items
KM (Air Malta) 180	Malta – Frankfurt	1 item
PA 647	Berlin – Frankfurt	1 item

This arrangement makes it clearer what has actually happened. Flight A has been attributed to a flight from Australia to India, which doesn't actually go to Frankfurt. The eleven items of flight B have been split 5-and-6 between a long-haul flight from India and a local flight from Bavaria. Flight D has been matched to KM180, the flight all the fuss is about. Finally flight H has been matched to one of the Berlin shuttles, the one with the PTM telex documenting 21 items of transfer luggage taken directly across the tarmac in a wagon.

The two items of flight A were coded together at 11.31. The flight number on the worksheet for that time is indeed AI465, a long haul flight that doesn't go to Frankfurt. The handwriting on the worksheet is perfectly clear with no alteration or ambiguity, but it refers to a flight number which designates a route from Sydney to Bombay, with a stopover at Singapore.

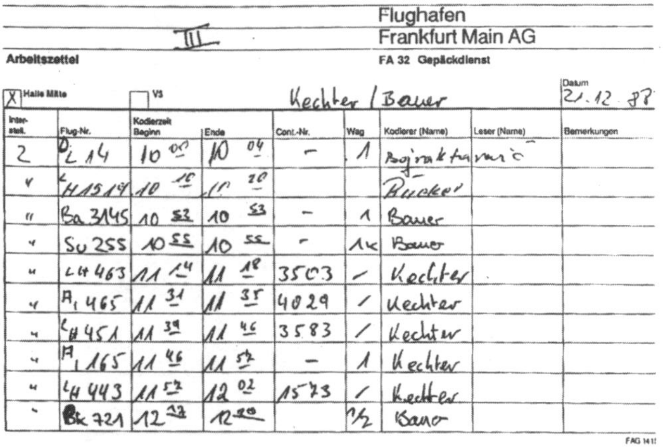

						Flughafen Frankfurt Main AG			
Arbeitszettel						FA 32 Gepäckdienst			
☒ Halle Mitte		☐ V3				*Kechter / Bauer*			Datum 21.12. 88
Inter- stell.	Flug-Nr.	Kodierzeit Beginn	Ende	Cont.-Nr.	Wag	Kodierer (Name)	Leser (Name)	Bemerkungen
2	PL 14	10 00	10 04	–	1	Bojrak tuvaric		
"	HA1519	10 16	10 20			Rucker		
"	Ba 3145	10 53	10 53	–	1	Bauer		
"	Su 255	10 55	10 55	–	1k	Bauer		
"	LH 463	11 14	11 18	3503	–	Kechter		
"	AI 465	11 31	11 35	4029	1	Kechter		
"	LH 451	11 39	11 45	3583	1	Kechter		
"	AI 165	11 46	11 52	–	1	Kechter		
"	LH 443	11 53	12 02	1573	1	Kechter		
"	BK 721	12 22	12 30		1½	Bano		

FAG 1411

Flight A >

Figure 38
Worksheet for coding station HM2, late morning.

There was a flight with a similar number, AI165, which did fly into Frankfurt and was being unloaded at about that time, indeed Richard Kechter who was coding at HM2 at the time coded a wagon from that flight just over fifteen minutes later. A mistranscription couldn't be completely ruled out, despite the neatness of Kechter's handwriting and coding sheets, but an alternative suggestion which was put forward was that a container of luggage from AI465 had been transferred to AI165 at Bombay, as the latter flight left that city a few hours after the former flight landed. However this conundrum was never satisfactorily resolved.

The main problem was that there wasn't a sniff of a passenger or so much as a pencil case scheduled to transfer from either of the Air India flights to the Pan Am flight.

AI165 was involved again when attention turned to flight B, the most striking feature of the printout, the group of eleven items coded in quick succession at HM4 at 11.59–12.00. This is where Fuhl's report becomes truly surreal. Even without access to the worksheets or timetables, one glance at this group of items is all that's needed to realise that it was a discrete batch of luggage being shot into the system one after the other without any intervening items for other destinations. The fact that the computer clock clicked from 11.59 to 12.00 in the middle of all this is neither here nor there.

Perhaps this was a package holiday, or another TV crew? There was no large organised group on PA103A, and no TV crew either, but whatever that luggage was, the answer must be a group of items for the feeder flight being coded as a discrete batch.

This stunningly obvious conclusion doesn't seem to have occurred either to Jürgen Fuhl or to Kurt Berg. When they saw what was written on the relevant worksheet (below), common sense appears to have gone right out the window.

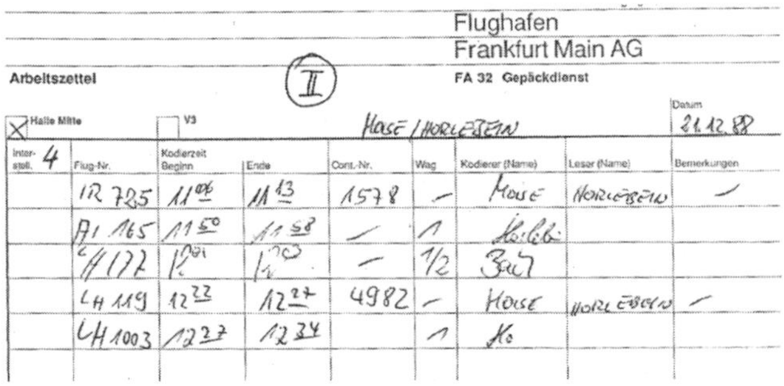

Figure 39
Worksheet for
coding station HM4,
late morning.

There is *nothing* recorded on this worksheet as being coded between 11.59 and 12.00. A wagon from flight AI165 was coded between 11.50 and 11.58, then there was a three-minute gap, then a half-wagon was coded from flight LH177 from 12.01 to 12.03.

Fuhl has split the eleven items between the two flights, with the five items carrying the 11.59 time stamp allocated to AI165 (a long-haul international route from Bombay in India flown by another Boeing 747 Jumbo) and the six carrying the 12.00 time stamp to LH177 (a short domestic route from Nürnberg in Bavaria flown by an Airbus 310).

It was accepted that the times on the worksheets (often taken from the coders' wristwatches) might vary slightly from the computer clock, but the maximum discrepancy was only about three minutes, and that would only happen later in the day as the computer clock drifted. This is not late in the day, but it looks as if Fuhl decided to allow for a bit of wiggle-room on the timings to attach each of the eleven items to its chronologically nearest flight.

This is quite *astoundingly* stupid. First, it assumes that the drifting computer clock might be a minute ahead of the coders' watches one moment, and a minute behind it the next. Second, it assumes that a coding rate of no more than ten seconds per bag can be maintained even when the baggage handlers are switching from one flight (and one wagon) to another, and in fact switching jobs, as the signatures show that the flights were coded by two different people.

Third, it assumes that an unusually large number of items for PA103A were present on *both* consecutive flights, and somehow all those on AI165 magically clustered at the end of its coding window, while those on LH177 equally magically clustered at the beginning. Fourth, it assumes that the coders who accomplished this prodigious feat were quite unaware of their achievement, and calmly allowed themselves a couple of minutes break between the flights when completing the paperwork. And if there was any doubt at all about the reasoning employed, or that this was more than a fleeting early hiccup, here it is laboriously typed up in an extract from a report dated *26th October 1989* (with a typo in the KM180 coding times just for good measure).

009/206	13.07	14.04 – 13.10	KM 180
076/HM2	11.31	11.31 – 11.35	AI 465
076/HM2	11.31		
072/HM4	11.59	11.50 – 11.58	AI 165
072/HM4	11.59		
072/HM4	11.59		
072/HM4	11.59		
072/HM4	11.59		
072/HM4	12.00	12.01 – 12.03	LH 177
072/HM4	12.00		
072/HM4	12.00		
072/HM4	12.00		
072/HM4	12.00		
072/HM4	12.00		

Figure 40

Extract from internal BKA memo by KOK Siegburg, tabulating the allocation of transfer trays to incoming flights as it was understood in late October 1989.

The worksheet match for flight D was the Malta flight, KM180, but flight H was another howler. The straightforward match for this flight, the single tray 5620, was LH1071 from Warsaw, coded on the same worksheet as the three legitimate items of flight G. (This worksheet is reproduced as figure 10.) Fuhl's original February report matched this tray to the Berlin shuttle PA647, which did indeed have legitimate luggage for PA103A. However, PA647 was coded at HM5 from 15.38 to 15.42, while tray 5620 was coded at HM3 at 15.44. It is entirely unclear why this mistake was made in the initial analysis of the printout, but it did make the reconciliation look marginally better than it actually was. It also prevented anyone from noticing there was also an "unaccompanied item from Warsaw" until after the investigation was already committed to Malta and entirely uninterested in stray luggage trays from behind the rapidly-collapsing iron curtain.

★　★　★　★　★　★　★

Although the Scottish detectives had eyes only for KM180 when they were finally shown Fuhl's report in August, the German police seem to have realised that the other thirteen or so unidentified trays on the printout complicated the issue. Fuhl was sent back to check his working.

Tray 5620 was almost immediately reallocated, correctly, to flight LH1071 from Warsaw, and it was confirmed that just as with KM180, there was no record of any legitimate luggage being carried on that flight tagged to be transferred to PA103A.

There was no instant rethink of the first thirteen incoming trays. The amount of time and effort expended by German detectives dredging through the Air India and Lufthansa paperwork in pursuit of these elusive thirteen items is phenomenal. Memo after memo lists the passengers who travelled on these flights, their onward journeys, and the luggage they carried. Well over half the passengers on LH177 continued on to the USA by a variety of routes (although nobody waited nearly five hours for PA103) and the FBI was enlisted to follow these people up. This exercise continued into 1990, with memos about LH177 even cropping up in 1991, long after the penny had finally dropped. All inquiries drew a complete blank.

By this time Fuhl had an assistant, an officer named Siegburg, and it was Siegburg who first suggested that perhaps these thirteen trays might represent *something not recorded on the worksheet by the coder*. It was some time in December 1989, almost a year after the disaster, before they found out about the *Fehlerbahn* ('error track') and the *umgebuchtes Gepäck* ('re-booked luggage'). How was the automated baggage handling system set up to cope with luggage which had missed its intended connection, or which had arrived at Frankfurt in error?

The answer was the *Fehlerbahn,* a track in the system which delivered such luggage to a particular station in the central hall to be dealt with. The computer was programmed with the expected departure times of all the flights, and this was updated in real time, so that an algorithm could determine whether or not any particular piece of luggage was able to catch its intended flight. Anything coded after its flight had departed, or within too short a period before the departure time, was diverted down this track for re-booking. The same arrangement coped with illegible tags and luggage that shouldn't have been in Frankfurt in the first place.

Once delivered to the central hall, luggage from the *Fehlerbahn* would be evaluated by the baggage handling staff to figure out which flight it should be sent on to get it back on track to its intended destination. It would then be re-tagged and coded back into the system. Crucially, such luggage was frequently not recorded on the worksheets, especially single items and small batches, which were not subject to additional billing charges.

In fact, the detectives might have figured out what the eleven-item group was at a much earlier stage, if they had simply put two and two together. Although there were twenty-five transfer items on the printout, Maier had only x-rayed thirteen interline items. That rather suggests that twelve of the transfer items had arrived in Frankfurt on Pan Am incoming flights. Once the mistaken attribution of tray 5620 to PA647 was corrected, only a single item on the printout was identified as online. And then there was a group of eleven items in a single batch. Which flights tended to be carrying batches of luggage this size for transfer to the Heathrow flight? The Berlin shuttles, obviously. Why might eleven items from a Berlin shuttle have arrived nearly five hours before the Heathrow flight left? Is it possible that a delayed shuttle from Berlin caused a batch of online transfer luggage to miss its connection to the previous Heathrow flight?

That is exactly what had happened on 21st December. The late morning Berlin shuttle, PA637, was delayed and didn't come on-block until 10.42. Pan Am 107 which flew Frankfurt–Heathrow–Washington left at 11.00, and eighteen minutes wasn't long enough to get the luggage across. The earliest BKA memo to refer to PA637 is dated 13th December 1989, over ten months after the printout had been handed over to the police. This memo notes the late arrival of the shuttle flight, carrying ten passengers booked on PA107 to Heathrow.

Glory hallelujah!

Nine of the ten passengers sprinted for the departure gate and made the connection, but without their luggage. That luggage, and the tenth passenger, had to wait for PA103. The passenger manifest revealed that only three of these people had checked-in luggage on the flight, four items in total, and all three were among the group who caught PA107.

The problem was, none of this was discovered until nearly a year after it happened. Inquiries with Pan Am at Frankfurt revealed that the records documenting luggage that failed to make its connection and had to be re-booked were no longer available. After failing to preserve the computer dataset in the last week of 1988, the German investigators had also managed to lose a second set of evidence vital to the analysis of the baggage transfers.

Jürgen Fuhl's report explained. *Bei der Pan Am 'Lost und Found Abteilung' sind die Unterlagen für Umbuchungen wie DV-Message und Arbeitskladde nicht mehr auffindbar. Dieses bestätigte Pan Am auch der Statsanwaltschaft Frankfurt Main auf anfrage.* "At the Pan Am lost and found department, documentation of the transfers, such as computer messages or workbooks, was untraceable. This has been confirmed by Pan Am to the state prosecutor of Frankfurt Main at his request." I'll just bet *that* was an interesting conversation.

Fortunately, some records had been preserved at Heathrow. A lost luggage list for 21ˢᵗ December turned up just ten items from various flights that had missed a connection for PA107 that day, and telex messages still existed detailing the steps taken to reunite these with their owners. Disappointingly, only two of the four PA637 items, the suitcases belonging to Fiona Leckie and Thomas Trautmann, were unequivocally documented as having arrived at Heathrow on PA103. Two suitcases belonging to the third passenger in the group, Gerd Pilz, had no clear record of a flight of arrival and one of them seemed to have been lost. Of the other six items, four were recorded as arriving on morning flights on 22ⁿᵈ December and the remaining two again had no clear arrival record.

Fuhl tracked down all the passengers involved and interviewed them. He was able to convince himself that Mr. Pilz's luggage had indeed arrived at Heathrow on the PA103 feeder flight, but that was all.

There were of course further sources of information to be tapped – the passenger manifest for PA103 itself, and the records of luggage actually found on the ground at Lockerbie. Additional items were recorded there that must have been transferred to PA103A at Frankfurt from other incoming flights, and the Scottish police had known about these since early 1989. Once he finally realised that the coding worksheets weren't the be-all and end-all of the luggage tracing exercise, Fuhl got on to it.

Adolf Weinacker was a no-show passenger for PA103 who had managed to find an earlier flight out with Lufthansa as described in chapter 3. One of his suitcases and some papers from the other were recovered at Lockerbie, and he was interviewed about his journey and his re-booking at an early stage in the investigation. The FAA inquiry conducted in January 1989 knew about his luggage and included it in their reconciliation of the thirteen x-rayed interline items. Jürgen Fuhl didn't find out about it until 1990.

Fuhl matched the two Weinacker cases to the pair of items coded at 11.31 at HM2, the ones that appeared to have come from the mysterious AI465 container. It seems his thinking was that these re-booked items had been entered into the system at HM2 perhaps half a minute before the coding for that container began, and so appeared with the time stamp corresponding to the beginning of its coding window. It is unclear why he chose this option rather than assuming that these cases were more of the eleven-item batch, as Mr. Weinacker's incoming flight landed at almost the same time as PA637, nevertheless it is a reasonable enough assumption.

Alternatively, though, since at the end of the day four items from the eleven-item batch were never traced, one might observe that the two items apparently originating from Bombay were never conclusively identified.

One more unaccompanied transfer item was found at Lockerbie. That was a 'rush tag' suitcase belonging to Pan Am pilot John Hubbard, one of two sent from Berlin Tegel to Seattle via Heathrow. As discussed in chapter 3, it was unclear how either case had got to Heathrow, or how the case that was found on the ground came to be on PA103. The conclusion of the Scottish detectives was that the misrouted case had been on the feeder flight, which was almost certainly correct, and although Fuhl didn't appear to understand the reasoning he accepted the conclusion. What he didn't seem to realise was that if one case had travelled to Heathrow on the feeder flight, the other had almost certainly done the same. Thus Mr. Hubbard's rush-tagged cases almost certainly account for two of the eleven-item group, having been transferred to the feeder flight from PA637 in the same way as the passenger items.

The final discovery related to a passenger who was actually a Lockerbie victim, also discussed in chapter 3. Although Kenneth Gibson was recorded on the PA637 passenger list as having no hold luggage on the plane, he was seen at Berlin checking in a maroon suit carrier. The suit carrier wasn't recovered at Lockerbie, but Derek Henderson was certain enough of its existence to have included it in his overall baggage reconciliation report.

Further inquiries taking in another seventeen passengers who arrived at Frankfurt on other incoming flights drew a blank. These people either had no checked-in luggage, or they had collected their suitcases at baggage reclaim and re-checked them as Frankfurt-origin items. And that was it. Seven of the eleven-item group seem to have been traced, plus the two 11.31 items. Four of the eleven-item group plus the two later mystery trays were never accounted for.

*   *   *   *   *   *   *

Fuhl's final report suggests he rather lost the will to live about that point, at least as far as the items coded in the central hall were concerned. Given that re-booked luggage was being entered into the system there without any record being made on the coding sheets, that explanation could be co-opted for all five, with a bit of luck.

The likelihood is that the rest of the unaccompanied items in the eleven-item group, like the Hubbard cases, were rush-tagged luggage being sent from Berlin to Heathrow via PA637 and Frankfurt, either to be collected there in due course, or to be transferred to other outgoing flights. There is no record of any inquiry at Berlin Tegel airport as to whether that might have been the case, but this is one more area where the requisite information is likely to have been lost as a result of the twelve-month delay in figuring out the PA637 connection.

Rush-tagged luggage offloaded at Heathrow could also be the explanation for tray 5620. However, there was no record of anything like that being carried on LH1071, and although that flight, like PA637, was not investigated until many months after the event, Lufthansa appears to have retained paperwork longer than Pan Am evidently did. It is possible, though, that a stray re-booked item was casually included with the LH1071 batch at HM3 – it wouldn't make any difference whether it was coded separately or tossed in with a batch already being coded, as nobody would be recording it on a worksheet either way.

That possibility should also have put tray 8849 to bed once and for all, except that re-booked luggage was not normally entered in the V3 hall, which makes that one more difficult to explain away. However, no evidence was ever presented to show that this was impossible, either. The only witness called by the defence in relation to the baggage handling was Lawrence Whittaker, an FBI agent who had been conducting investigations at Frankfurt airport in September of 1989. During that visit he observed something in the V3 hall of interest to the defence.

> There was a -- an individual who appeared to be an airport worker. He was dressed in clothing appropriate to the area, carrying a suitcase, to the best of my recollection, a single suitcase, who approached a coding station or a baggage entry input station near where we were standing and placed it in a bin, one of the luggage bins on the track, used the keypad to encode what I assume was a destination, and sent the bag on its way. And then he wandered off. […] His behaviour was very consistent with what you would expect from a baggage handler or an employee who was about his normal course of business.

Under cross-examination Mr. Whittaker acceded to the suggestion that even though he had not seen the man write anything on a worksheet, he could not be absolutely certain that he hadn't done that. Much was also made of the fact that the coding station was not dealing with an incoming flight at the time. Nevertheless, the question arises, what was that suitcase? A single transfer item from a flight, being carried by hand rather than on a wagon? Or a stray, misrouted or re-booked item being entered into the system in the V3 hall? This aspect was not explored in evidence.

Another possibility Fuhl came up with related to an ambiguity in the KM180 coding time window, and luggage from another Lufthansa flight, LH669 from Damascus, which was being dealt with in V3 at the same time as the KM180 wagon. Yaser Koca's handwriting is unclear (see figure 10), and although the end time for the KM180 coding window is usually given as 13.10, it is equally possible that the worksheet reads 13.16. While five to six minutes is just about right for the coding of thirty items of luggage, twelve minutes is an improbably long time. The suggestion was made that some of the Damascus luggage had been coded at station 206 either with or immediately following the KM180 batch, without a separate record being made, this possibility being suggested by an apparent discrepancy in the number of wagons recorded as being received and coded for that flight.

There were several things wrong with this proposition, namely that there was no record of any luggage being carried for PA103A on LH669 either, that such discrepancies in wagon numbers were not especially uncommon and were usually due to luggage unloaded for customs inspection being re-packed into fewer wagons than originally utilised, and that the 13.07 coding time of tray 8849 was still more compatible with KM180 than a wagon coded immediately after it. Although he incorporated it into his report Fuhl realised that it didn't really fly.

He had no idea what was in trays 8849 or 5620, or where they had come from. The surviving paperwork was simply not capable of solving the mystery.

$$* \quad * \quad * \quad * \quad * \quad * \quad *$$

A final anomaly relates to the total luggage count for the flight, depending on which way you add it up. As noted on page 195, the total from the baggage records was 136. This tally includes the nine unaccompanied items documented above, and the six unidentified trays. This would suggest there were 121 accompanied items on the feeder flight. However, in total only 118 items are recorded on the passenger manifest, a discrepancy of three.

One of these is explained by Kenneth Gibson's case, which wasn't recorded on the passenger list because the check-in clerk thought it had gone ahead on PA107 when she was dealing with Ken's reservation. A second is explained by a mistake on the passenger list, with only two items being recorded against Karen Noonan's name, although she had checked in three holdalls at Vienna. The remaining one-item discrepancy remains a mystery.

Either there was another mistake on the passenger manifest which hasn't been reported, or there was a rush-tag item somewhere among the Berlin shuttle luggage transferred across the tarmac. Jürgen Fuhl's investigation doesn't analyse the Frankfurt check-in luggage or the PA647/PA649 luggage in sufficient detail for this to be figured out.

Appendix B

THE PERVERSE PCB PAPER-TRAIL

Gathering the widely-strewn debris from the plane was a monumental task. It was made more monumental by the Scottish rules of evidence, which dictate that everything must be attested to by two witnesses. If the searchers had had to move in pairs, both signing a production label every time they picked something up, they would still be out on the moors today.

A compromise was worked out. Searchers, who included local volunteers and mountain rescue teams as well as policemen, would work in teams of ten, each with a team leader whose function was to act as the second witness for everything picked up by members of their team.

At least, that was the theory. In practice members of the public were showing up with items from all over the place, sometimes without any clear indication of where the stuff had been found, and souvenir-hunters were making off with assorted unconsidered trifles. The weather was wet and chilly, making writing – in particular producing a recognisable signature – pretty much impossible much of the time. There was no heavy snow, which would have been disastrous, but there was little more than six hours of daylight per day.

Further east, into England, where light debris had been blown, nobody was even making the effort. Local residents were asked to pick up anything that had fallen on their land and turn it in to the police station. In Scotland, in the main sectors where significant wreckage had fallen, it was supposed to be more meticulous. This wasn't always achieved.

In 2008 the BBC filmed a reconstruction of how they imagined the fragment of shirt collar which was later dubbed PI/995 was found. The programme depicted two yellow-clad policemen standing in a forest, gazing with interest not just on an oversized piece of grey cloth, but on an implausibly green mock-up of the PCB fragment itself.

The Conspiracy Files: Lockerbie
BBC2, 31st August 2008

NY 502 858 – field beside
Blinkbonny farm, with Newcastleton
Forest on the horizon

Figure 41
The finding of the scrap of grey shirt collar, PI/995 – fantasy and fact.

The reality was very different. The grid reference given for the recovery of the scrap of collar is a spot in the middle of a large field of rough grazing beside Blinkbonny Farm, near Newcastleton, Roxburghshire, close to the border with England. In court, DC Thomas Gilchrist testified that his interpretation of the label on the bag containing the scrap of collar was that he had found it at that grid reference on Friday 13th January 1989. However, the documentation contained several anomalies.

Although recorded as found on 13th January, PI/995 was entered into the log at the property store, the Dextar warehouse in Lockerbie, on 17th January. Items logged before and after that item were recorded as being found on 17th January, finder unknown.

The countersignatory on the label was DC Thomas McColm. McColm comes in for bitter criticism in DC John Crawford's account of the investigation because of his skill in wangling indoor jobs in the production office and avoiding the outdoor fingertip searches. Crawford also describes him as having a very cavalier attitude to continuity and documentation of evidence. While it's not inconceivable he was out in the field on 13th January with Gilchrist, it's also possible that the label was completed retrospectively in the production office, and that the signatures do not accurately record the personnel who actually picked the thing up.

Another anomaly is the appearance of the production label itself. At first glance, it appears to read "DEBRIS (CHARRED)", despite the item inside being merely a scrap of cloth – its various interesting contents weren't discovered until four months later, at RARDE. Close inspection, however, reveals that the word "DEBRIS" has been formed by over-writing the original text, which was the word "CLOTH".

Figure 42
Production label (left),
with detail of
alteration below.

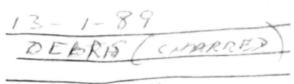

The alteration is quite skilfully done; hardly the sort of thing someone would fiddle with in a windy field. It's also quite improper. If something has to be altered, correct procedure is to cross out the mistake in such a way as to leave the original text legible, and add the correction above or below. Nobody seems to have noticed this until Richard Keen questioned Gilchrist about it in the witness box at Camp Zeist. Gilchrist had no recollection of making the alteration and could not explain it.

The SCCRC investigation found nothing sinister in these anomalies, concluding that the alteration had been made by DC Gilchrist more or less at the time the label was originally filled in, and that the other signatures were in order. A possible explanation may be that the scrap of material was originally scooped up in a hurried sweep of a freezing, darkening field, and not even sorted until the aggregate was delivered to the property store. Subsequently, after its importance to the inquiry was appreciated, it may have been decided to represent the original recovery as more meticulous than had actually been the case. This might explain contemporary reports of Gilchrist being irrationally nervous before his scheduled appearance in the witness box, and the judges' description of his evidence as "at best confusing, at worst evasive".

The label certainly doesn't inspire confidence, but what about the evidence itself?

★ ★ ★ ★ ★ ★ ★

The bag containing the cloth eventually found its way to the RARDE laboratory in Kent, where the tale of confusing and suspect paperwork continues. Hayes recorded in his notes that he opened the bag and examined its contents on 12th May 1989.

His notes from that day, reproduced opposite, detail these findings and the new numbers he allocated to the various fragments. He was most interested in the wad of paper, which he teased out into its individual leaves and sketched. It was numbered PT/2, perhaps to correspond with the reference copy of the Toshiba manual which was already in the system as PT/1. The rest of the debris was all lumped together as PT/35, with the pieces of black plastic becoming PT/35a, the PCB fragment becoming PT/35b and the shard of speaker mesh becoming PT/35c.

This photograph shows the collar itself, the pieces of plastic and mesh, the wad of paper still packed together (bottom centre), and the PCB fragment – which never really looks green in the photographs, mainly because the green solder resist coating was on the reverse side.

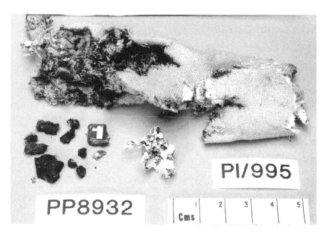

PI/995

PP8932

Cms

Figure 43
Lower half of photograph 117 from the Joint Forensic Report – the upper half, shown in figure 42, shows the production label.

Hayes then proceeded to have detailed photographs taken of both sides of the scraps of paper. The PCB fragment remained unsketched and the only photograph taken of it was the composite one shown above. In the latter half of May Hayes and Feraday became extremely interested in fragments of PCB from the Toshiba radio in their continuing quest to pinpoint the exact model involved, but PT/35b continued to be ignored. Certainly it wasn't from the radio, being made of fibreglass while the radio PCBs were phenolic paper, but why oh why did nobody seem at all interested in something which was obviously very close indeed to the explosion and might well have been part of the IED itself?

EXAMINATION

Ref. PP 8932   **Date** 12/5/89

PI/995   Plastic bag, attached i.d. label marked "Debris (charred)".
Contents?

Photo ✓   A portion of the ? neckband of a grey? shirt, severely explosion damaged with localised penetrations and blackening.

Trapped in the grey material within the blackened area were :—

a) several fragments of black plastic ~~sheet~~.

below PT/35   b) a fragment of a green coloured circuit board

c) small fragments of metal + wire

(PT/2) → d) a multilayered fragment of white paper bearing writing in various languages.

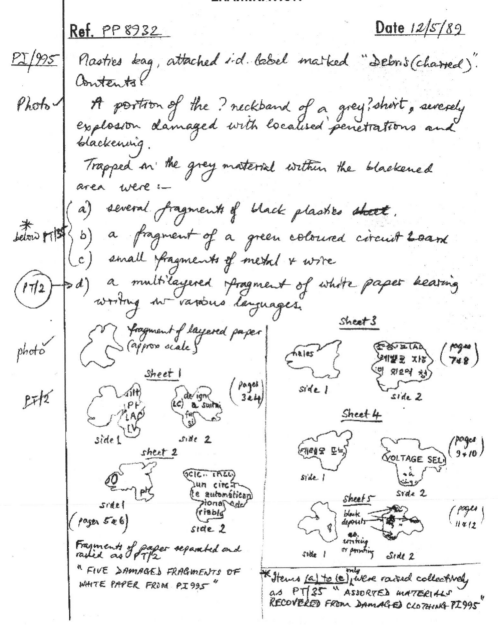

photo

PT/2

fragment of layered paper (approx scale)

Sheet 1   (pages 3 & 4)

Sheet 2   side 1   (pages 5 & 6)   side 2

Fragments of paper separated and raised as PT/2

"FIVE DAMAGED FRAGMENTS OF WHITE PAPER FROM PI 995"

Sheet 3   holes   side 1   side 2   (pages 7 & 8)

Sheet 4   side 1   VOLTAGE SEL   side 2   (pages 9 + 10)

Sheet 5   black deposit   no writing or printing   side 1   side 2   (pages 11 & 12)

*Items (a) to (e) only were raised collectively as PT/35 "ASSORTED MATERIALS RECOVERED FROM DAMAGED CLOTHING PI 995"

Figure 44
Page 51 of Hayes's examination notes, dealing with the shirt collar PI/995.

The page number on Hayes's notes, 51, looks uncontentious. However, it's not the only "page 51". A second page was also originally numbered 51, but the 1 has been over-written with a 2. The over-written alterations continue as far as page 56 (changed from 55), then page 57 shows no sign of alteration. This not unnaturally has given rise to suspicions and indeed accusations that the new "page 51" was a later interpolation aimed at providing a back-dated provenance for fabricated evidence which was in reality introduced at a much later date.

Other anomalies tend to support that interpretation, including inconsistencies in the sequence of the allocated production numbers, and in the dates on the surrounding pages.

The notes for 14th March end on page 44. Pages 45 to 48 all detail the examination of the reassembled baggage container, and all four sheets are dated 27th February. The March sequence picks up again on page 49, which is dated 15th March (a Wednesday). However, that examination occupies just over half the page, at which point a new date appears for a new examination, 15th May (a Monday). Pages 50 and 51 are dated 12th May, which was the previous Friday, then 15th May reappears on page 52. One might speculate that a task laid aside on 15th March was resumed on 15th May on the original page, but that two pages of additional material were later inserted and given the date of 12th May.

Hayes himself, at Camp Zeist, initially could give no explanation for the renumbering, describing it as an "unfathomable mystery". However, he then proceeded to provide one. The pages, he said, were loose leaves which originally had not been numbered at all. The numbers were added later, and it was possible that he had accidentally numbered two pages as "51", then on realising his mistake gone back and corrected himself. He was never asked about, or offered any explanation for, the dating inconsistency.

In fact the muddle described above merely exemplifies the general shambles of Hayes's page numbering 'system'. Numerical order and chronological order frequently do not coincide, and interpolated pages are common. Sometimes sequentially-numbered pages appear in the middle of something unrelated, even splitting a sentence, and sometimes extra pages are inserted such as 6a and 36a. The extra pages are sometimes dated chronologically in context, and sometimes months later.

This is no way to keep laboratory notes, particularly forensic notes that may be required as court productions. Normal laboratory practice in the days before notes were typed directly into computers was to keep a hard-bound notebook and record every examination and experiment in order, with the date. The structure of these books makes it virtually impossible to remove or interpolate pages undetectably.

In this context it is interesting to note that more than a decade previously the RARDE laboratory was indeed in the habit of using normal bound laboratory notebooks. This was highlighted by the inquiry into the wrongful conviction of the Maguire Seven by Sir John May which began its work in October 1989, the month after Thomas Hayes, PhD in forensic science, left RARDE to retrain as a chiropodist. Initially only selected extracts from the notebooks in question had been supplied to the May Inquiry, however Sir John later requested and was provided with the complete books.

Sight of the complete notebooks allowed the Inquiry to understand that the RARDE scientists dealing with the case, who included Thomas Hayes, had withheld certain important results from the original trial, and been less than candid in their evidence in court. Sir John stopped short of finding that there had been a conspiracy among the scientists to mislead the court, nevertheless Hayes and his then superior Douglas Higgs came in for some stinging criticism. A picture emerged of an institutional culture prepared to massage figures and cherry-pick results in support of the prosecution case. This culture appeared to stretch back at least to the time of the Judith Ward trial in 1974. Hayes was unable to state in court exactly when RARDE had switched from using standard laboratory notebooks to loose leaf sheets, however it had been some time after the Maguire Seven case but before the Lockerbie investigation.

In the absence of proper laboratory notebook procedure, the SCCRC commissioned specialised tests of the individual pages of Hayes's notes. This involved a method known as ESDA, which detects indents in the paper caused by another page having been written while on top of the page in question, such as might happen when a pad of paper is being used a sheet at time. The Commission took the view that these tests confirmed that the pages had been written in sequence, but the results on which they based that conclusion do not appear to support it.

The results showed that from (new) page 53 right up to page 59, everything was hunky-dory. The eight pages *following* the disputed page appeared all to have been written in sequence, tending to disprove the suggestion that an original page 56 had been removed in order to make room for the new page 51. The disputed page 51 also bore the imprint of page 50. This appeared to satisfy the Commission that there had been no interpolation. However, that may not be a valid conclusion.

The crucial page in this respect is in fact page 52. Which imprint does it bear? Page 51, as would be expected? Or an earlier page in the sequence? In fact, neither. Disturbingly, the imprint on page 52 is of examination notes from an unrelated case Hayes had been dealing with around the same time. The date is partially legible, the 17th of a month.

Also relevant would be the imprint on page 50. Page 49 contains material written on two different dates, two months apart. Which day's entry, if either, appears on page 50? We don't know. That information is not included in the SCCRC report.

It is extremely difficult to understand why the SCCRC accepted these findings as evidence that no interpolation had occurred. In particular it is extremely difficult to understand why they accepted assurances from Dr. Hayes that he might have worked on the unrelated case between 12th and 15th May. First, the 13th and 14th of May are not the 17th of any month. Second, in 1989 they were a weekend. Third, Hayes had been instructed on 5th April to devote himself entirely to Lockerbie and not to work on any other cases. While the ESDA results show that pages 50 and 51 were written together, and that no 'old' page 56 was removed, they leave the possibility entirely open that pages 50 *and* 51, the two dated 12th May which appear in the middle of material dated 15th May, were later interpolations.

The confounder is of course the enormously disorganised pagination throughout the examination notes, combined with the use of loose-leaf pages. Almost any anomaly can be explained *somehow*, perhaps by suggesting two pads were in use simultaneously, especially if an inquiry is predisposed to see no evil. Nevertheless the ESDA investigation commissioned by the SCCRC does not by any stretch of the imagination provide reliable proof that page 51 was written on 12th May 1989.

A similar difficulty arises when considering the provenance of the photograph shown in figure 44 (photograph 117). This must have been taken *during* the examination described on the disputed page 51, showing as it does the process after the debris has been removed from the collar but before the wad of paper was separated. Can the negative of that photograph be reliably dated?

Once again the SCCRC discovered laboratory procedure which was contrary to best practice. In the days before digital photography, it was *de rigeur* when dealing with developed film relating to cases likely to come before the court for films to be kept intact in their rolls, not cut into individual negatives. The reason for this was to be able to show that the photographs were taken in sequence and nothing extraneous has been introduced or substituted.

At RARDE, all films were cut into individual negatives, each stored in its own little sheath, which was stamped with the date the film had been developed. The negative of photograph 117 was date-stamped 22nd May 1989. That's all very nice, and the reference number matches up with an original print on file, too. However, once the negatives have been separated, any filing system of that nature can be tampered with. All that is necessary is to substitute a new negative and print for a picture that can be dispensed with.

Hard-bound laboratory notebooks are used for a reason. Photographic negatives are kept in their original rolls of film for the same reason. In order to be able to prove provenance, if this is challenged or malpractice is alleged. The

RARDE laboratory in 1989 was systematically non-compliant with both procedures. As a result it is *not* possible to prove provenance, of either page 51 or its accompanying photograph. This is a shocking state of affairs.

The corollary to this, of course, is that it is equally impossible to prove that malpractice has occurred. Another May Inquiry would be unable to discover the details of additional tests and embarrassing raw data that led to Thomas Hayes and Douglas Higgs being so severely criticised by that report. It is left to the discretion of the investigating body to decide if inability to prove provenance should be regarded as incriminating, or if inability to prove malpractice should be regarded as reassuring. The SCCRC appears to have taken the latter view.

Something which might support the authenticity of photograph 117 is the record of the examination of the scraps of the radio manual. Feraday testified to being more interested in these than in the PCB fragment when the collar was first examined. Which doesn't seem very sensible, but then what about the RARDE investigation does? The photograph was apparently taken before the pages were teased apart, so if there is a reliable provenance for these scraps being examined in May 1989, this would provide strong support for the contention that 117 was indeed taken that month. Unfortunately this is not something the SCCRC looked into.

On the other hand, only one side of the wad of paper appears in the photograph. Is that all five pages, or only one? Once a suspicion is kindled, it can be difficult to extinguish.

★ ★ ★ ★ ★ ★ ★

The reason 'photograph 117' occupies such a crucial position is that it is the only photograph showing PT/35b which even *might* have been taken before September 1989. Despite the fragment appearing to sit there in the photo shouting "look at me, I'm a freaking great CLUE", despite Feraday testifying to the SCCRC that he remembered its discovery in May 1989 because Hayes had called him into his office to see it, and despite both forensics officers being extremely keen on blast-damaged PCBs in general, nobody paid any further attention to it. No individual photographs were taken, and nobody tried to find out what it was. It seems to have been filed away and forgotten about for four months.

It next surfaces in a memo dated 15th September from Allen Feraday to DI William Williamson, who was working on the Lockerbie investigation. This *billet-doux* is commonly known as the 'lads and lassies memo' (figure 45).

Feraday had only just returned to Kent from a visit to Lockerbie, where memos indicate that he had been looking through the stored debris for more fragments of PCB which might be a match for another fragment designated PT/30, a part of one of the Toshiba circuit boards. The Toshiba circuit boards were quite distinct from PT/35b, being of a different material and showing a distinctive orange/brown colour on one side. In context, it seems that Feraday is sending Williamson pictures of something they have been discussing during the visit, something rather different from the Toshiba PCBs.

Although the production number PT/35b is not mentioned, the description of the fragment as green and the careful drawing of the 0.6-inch diameter curvature of the cutaway corner identify the item under discussion beyond any doubt. Exactly why this matter assumed such urgency at that moment when the thing had been sitting unregarded at RARDE for four months has never been explained. Apparently it was now so urgent that Feraday could not even

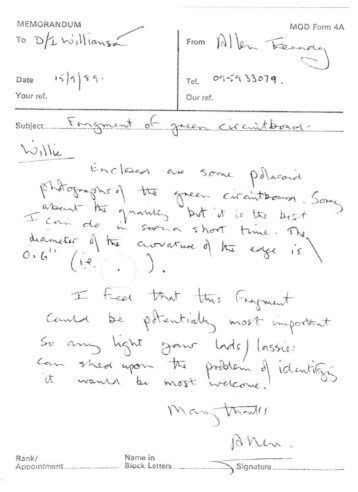

Figure 45
'Lads and lassies' memo from Allen Feraday to DI William Williamson, 15th September 1989.

wait over the weekend (15th September 1989 was a Friday) to have good quality photographs taken, Hayes having singularly failed to do that in May, and had to snap a couple of quick (and undateable) polaroids.

And yet, despite the urgency, there is no evidence at all of Williamson's 'lads and lassies' having looked at any polaroids of PT/35b in September 1989 with the object of identifying its provenance. Memos written by two Scottish police officers consistently refer to investigations relating to PT/30 taking place at about that time, mainly involving efforts to locate further fragments from the same board. Nevertheless Allen Feraday represented to the SCCRC that the entire exercise was in fact in relation to PT/35b. Eventually the Scottish officers appear to have concurred.

According to the RARDE photographic archive Feraday did indeed have high-quality photographs taken of the fragment immediately afterwards, with their negatives marked as being developed on 22nd September. The photographs are high resolution and show the tiny fragment in impressive detail (see plate 8), but the unreliability of the provenance accorded by that archive has already been remarked on.

The entire episode seems irretrievably mired in confusion. The SCCRC accepted that the PT/35b narrative was the true one, but this decision was largely informed by their having already decided that the 12th May provenance recorded by page 51 of Hayes's examination notes and photograph 117 was genuine. Is it possible that the 'lads and lassies' memo was a complete re-write of a memo originally referring to PT/30, forming a complementary strand of an elaborate attempt to provide a retrospective provenance for the green fragment? Once again the paperwork is highly suspect and invites an answer in the affirmative. But at the same time the contention that the Scottish police officers were confused about the production number of the fragment in question is not wholly incredible.

Feraday represented to the SCCRC that during 1989 he had been concerned to keep the investigation of PT/35b in-house, just as Stuart Henderson wanted to keep it in-house in 1990. However, while there is ample evidence of a strenuous and diligent effort by the Scottish police to identify the fragment in the early months of 1990, there is no evidence that either Hayes or Feraday did anything at all with it in 1989. Where are *their* metallurgy tests, fibreglass analysis, copper assays and so on? In April and May 1989 Feraday travelled round Europe and eventually to Japan to determine the exact model number of the Toshiba radio-cassette player from a few fragments of its circuit board, but the green fragment seems to have languished unremarked in the store room. What was to become the biggest clue of the Lockerbie case was apparently completely overlooked.

The serial irregularities in its paperwork weren't something that worried the judges, though.

> While it is unfortunate that this particular item which turned out to be of major significance to this enquiry despite its miniscule [*sic.*] size may not initially have been given the same meticulous treatment as most other items, we are nevertheless satisfied that the fragment was extracted by Dr Hayes in May 1989 from the remnant of the Slalom shirt found by DC Gilchrist and DC McColm.

One wonders if the same latitude would have been accorded to a clue which turned out to be of major significance to the case for the defence.

ACKNOWLEDGEMENTS

Particular thanks are due to George Thomson and John Ashton, who provided access to reports, memos and witness statements not referred to in court, and also to the photographic productions from the Joint Forensic Report and elsewhere. Much of the material in chapter 9 is sourced from John Ashton's 2012 book *Megrahi: You Are My Jury*.

I am also grateful to Barry Walker and Dr. Jim Swire for providing access to the letter from DS Emerson of the Metropolitan Police and the email from DCS Patrick Shearer of the Dumfries and Galloway Constabulary respectively.

Thanks are also due to the many people who have discussed the case with me both online and in real life, chewing over various plausible and less-than-plausible theories and providing a range of insights and analyses. These include Professor Robert Black, Robert Forrester, Eddie McDaid, Adam Larson, Paul Feeney, Barry Walker, and also the online personas of 'Ambrosia', 'CTB', 'LittleSwan', 'Pete2' and 'SM'. If anyone has been forgotten, sincere apologies are offered.

Finally, this entire undertaking would have been impossible without digital data storage and retrieval, which allowed documents to be shared and accessed without the need to source multiple paper copies, and the internet itself, which drew together such a wide range of disparate characters with an interest in the case, although separated in many cases by thousands of miles.

ILLUSTRATIONS

The vast majority of the images in this book are taken from Crown productions; principally the Air Accident Investigation Branch report into the crash of Pan Am 103 (1990) and the Joint Forensic Report by RARDE (1991), plus other police and forensic reports and memos.

Figure 22 (first image) and figure 41 (first image) are stills from BBC programmes as detailed in the text, and BBC copyright is hereby acknowledged. Figures 9, 18, 20, 22 (second image) and 33 were prepared for this book by Adam Larson.

Figure 41 (second image) is the author's copyright.

SUPPORTING DOCUMENTATION

The author maintains a web page at www.vetpath.co.uk/lockerbielinks.html, which provides an index of links to much of the primary documentation in the case.